NANCY BUBEL'S

HANDBOOK OF GARDEN PROJECTS FOR ALL SEASONS

◆ Welcome Beneficial Insects ◆ Grow Herbs on Your Kitchen Windowsill ◆ Attract Birds ◆ Brighten a Shady Spot with Perennials ◆ Cut Salad Greens All Summer ◆ Craft a Cornhusk Wreath ◆ And Much More!

Illustrations by Carol Inouye

Rodale Press, Emmaus, Pennsylvania

Printed in the United States of America on acid-free ♾, recycled ♻ paper

This book contains revised versions of material that appeared in *Country Journal*, *Horticulture*, *The Mother Earth News*, and *Organic Gardening* magazines.

This book is being published simultaneously by Rodale Press as a book entitled *52 Weekend Garden Projects 1993.*

Executive Editor: Margaret Lydic Balitas
Senior Editor: Barbara W. Ellis
Editor: Sally Roth
Associate Editor/Senior Research Associate: Heidi A. Stonehill
Copy Manager: Dolores Plikaitis
Copy Editor: Nancy N. Bailey
Indexer: Cheryl Namy

Cover and book design by Lynn N. Gano
Layout by Linda J. Brightbill
Art Director: Anita G. Patterson
Cover and interior illustrations by Carol Inouye

If you have any questions or comments concerning this book, please write:
Rodale Press
Book Readers' Service
33 East Minor Street
Emmaus, PA 18098

Library of Congress Cataloging-in-Publication Data

Bubel, Nancy.
[Handbook of garden projects for all seasons]
Nancy Bubel's handbook of garden projects for all seasons/by Nancy Bubel; illustrations by Carol Inouye.
p. cm.
Rev. ed. of: 52 weekend garden projects. 1992.
Includes bibliographical references and index.
ISBN 0-87596-572-5 paperback
1. Gardening. I. Bubel, Nancy. 52 weekend garden projects, II. Title. III. Title: Handbook of garden projects for all seasons. IV. Title: Garden projects for all seasons.
[SB453.B867 1993]
635—dc20 92-32798
CIP

Distributed in the book trade by St. Martin's Press

2 4 6 8 10 9 7 5 3 1 paperback

For our grandchildren, gardeners all:
Ansel Bubel
Carolyn Bubel
Nicholas Boerio

Other Books by the Same Author:

The Adventurous Gardener
The Country Journal Book of Vegetable Gardening
52 Weekend Garden Projects 1992
The New Seed Starter's Handbook
Root Cellaring (written with Michael Bubel)
Vegetables Money Can't Buy
Working Wood (written with Michael Bubel)

CONTENTS

INTRODUCTION

"However small it is on the surface," Charles Dudley Warner said of his garden, "it is 4,000 miles deep, and that is a very handsome property."

Gardening gives us a sense of depth—indeed, a heightened appreciation of every dimension. We look up to see scudding clouds, gathering snow, hoped-for rain, warm sun. We look around us more than we did before we took up hoe and spade, observing leafing trees, blooming wildflowers, ripening fruit, budding tulips. Everything in the world around us seems more vital, more meaningful when we notice it while digging and planting: useful weeds, intricately patterned insects, filigreed stalks of last year's broccoli. The earth, too, has a new depth for us when we find out how much is going on in the soil under our feet, how many creatures live and interact there, how last year's decayed leaves and stalks cycle into the hopeful green buds of this new spring.

Being at home, with the garden (however small) around us, we can explore all these dimensions—planting trees, starting seedlings, gathering flowers, snipping herbs, providing for the birds, harvesting good food. We don't need trumped-up "events" to fill our calendars. There's a lot going on right here around us.

I hope you'll find this book a helpful guide to having good growing times on your home place, to exploring some new dimension, to seeing possibilities in the space you call your own. If even that little plot between the back porch and the garage is 4,000 feet deep, then it's worth developing with some weekend project of your choice.

Happy gardening!

PART ONE

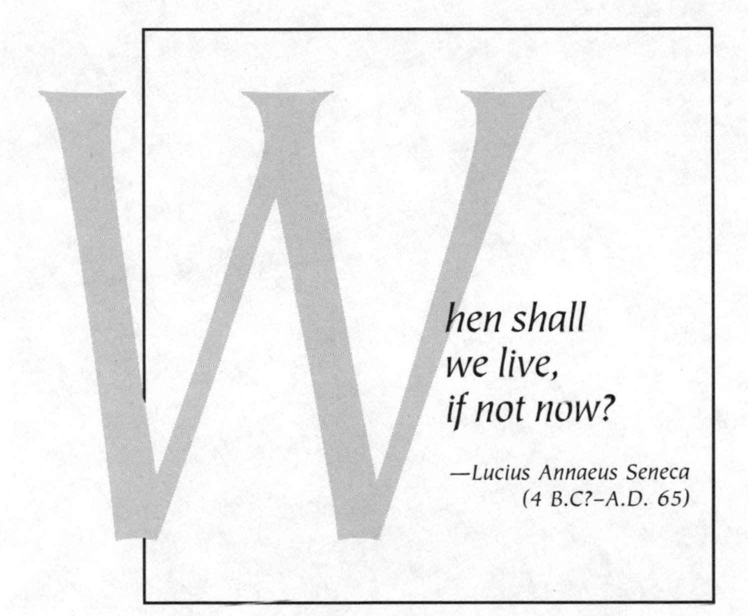

When shall we live, if not now?

—Lucius Annaeus Seneca (4 B.C?–A.D. 65)

SPRING

CHAPTER ONE

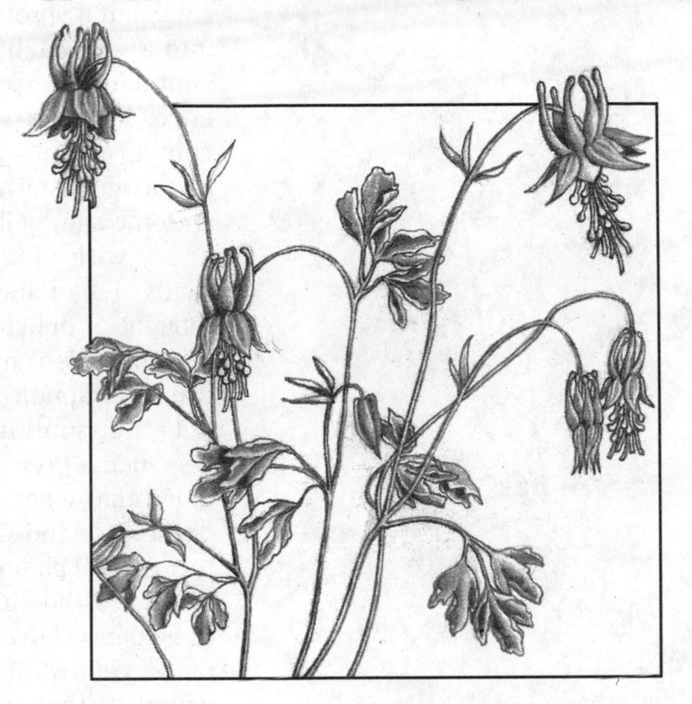

Plant Flowers That Volunteer

The first volunteer plant I ever met was a rose-colored columbine that perched improbably in the crevice of the low stone wall in our first yard where I would never have dared to tuck a living plant. It was so right for that spot, with its graceful blue-green foliage and airy blossoms dancing in the breeze, that I began to appreciate the special wisdom of self-sown plants.

The following year, a bird dropped a sunflower seed by our front

Flowers that self-sow are a pleasure in the garden, skipping around from year to year and turning up where you least expect them. By happy accident, this columbine found a roothold in our stone wall.

gate, and it sprouted into a stout-stalked, commanding presence. It was a welcoming plant—yellow as gold, turning with the sun, quilted later with plump seeds. I had never thought of punctuating our garden entryway so dramatically, but the sunflower was such a great addition that when the house door and shutters needed painting, we chose the shade of golden yellow (Indian yellow, they called it) that most closely approximated the glowing shade of a blooming sunflower. (Shocked the neighbors, who were accustomed to conventional green, black, or red shutters, but they were very nice about it.)

After that, I began to expect surprises in the garden. And I've found another gardening pleasure: In addition to the capricious volunteers that come unbidden, we can have the additional fun of planting varieties of flowers that we know will self-sow. Random happy accidents still occur, and by giving nature a gentle nudge, you can enjoy more of them.

Creating Happy Accidents

Volunteer flowers can make gardening more fun in several ways. You might find that you can depend on them to brighten a formerly

MEET THE VOLUNTEERS

Here are some reliable self-sowing flowers that have reseeded in my garden. Experiment. You might find that others will self-sow for you, too. I know gardeners who have had volunteer annual candytuft (*Iberis umbellata*), marigolds, morning glories, poppies, zinnias, and others.

Ageratum houstonianum (ageratum)
Alcea rosea (hollyhock)
Antirrhinum majus (snapdragon)
Aquilegia spp. (columbines)
Borago officinalis (borage)
Calendula officinalis (pot marigold)
Centaurea cyanus (cornflower, bachelor's-button)
Cleome hasslerana (cleome, spider flower)
Consolida ambigua (rocket larkspur, annual larkspur)
Coreopsis lanceolata (lance-leaved coreopsis)
Coreopsis tinctoria (calliopsis)
Cosmos bipinnatus (cosmos)
Cosmos sulphureus (yellow cosmos, Klondike cosmos)
Eschscholzia californica (California poppy)
Linum perenne (blue flax)
Lobularia maritima (sweet alyssum)
Myosotis sylvatica (garden forget-me-not)
Nicotiana alata (flowering tobacco)
Nigella damascena (love-in-a-mist)
Portulaca grandiflora (rose moss)
Viola tricolor (Johnny-jump-up)
Viola × *wittrockiana* (pansy)

utilitarian patch of ground by the garage. They can fill in between perennials in a flower border, skipping around from year to year in a kind of annual re-embroidery. Or you can toss seeds of self-sowing plants on rocky areas or other hard-to-dig places.

Once a few plants get a toehold, they often multiply year after year. When you find that certain flowers self-sow reliably for you, you might even consider planting a nursery bed from which you can transplant seedlings to other parts of the garden—an easy and thrifty way to get more plants. I do this every year, especially with pot marigold (*Calendula officinalis*), spider flower or cleome (*Cleome hasslerana*), flowering tobacco (*Nicotiana alata*), and Johnny-jump-up (*Viola tricolor*).

REMEMBER THE BIRDS AND BEES

Remember that seed shed by hybrids may produce plants that are different from the parents. Hybrid dwarf ageratum, for instance, may revert to its tall-species parents when it self-sows. Try my favorite ageratum, 'Bavaria', instead—an open-pollinated powder blue flower with a white center. Open-pollinated flowers, not hybrids, are the best for starting a garden of volunteer flowers that will be like the original ones, though flower color may vary from year to year.

Whether you're hoping for big dividends or are just curious to see what will happen, here are a number of things you can do to encourage self-seeding flowers to perform their magic in your garden.

- Let at least some flowers form seed heads. As our experienced gardening neighbors told us when we were planting our first garden, "The Lord loves a dirty garden." If you're not too neat about removing all spent flowers and the resulting seed pods or heads, your willing volunteers will multiply.
- Learn to recognize the young seedlings of your favorite self-sowing plants so you won't pull them up unintentionally when weeding. Check for volunteers in the grass near flower beds and borders.
- Wait, if possible, before digging up ground around your self-sowers in early spring. Give those hoped-for volunteers a chance to germinate.
- Scatter some seeds yourself, in likely and in unlikely places, any time in early spring. And in fall, as you clean up the garden, collect and sow seeds. Many flower seeds that volunteer well will germinate better after exposure to cold.

- If you get a thick stand of volunteers, weed and thin them as you would any other garden plant, to give them space to grow.
- Transplant small volunteer seedlings to garden spaces where you want them to grow. For example, I often move seedlings of tall-growing cleome (*Cleome hasslerana*)—which some call spider flower, but I call lace flower—to the back of the bed or to other places where tall plants would look good.
- Many self-sowing flowers, such as cornflower or bachelor's-button (*Centaurea cyanus*) and California poppy (*Eschscholzia californica*), resent transplanting. If you must move them, do so while the plants are still very small and take a good scoop of ground along, to avoid disturbing the roots.

CHAPTER TWO

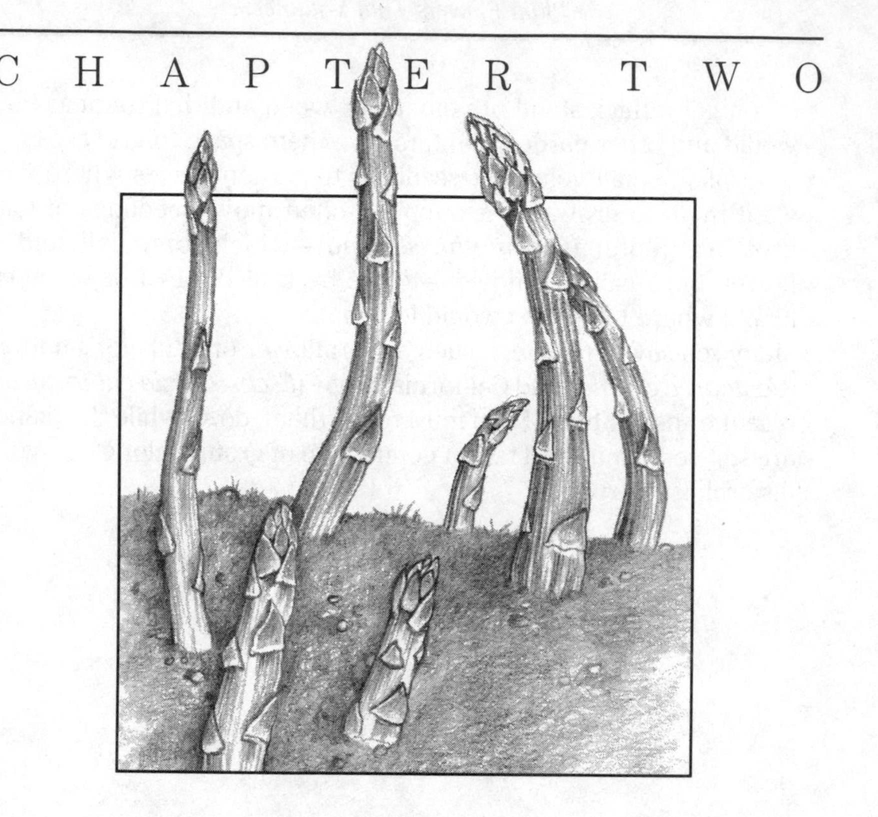

Start an Asparagus Bed

Asparagus is truly gourmet food—tender, delicately flavored, and attractive on the plate. It's even low in calories. A well-planted bed of this perennial vegetable can be one of your most dependable sources of good, fresh garden food—an easily managed luxury that starts producing in early spring, just when you need it most, and continues until the summer.

Many people who might otherwise be harvesting baskets of tender green spears have left asparagus out of their garden plans because of the mistaken notion that they must dig practically to China to prepare the bed. But it's really not necessary to go to the traditional extremes of digging and trench filling in order to raise a good crop of asparagus. The new shallow-planting method works very well indeed and is certainly easier on the back.

One Planting, Years of Eating

A bed of asparagus can remain productive for at least 20 to 30 years (ours is 19 years old and still going strong), so choose the spot with care. Asparagus needs full sun. It appreciates humus-rich garden soil, slightly acid or near neutral, and needs good drainage. Sandy loam is excellent for asparagus, but you can have a fine bed of it in clay, too, by adding compost to the soil to improve drainage.

Plant asparagus crowns as early in the spring as you can work the ground. Wait until the soil is dry enough so that it crumbles in your hands instead of packing into a dense, muddy ball. Buy crowns from your local garden center or order them by mail from seed companies. Or perhaps you know another gardener who could give you some. Asparagus roots look like string mops, topped by several small, dry buds that constitute the crown of the plant. Buy only one-year-old crowns. The older, more expensive two- or three-year-old crowns often start out more slowly because they suffer greater transplant shock.

If you have plenty of patience, you can even start asparagus from

BOY OR GIRL?

Asparagus, a member of the lily family, has both male and female plants. The females sport red berries full of seeds in autumn. The females' spears are thinner than the males', and female plants are less productive than male plants. The cultivars 'Mary Washington' and 'Roberts Strain', both nonhybrids, are time-tested and reliable. 'Jersey Giant' and 'UC 157' are two high-yielding hybrids that produce thick, all-male spears.

seed. Soak the seeds for a day or two to hasten germination, then plant them in peat pots. One seed per pot is all you need. In about 10 to 12 weeks, when the little ferns are a manageable size, move them to a permanent spot in the garden. In three years, the spears will be ready for picking.

Out of the Trenches

There was a time when the planting of an asparagus bed called for heroic measures like digging trenches 3 feet deep. That's an effective—if strenuous—way to plant asparagus, and there's nothing wrong with it. All that effort is not really necessary, though.

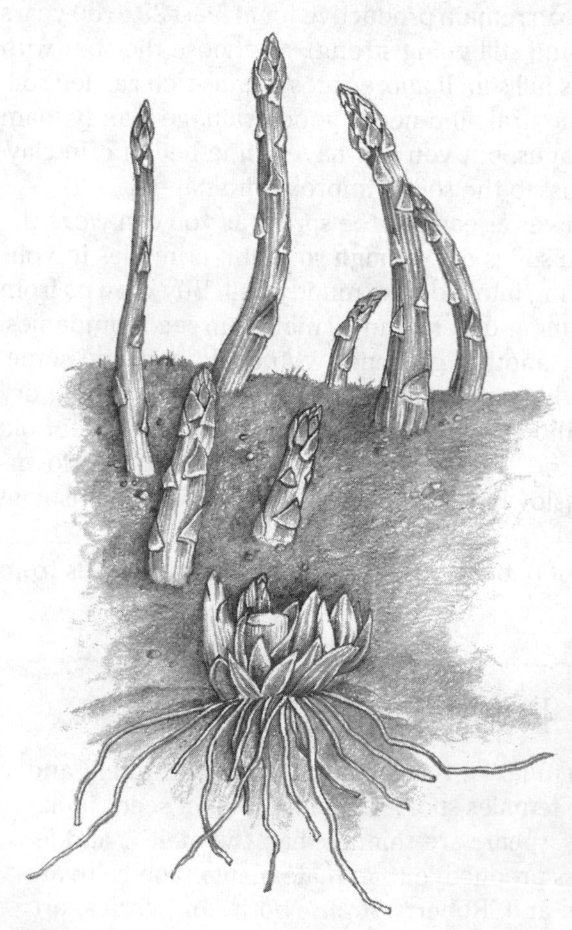

Asparagus roots may look like string mops, but they'll soon be producing tender, tasty spears year after year.

Gardeners who have examined the evidence have concluded that asparagus may be planted much more shallowly, and research studies have confirmed the effectiveness of shallow planting. Plantings made just under the soil surface—4 to 5 inches deep—do very well. Deeper-planted crowns will erupt somewhat later in the spring. You can stagger your harvest by digging crowns in at different levels, say, 8, 6, and 4 inches deep.

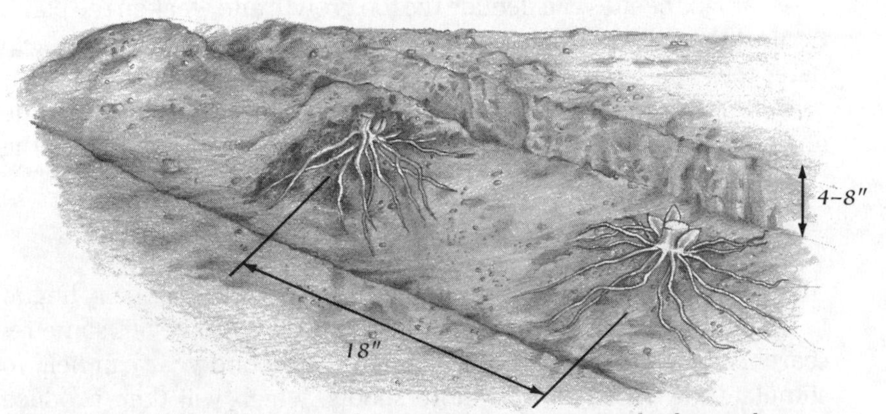

No need to dig to China to plant asparagus—research shows that asparagus planted shallowly does just as well as traditional deep-trench plantings.

Traditional deep digging loosened the soil under the crowns of the asparagus plants, and that probably accounted for much of the success of the method. Asparagus really puts forth when it has good drainage and well-aerated soil. If you want to give your plants a good start, you can achieve a similar effect by rotary tilling thoroughly before planting or by building a raised bed for your asparagus. Plant the crowns in a shallow trench, or plant them on the surface of the prepared area and build up a raised bed of loose soil above them.

Soak the dry asparagus crowns in water for 1 to 2 hours before planting. Then spread out the strands on each root clump so that they'll be in contact with the soil, not tangled with each other. Figure on providing about 6 square feet of soil for each root clump. If your rows are 4 feet apart, space root clumps 18 inches apart. If your rows are 6 feet apart, plant the clumps every 12 inches. Keep the bed or row at least 3 feet away from any other garden perennial.

Add soil gradually as the plants grow, filling in the trench or building up the mound 1 inch at a time over the course of a month or two. Keep weeds under control while the plants are young, and water the new bed if the season is dry. Mulch will help to control weeds and retain moisture—and will help to gradually feed those prodigious roots, which may range as far as 5 to 6 feet in each direction. Give your asparagus patch a yearly topdressing of well-rotted manure or other fertilizer, either in fall or after picking season ends in spring.

Asparagus beetles can denude the top growth and weaken the plant. Control them by handpicking. Planting tomatoes nearby may help deter these pests. In case of a severe infestation, cut down the ferns as soon as picking ends for the season. Dust the bed with rotenone and then let the new ferns grow. This is a good time to fertilize the bed.

Picking Your Reward

Picking—the moment we're all waiting for—has traditionally begun in the third year (two years after planting). Now, however, some researchers maintain that light picking in the second year can help to stimulate the production of more shoots, which will then produce more food for the plant.

If you decide to start picking in the second year, stop after two weeks. Pick for only two to three weeks in the third year. In the fourth year, you can pick for a month or six weeks, as long as the spears remain large enough. Don't pick any spears that are thinner than a pencil. After the fourth year, you can pick for eight weeks, as long as the spears maintain their size. In a young bed, you can probably stretch that to ten weeks. In my older asparagus bed, though, I find that spear size stays larger if I pick for only eight weeks.

Snap off the spears with your fingers. Using a knife can injure the crowns. After picking season ends, let the ferns grow and overwinter in the bed. Cut them down in very early spring.

Each spring, we eat asparagus almost daily for about two months—steamed for dinner, served with toast for lunch, or cut raw into a salad. (We eat some raw right out there in the patch, too.) I freeze extras for winter soups. We never tire of it. Can you imagine ever having too much asparagus?

CHAPTER THREE

Edge a Bed with Coral Bells

If you have a path or flower bed that needs edging or a semi-shady corner that could use a dose of charm, let coral bells (*Heuchera sanguinea*) spread their skirts along your path or add a graceful note of dainty, breeze-blown color. Hardy but never invasive, their neat rosettes of rounded leaves are sturdy and attractive. The tiny bell-shaped flowers are borne in airy clusters atop 12- to 18-inch stems from May until July. They provide accents of intense or

Old-fashioned coral bells (*Heuchera sanguinea*) add a charming scalloped border to flower beds. Their graceful stems of bright, long-lasting flowers attract hummingbirds.

delicate color in white, pink, crimson, or coral red, depending on the cultivar. The graceful, wiry stems are strong but responsive to a breeze, producing an interesting shifting and blending of color areas against greenery or in a gaily colored flower bed.

In a city garden, I once had a bare strip of ground 5 feet long and 1 foot wide, bounded by a hedge and dropping off to a low rock wall. The coral bells I planted in that strip soon hid the scraggly hedge base and softened the rock edges, transforming a bleak odd spot into an attractive welcoming garden that greeted visitors on their way in the gate and made a delightful view from our living room windows. In a friend's garden, a long, wide perennial border edged with coral bells has a cottage garden effect.

Even when coral bells aren't in bloom, they add a pretty scalloped boundary to beds and borders. The leaves resemble those of a geranium and are often shaded in darker green around the veins. In fact, the compact mounds of leaves are nearly evergreen, retaining their green color long after other perennial leaves have turned to mush from fall frosts.

Easygoing and Adaptable

Coral bells are among the easiest and most versatile perennials you can grow. My first planting was made in the most casual way, without enriching the soil or mulching, but the plants grew and bloomed well. I think they appreciated the good drainage provided by the low stone wall beneath them. They won't survive wet, soggy soil over winter.

Although they don't require rich soil, coral bells grow bigger and better in soil enriched with compost, producing handsome, bushy clumps. Easygoing coral bells will grow and bloom in either full sun or partial shade.

For such easy-to-please plants, coral bells are remarkably unaggressive. They don't self-sow, and their roots don't ramble. They do tend to develop a high, woody crown after five to six years in the ground, but that is easily remedied by dividing the plants. Division gives you a chance to extend your border, too. If you have a single healthy clump of coral bells and want to establish a row of them as an edging, you're closer to your goal than you might think. Here's how to divide an established plant.

1. Examine the plant. You'll see that it is composed of eight or ten brown stalks projecting from the roots, each stalk bearing leaves and, in season, one or more flowered stems.
2. Take advantage of an overcast, showery day in spring or early fall to do your propagating by division. Break off several of the cigarlike stalks. Make sure each stalk retains at least a few roots.
3. Plant the divisions in good garden soil, 10 to 12 inches apart. Cover the entire brown stalk with a few inches of soil, leaving only the leaves exposed. Firm into place.
4. Water the new plants well and keep them moist until new roots develop. In the North, mulch plants if winter snow cover is sparse.

Once you have a supply of plants built up, you can gain a few more to fill in corners by simply breaking off the projecting stalks, without

GROWING CORAL BELLS FROM SEED

If you want a lot of coral bells, start some from seed. You'll get about 1,000 of the tiny seeds in an average packet. You can plant the seeds in fine soil in the garden in late spring, around the time of your last frost. But it's easier to keep track of the tiny scallop-edged seedlings if you start them indoors. Scatter the seeds in a flat, or sprinkle a few seeds into individual pots. At about 55°F, they'll germinate in 10 to 15 days. If you planted in flats, move small clumps of four or so seedlings to small pots for the first transplanting. Separate them later when they're about 1 inch high, replanting in individual pots. Plant in a nursery row in the garden around the time of the last spring frost. This year's seedlings will bloom next year.

digging the plant. I've found that if I keep these new starts moist enough, I lose very few of them. Those that I plant in spring sometimes bloom the same year and, two years later, can be borrowed from to make more new plants.

As if ease of culture, graceful charm, and adaptability aren't enough, coral bells are also disease and insect resistant. I can't recall ever seeing an infested or diseased coral bell plant in my garden. I do, however, have happy memories of watching hummingbirds visit my coral bells—an extra dimension of beauty added to an already lovely plant.

CHAPTER FOUR

Blanket Bare Spots with Groundcovers

Groundcovers are green—and sometimes blooming—blankets for those odd spots on your home grounds. A good groundcover can make your place look great and simplify your maintenance chores. Established groundcover plantings need no mowing and little or no weeding. They can solve all sorts of yard puzzlers, from steep banks to tree-shaded areas where grass won't grow to bare spaces around leggy shrubbery.

Groundcovers prevent soil erosion, conserve moisture, and shade

Good groundcovers can be pretty as well as practical. The dainty white flowers of Allegheny foamflower (*Tiarella cordifolia*) and the handsome speckled foliage and blue-pink flowers of lungwort (*Pulmonaria saccharata*) are a good combination for a shady corner. Foamflower foliage holds its green well into winter.

out weeds. Shrubs like rhododendrons, mountain laurel (*Kalmia latifolia*), and azaleas (*Rhododendron* spp.), whose roots are sensitive to disturbance, grow better with groundcovers around their feet than with bare ground that must be cultivated. Clematis (*Clematis* spp.), too, appreciate a living mulch over their roots to keep the soil cool. Groundcovers also make good carpets for beds of spring-blooming bulbs, which pop through in spring and then die back, leaving the groundcover to fill in.

Not Just a Pretty Face

The best groundcovers need little care, root readily, and grow quickly without being invasive. They look good all year and grow thickly enough to discourage weeds. That's a lot to expect of any plant, but there are plenty of good candidates.

Many groundcovers bloom, and some are even evergreen. Plant forms can range from the flat, ground-hugging mats formed by ajuga (*Ajuga* spp.) to taller, airier, but still carpetlike pachysandra. All have in common a dense habit of growth and a strong, soil-binding root system. Here are some attractive perennial groundcover plants, with a bonus of pretty bloom, that you might like to try in your landscape. All do well in Zones 4 through 10, unless otherwise noted.

Sun Lovers

Plant these groundcovers in a sunny spot and watch them flourish.

Iberis sempervirens (Perennial Candytuft)

Candytuft's clusters of spring-blooming white flowers punctuate mounds of slender, dark green leaves. It does best in rich soil, in sun or part shade. Space plants 6 to 8 inches apart. Candytuft tends to be evergreen, or nearly so. If old plants become woody, shear them back after flowering to 4 inches high to encourage new growth.

Phlox subulata (Moss Pink)

Only 6 inches high, these ground-hugging carpets form masses of pink, white, or lavender flowers in spring. Moss pinks are great for slopes, rock gardens, and a welcoming patch by the mailbox. They spread fast in rich soil, though even ordinary soil will do. May be hardy to Zone 2.

Potentilla spp. (Cinquefoils)

Cinquefoil has sprawling stems of strawberry-like leaves, topped by golden yellow flowers in spring. It forms mats or low mounds, from 2 to 12 inches high, depending on the species. Plant in ordinary well-drained, even dry, soil. Most species are hardy in Zones 4 through 8; some are hardy to Zone 3.

Shady Characters

These plants do best when kept out of full sun. Most prefer partial shade, and some thrive even in dense shade.

Ajuga reptans (Ajuga)

Ajuga, or bugleweed as it's also called, forms a dense mat 2 to 6 inches high with oval, bronze or purple-tinged green leaves and short

ARTFUL ARRANGEMENTS

A bed of periwinkle under trees is a classic, but you can have fun thinking of new places and creative combinations for your groundcovers. You might like to try one of these.

- *Ceratostigma plumbaginoides* (leadwort) mixed with *Vinca minor* (common periwinkle) in a handkerchief-size, city front yard that's too small to mow
- *Convallaria majalis* (lily-of-the-valley) on the north side of the house where few other flowering plants will thrive
- *Lamium maculatum* (spotted lamium) to soften and fill around a border of hollyhocks
- *Phlox subulata* (moss pink) in that hard-to-mow spot around the mailbox
- *Vinca minor* (common periwinkle) along a semishady stone wall where daffodils bloom in spring

spikes of small blue flowers in early summer. It accepts poor soil and partial to deep shade. This popular groundcover spreads rapidly; use a strip of sunken edging to keep it out of the grass. Plant starts about 1 foot apart. Although ajuga has a tendency to develop scattered dry, brown spots, these are easily repaired by transplanting rooted stems from elsewhere on the plant. Leaves are evergreen, or semi-evergreen in the far North.

Asarum europaeum (European Wild Ginger)

Glossy, rounded leaves form a 4- to 6-inch-high mat that conceals the maroon, bell-shaped flowers that blossom in spring. (Our native wild ginger, *Asarum canadense,* which has silky-looking, rather than glossy, leaves and similar flowers, also makes a good groundcover.) Plant ginger in humus-rich, woodsy soil or rich garden soil, in partial to deep shade. It's a good edging plant and makes a handsome border around a bed of another, slightly taller groundcover plant. Hardy to Zone 8.

Convallaria majalis (Lily-of-the-Valley)

Loved by children who often pick these flowers for Mother's Day bouquets, lily-of-the-valley's sweetly fragrant white bells stand out against the smooth, pointed leaves. Grow it in humus-rich soil, in shade or partial shade. Plant the pips about 1 foot apart, ½ to 1 inch below ground level. This plant does best in cooler areas, to Zone 8.

Lamium maculatum (Spotted Lamium)

The pink flowers of spotted lamium, or spotted nettle, bloom from spring through fall above mintlike leaves brushed with patches of silver. It reaches about 8 inches tall. Plant spotted lamium in rich, moist soil, in shade to partial shade. Space plants 10 to 12 inches apart. The cultivar 'Beacon Silver' spreads readily but stays neat.

Pulmonaria saccharata (Bethlehem Sage)

This borage-family member bears clusters of pink-budded flowers that turn blue as they open, above handsome speckled leaves. Also called Bethlehem lungwort, this pretty plant is one of the first to bloom in spring. It likes a good supply of humus but adapts well to varied

WATCH OUT FOR GOBBLERS!

Some plants cover ground all too well, by leaps and bounds—clambering beyond boundaries, enveloping porches, and twining up trees. Many of these super-enthusiastic plants have their place. Crown vetch (*Coronilla varia*), for example, does a fine job of preventing erosion on roadside banks and pond perimeters. If you have large open areas that need cover, it can be a good choice. But in your front yard, it's likely to gobble the petunias and the grass once it gets going

Honeysuckles (*Lonicera* spp.) ramble and climb vigorously and are hard to mow down once spread. We're glad to have some growing along our lane, but wouldn't want it in our yard. Kudzu (*Pueraria lobata*), famous for its galloping ground consumption, has taken over acres of land in the South. Common matrimony vine (*Lycium halimifolium*) and its cousin Chinese matrimony vine (*Lycium chinense*) are two more ground-gobblers to avoid. On a smaller scale, don't let anyone give you a start of ground ivy (*Glechoma hederacea*). This creeper is attractive but watch out: It roots as it spreads, making it difficult to eradicate completely. It can take over a garden if left unchecked for a season.

conditions. Plant in well-drained soil in partial shade, allowing about 10 inches between plants. It grows 8 to 10 inches tall.

Tiarella cordifolia (Allegheny Foamflower)

Foamflower spreads by sending out runners. It's a wonderful groundcover for a woodsy setting or under tall shade trees. Spikes of dainty, white, May-blooming flowers nod over slightly hairy basal leaves that resemble those of the maple. Leaves stay green well into winter. Allegheny foamflower appreciates humus-rich, moist soil and light shade, and grows well in Zones 5 through 8. Mulch with leaf mold. Space new plants 8 to 12 inches apart.

For Sun or Shade

These flexible groundcovers take happily to sun or partial shade.

Ceratostigma plumbaginoides (Leadwort)

Surprisingly intense blue flowers top these 6-inch-tall charmers in August and September, and foliage turns a deep, rich red in the fall. Grow leadwort in ordinary garden soil, in sun or partial shade, spacing plants 10 to 12 inches apart. Good drainage is essential.

Sedum spp. (Sedums)

Fleshy-leaved sedums, in many species and cultivars, are drought-resistant, low-maintenance plants, and they spread quickly. Good drainage is a must. Among the low-growing forms of sedum are species with yellow, white, or pink flowers. *Sedum acre,* with small leaves and yellow flowers, grows 4 inches high in any well-drained soil, in sun or partial shade. Some species are hardy to Zone 3.

Veronica spp. (Speedwells)

The low-growing speedwells make good groundcovers in moist, well-drained soil. They'll thrive in Zones 4 through 8. *Veronica prostrata* 'Heavenly Blue' is a wonderful blue-flowered plant, with short wands of deep sky blue flowers in spring and summer. It reaches a height of 6 inches.

Vinca minor (Common Periwinkle)

Periwinkle, or myrtle, bears glossy leaves on trailing stems. The stems root where they touch the ground, forming a 6-inch-high evergreen mat. Violet-blue flowers, like little pinwheels, appear in the spring. White and rose-colored cultivars of vinca are also available. Periwinkle does well in any soil, in shade or sun, but spreads faster in good soil with steady moisture. Space starts about 10 to 12 inches apart. Periwinkle is excellent for holding banks of soil in place, and it makes a wonderful background for daffodils.

Making the Bed

Like any other plants, your new groundcover starts will produce stronger and more extensive roots if they're planted in loose ground well supplied with humus. When possible, loosen the soil to a depth of 6 to 8 inches. Dig in some well-rotted manure or compost to provide nourishment and increase the soil's ability to retain moisture. If tree roots or other obstacles prevent your digging the entire area, then at least loosen and enrich each spot of soil where you intend to plant a rooted start.

Remove all weeds and strip off the sod if you're replacing grass. If the area you're planting is small enough to reach into without stepping into it, water the soil before planting. Otherwise, water after planting with a sprinkler or soil-soaking hose.

Planted about a foot apart, most groundcovers cover bare spots in only a year or two. Plant thickly for fast coverage and less weeding. To encourage rooting, keep new plantings well watered for the first year.

ONE FAMILY'S GROUNDCOVER PROJECT

Our daughter and her husband and son live in a suburb of hills and more hills, where no two houses are the same level. Their backyard slopes steeply enough for some wild sledding in the winter, but that slope makes for some tough mowing in summer. Their solution was to start a groundcover sampler on the bumpy part of the slope that's hardest to mow. (They kept the smoothest part as a sled run.)

Like most busy young families, they didn't have large blocks of time to devote to the project, so they proceeded gradually. Young Nick, their preschooler, is a born landscaper whose idea of fun is to scalp the grass from any even remotely diggable spot. This questionable talent came in handy when Nick and his mother spent several mornings stripping sod and loosening the soil.

They planted the new bed with moss pinks (*Phlox subulata*) and 'Nashville Star' daylilies, a fast-spreading cultivar. By the second spring, the phlox our daughter had set out as spindly, single-stemmed plantlets had spread into bushy clumps. The daylilies grew from two-leaved beginner plants to healthy thickets, and they even bloomed the first year.

Set the plants in place and firm the soil well around them. Water thoroughly. Rooted starts grown in a flat will suffer more root disturbance and may need to be shaded for several days after planting. Water the area once or twice a week for a month or two after planting unless it rains.

Spacing of transplants is a trade-off: If you plant thickly, you'll get quicker coverage of the ground, but it will cost more and you may need to thin after a few years. Plant thinly and you'll save money but spend more time weeding. If you're able to root cuttings from a friend's plants or to transplant your own starts from your own garden or nursery bed, you'll save money and have a nice, thick planting right from the start. It's generally good to plant small plants 8 to 12 inches apart. If you're planting a bare slope where erosion could be a problem, plant as thickly as you can and then spread a fine mulch of dry grass clippings over the area to break the force of rainwater.

Groundcovers need to root well before they can start to spread, so keep your new planting well watered to encourage rooting. Keep weeds pulled so the new plants won't be shaded or crowded out. Most groundcovers take at least a year to fill their allotted space.

CHAPTER FIVE

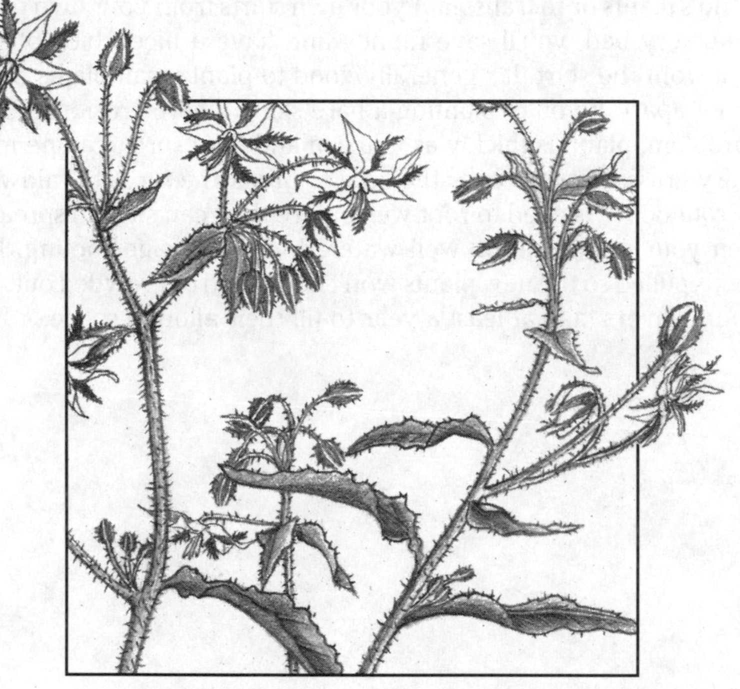

Raise Cooking Herbs from Seed

Growing herb plants from seed requires some patience, but it's a wonderful way to use your gardening skill to earn a whole patch full of aromatic culinary sprigs. It's immensely satisfying, too, to know that the generous borders of chives, the aromatic basil, even the pungent, bushy rosemary were successfully raised by your own hand. If you've always bought your herbs as nursery plants, why not try growing one or two of your favorites from seed this year?

NOT FROM SEED, PLEASE

Start with cuttings or young plants for tarragon and mints. True French tarragon (*Artemisia dracunculus* var. *sativa*), the only kind worth growing, does not set seed. If you see tarragon seed offered, it's Russian tarragon, an inferior woody plant without much flavor. Mints hybridize so readily that mint seed, even when offered by reputable dealers, often fails to be true to name. If you just want mint and don't mind what kind you get, then go ahead and plant mint seeds. But if you want curly mint, apple mint, peppermint, or other specific mints, buy plants.

If you've started flowers and vegetables from seed, then you should have no trouble with herbs. Those that are slow to germinate or slow to grow require an extra dose of patience. But many herbs are as easy to grow as annual flowers.

Some herbs, such as German chamomile and burnet, may be sown right in the garden. But many herb seedlings, such as those of rosemary, are tiny and slow growing, easily outdistanced by sprouting weeds in the garden. It's best to start and grow them indoors until they can hold their own. Plant herb seeds in a flat or in individual pots filled with damp vermiculite and keep them at the recommended temperature until you see sprouts emerging.

Some seeds need cold treatment in order to germinate. Plant them in damp moss, vermiculite, or potting soil in a small, shallow container. Enclose it in a plastic bag and keep it either in the refrigerator or in a protected—but cold—outdoor spot to chill for a month before bringing it to a warmer place for the seeds to germinate.

If you use flats, transplant into pots as soon as the seedlings develop their first set of true leaves. Plant the seedlings out in your herb garden in late spring.

A Garden of Good Tastes

Most of these agreeable herbs are easy and rewarding to start from seed. And if you end up with extras, herb plants are always a welcome gift to friends and neighbors.

Basil (*Ocimum basilicum*)

With so many wonderful basil varieties, from cinnamon and lemon to lettuce-leaf and dark opal, you're sure to find one or two just right for your garden and cooking style. There's even a fine-leaved basil that grows in a rounded shrubby form, like a 9-inch-high topiary tree. For kitchen use, 'Genova Profumatissima' is especially fine flavored.

Growing your own herbs from seed is satisfying and just as easy as starting flowers. Sprinkle seeds right in the garden for tall, blue-flowered borage. Mince the hairy leaves for a touch of cucumber flavor in chicken soup, or toss the starry blossoms in salads.

Basil is a frost-sensitive, 12- to 18-inch-tall annual that grows well in warm weather. The small seeds germinate within a week at 70°F. Start plants indoors about six weeks before your last frost date, or plant seeds directly in the garden after frost. For bushier plants, cut back the leafy tips every few weeks.

Borage (*Borago officinalis*)

This 2-foot-tall annual herb bears sky blue, star-shaped flowers and hairy leaves. Borage grows quickly, even in poor soil. You'll only have to plant it once because it volunteers readily.

Borage suffers from having its roots disturbed, so plant seeds right in the garden, starting a week or so before your last expected frost. Choose a spot in full sun. Seeds germinate in about five days at 70°F. Thin plants to about 15 inches apart.

READY FOR A CHALLENGE?

Hauntingly aromatic rosemary is one of the more temperamental herbs to start from seed, but it can be done. The seeds have a low germination rate and demand close attention to growing details. Bertha Reppert, who has grown countless rosemary plants from seed in her Rosemary House herb shop in Mechanicsburg, Pennsylvania, advises, "First, be patient. The seeds can take up to three weeks to germinate. Rosemary really demands sharp drainage, both in order to germinate and after germination. Soggy soil is sure death to seeds and seedlings. Avoid peat in your starting mix, and add vermiculite or sharp sand or both to improve drainage. But don't let the soil dry out, either. The safest thing to do is mist it, and also mist the young seedlings."

Rosemary seedlings grow slowly, but within a year you should have respectable thriving plants.

Burnet (*Poterium sanguisorba*)

An attractive perennial, burnet forms loose, rounded clumps of lacy leaves that have a refreshing flavor often compared with that of cucumber. The leaves are good in salads, and the 1- to 2-foot plant is decorative in the garden.

You can plant burnet seeds in the fall for spring seedlings or in early spring. Plant the seeds where they are to grow. Burnet likes limey soil and full sun, and does well on poor ground. Once established, it self-sows freely.

Chives (*Allium schoenoprasum*)

This clump-forming perennial is especially easy to grow from seed. Seedlings of common chives look like new grass at first, thin and thready. They soon thicken into the familiar tubular, quill-like leaves with a gentle onion flavor.

I usually start seeds indoors in January or February when I plant my onions, but chive seeds may also be planted in the open ground as soon as the soil is workable. They do well in sun and don't mind a bit of light shade. Unlike many other herbs, chives appreciate a generous dose of fertilizer each year.

Parsley (*Petroselinum crispum*)

Tangy parsley is a biennial that's planted annually. It will thrive in sun or partial shade, and prefers well-drained soil enriched with compost. Choose your favorite curly or flat parsley; both kinds are high in iron and vitamins A and C.

Parsley is a slowpoke. Its seed contains compounds called furanocoumarins that block germination, especially in the presence of sunlight. Soak parsley seeds overnight before planting and discard the water. Chilling parsley seeds before planting also seems to help. Be sure to cover the seeds.

You can plant parsley seeds in the garden as soon as your soil is workable, or start seeds indoors, using reusable cell packs. Or you can use peat pots to avoid root disturbance, and transplant pot and all to the garden. Presoaked seeds often sprout in two weeks at 70°F; seeds that haven't been presoaked may take three weeks or longer to sprout.

Sage (*Salvia officinalis*)

The soft gray-green leaves of garden sage make a good texture contrast for beds and borders as well as the herb garden. This hardy perennial herb grows readily from seed. Start indoors in early spring, or sow outside in midspring. At 60° to 70°F, seedlings will emerge in two to three weeks. Even the first tiny leaves show sage's characteristic pebbly texture.

Sage seedlings grow quickly. They prefer full sun and well-drained soil, and when well rooted outdoors, they tolerate drought. Waterlogged soil can kill them. Cut plants in midseason to encourage bushiness.

Thyme (*Thymus vulgaris*)

Pungent thyme, with its tiny leaves and creeping growth habit, is a slow starter and a slow grower. The seeds germinate in three to four weeks. Thyme seedlings and plants require good drainage and like a sunny spot. Seedlings need more frequent watering than mature plants, which don't mind dry soil, but avoid overwatering.

Thyme plants usually need to be renewed every three to four years. Older plants that become woody seem to be more susceptible to winter frost damage. Cut back three-fourths of the new growth during the growing season to keep the plant bushy.

C H A P T E R S I X

Design a Lettuce Bed

Gone, unmourned, are the days when "salad" meant a green cube of fruit-studded gelatin bedded on a pale iceberg lettuce leaf. True salads of mixed greens are appreciated more than ever these days, for their piquancy, for their splendid contribution of vitamins at low calorie cost, and for their ease of preparation.

Imaginative restaurant chefs are discovering what gardeners have

MORE AND BETTER LETTUCE

Lettuce does best in cool weather, but a careful choice of cultivars will carry you through the gardening year. Plant lettuce seeds outdoors in early spring, as soon as the ground can be worked. You'll have better lettuce, and more of it all season long, if you make frequent small plantings every two to three weeks throughout the season. Avoid planting when the soil temperature exceeds 80°F; germination may be poor. Wait until early fall.

Take care not to bury the seeds too deeply. Cover them with ¼ inch or less of fine, light soil. Keep your lettuce well watered; dry soil can cause a bitter flavor.

known for ages: There is a whole world of lettuces above and beyond the common iceberg type. You'll find salads of 'Bibb', romaine, or perhaps 'Craquerelle du Midi' on more and more menus these days.

This is a happy development for both the diner and the local market grower who supplies the restaurant. It's also a reminder to the rest of us that we're missing a lot if we plant only one or two kinds of lettuce, or if we sow merely once or twice in a season.

A Living Sampler

Lettuce you grow yourself is fresher than any you'll ever get in a restaurant or store, and you have a choice of dozens of different varieties with varying leaf form, color, texture, plant shape, and density. It's fun to arrange varied lettuce plants to form an interesting pattern in a bed or row.

You might plant tall cos lettuce in the center of a rectangular bed, surrounded by rows of a red-leaved lettuce, then a green head lettuce, and at the edge of the bed, a butterhead variety. Or you might plant solid patches of a succession of six or so kinds of lettuce in a wide row . . . a live lettuce sampler. A tiny semicircular bed by the back door, meant for easy snipping, could be so good to look at that you hesitate before removing a head!

Pick the Best Lettuce

A mix of lettuces with different colors, textures, and tastes makes an interesting garden and an interesting salad. Choose as many lettuces as you have room for, and remember to stagger plantings so you'll have fresh salad pickings all season long.

Most catalogs list four types of lettuce: looseleaf, romaine or cos, butterhead, and crisphead. A fifth, intermediate type, French crisp or Batavian, is available from some seed suppliers.

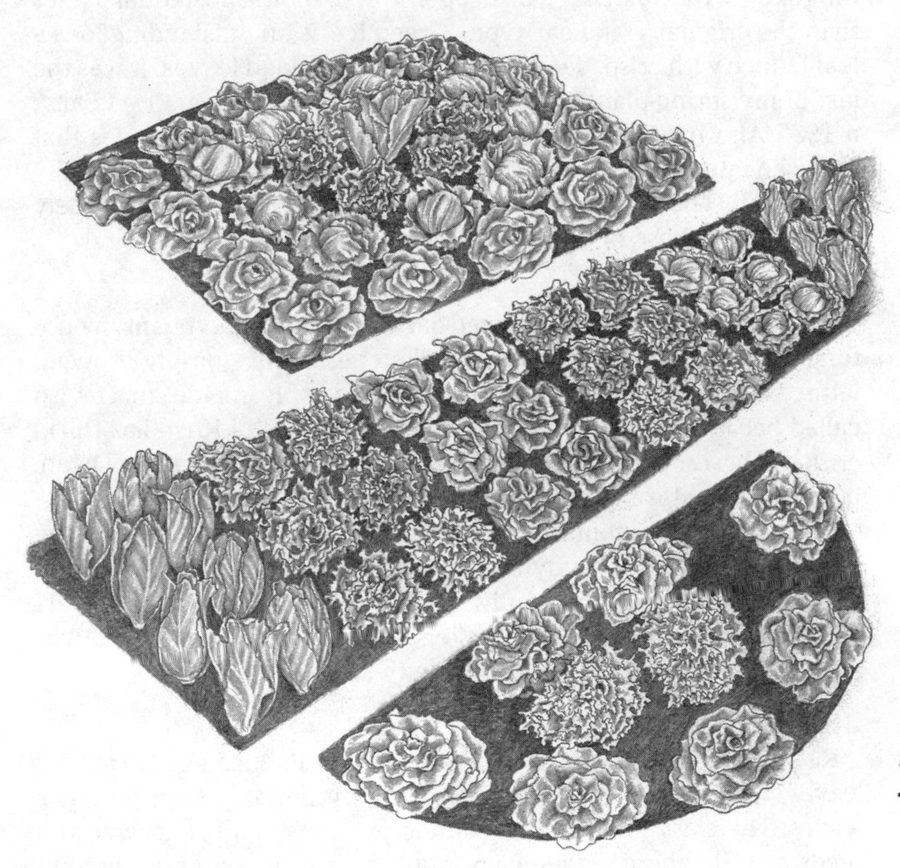

A lettuce bed adds interest to the garden when you plant it in an attractive design. Varied textures and colors of different lettuces make an attractive contrast. Try these designs, or create your own sampler.

Looseleaf

Looseleaf lettuce grows in an open rosette of loosely arranged leaves that do not head up. It is the earliest of the lettuces, ready in 40 to 45 days from seed. The distinctive leaf shapes account for the picturesque names of some older looseleaf lettuces like 'Deertongue' and 'Oak Leaf'.

The widely available 'Black-Seeded Simpson', which dates back to the mid-nineteenth century, is still beloved by many gardeners for its earliness, mild flavor, and good texture. The crinkled leaves are crisper than those of some smooth-surfaced varieties like 'Deertongue'. 'Royal Oak Leaf' has deeper green, more substantial leaves than the original 'Oak Leaf' type. 'Green Ice' is an outstanding looseleaf lettuce with crisp, deep green, heavily crinkled leaves. It was the last of my spring-planted lettuces to go to seed last year. 'Red Sails', a 1985 All-America winner, has deep burgundy-bronze leaves that make an interesting addition to the salad bowl. It performs especially well in fall. The leaves of 'Red Sails' are crisper and more intensely colored than those of the earlier 'Ruby', another red cultivar.

Romaine or Cos

This type of lettuce can be traced back to the early Egyptians, whose tomb drawings show recognizable sketches of this upright-growing lettuce with its long, 3- to 6-inch-wide leaves. Romaine, or cos (so called because it was grown on the Greek island of Kos), has thick, crisp leaf bases. The overlapping leaves form a loose, cylindrical head. It produces mature heads in 79 to 80 days from seed.

This lettuce is customarily used to make Caesar salad because the leaves have sufficient body to stand up to vigorous tossing. The flat leaves are convenient for sandwiches, too. I've tried newer cultivars like 'Cosmo' and 'Ballon', but my loyalty still lies with the old cultivar 'Parris Island', a tall, crisp romaine with large leaves.

Butterhead

Ready in 60 to 75 days, butterhead forms a soft, open head of tender leaves, with pale center hearts covered by darker green wrapper leaves. The classic butterhead cultivar is 'Bibb'. Lettuce grower and seedsman Shepherd Ogden calls it "the first American gourmet lettuce." 'Bibb' is delicious, but it bolts to seed in early summer much more readily than other types, so I grow it in the fall or in the greenhouse.

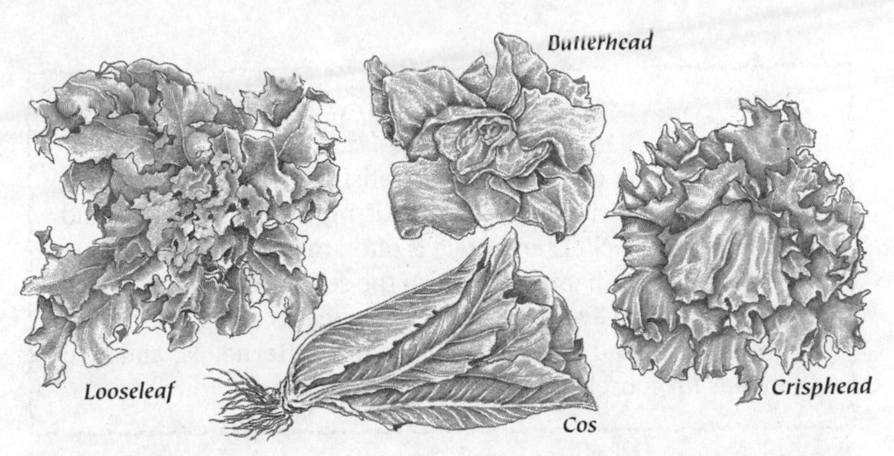

Choose lettuces in different colors, textures, and tastes for interesting salad pickings all season long. A careful choice of cultivars will carry you through the gardening year. Select from lettuce types like looseleaf, cos, butterhead, or crisphead.

'Buttercrunch', which is slower to bolt than 'Bibb' but similar in form, is a summer standby for many gardeners. 'Mescher', one of my favorite butterhead lettuces, is an heirloom variety formerly available only through a seed-saving exchange but recently introduced for sale by several seed companies.

If you're looking for a forcing lettuce for use in greenhouse, tunnel, or cold frame, try 'Magnet', a quick-growing, nonfussy butterhead. Most winter lettuces are butterheads, too. Both 'Winter Marvel' and 'Winter Density' survive Vermont winters. 'Brune d'Hiver' and 'North Pole' are also very hardy. These winter types should be planted in late summer. They're likely to bolt if seeded much earlier than the first week in September.

Crisphead

Crisphead lettuce is exemplified by the familiar 'Iceberg' found in every grocery store and salad bar. Its solid round head of tightly packed leaves is crisp and mild flavored, but much lower in vitamin content than either looseleaf or romaine lettuces. Butterhead lettuces, too, contain more vitamins A and C and more calcium and iron than crisphead. Crisphead grows more slowly than other lettuces, requiring 70 to 90 days to form usable heads.

Head lettuce was first recognized as a distinct type around the sixteenth century. It's less forgiving of heat and lean soil than leaf lettuce

ELBOW ROOM

Lettuce can be one of the most satisfying of garden crops if you give it what it needs: plenty of moisture, rich soil, and enough space. Lackluster lettuce is often the result of crowding. It's easy to let this happen, because the seeds are small and easily overplanted. Give each seedling space to grow: 12 inches between crisphead plants, 10 inches for butterheads, and 8 to 10 inches for looseleaf and romaine cultivars.

is, and it requires plenty of phosphorus to form solid heads. 'Ithaca', an early crisphead, has been a standard in my garden for years.

French Crisp or Batavian

These lettuces are looseleaf in form when young, but develop small, loosely wrapped heads when mature (55 to 60 days). The leaves are crisp, sweet, and mild flavored. 'Anuenue', developed by the University of Hawaii, is one of my favorite lettuces. I plant it late for a summer crop, and it's proved to be more heat resistant, darker green, and crisper than 'Kagran Summer' and more bolt resistant than 'Buttercrunch'.

CHAPTER SEVEN

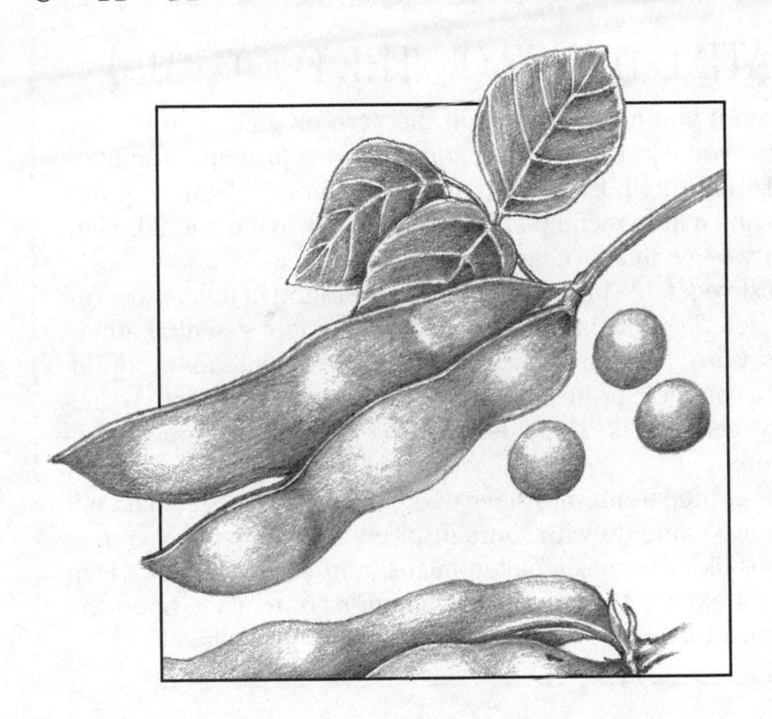

Grow Protein in Your Garden

When our grandparents were young, vegetables—often called "garden sass"—were customarily served thoroughly stewed in small, oval side dishes. This treatment was befitting of their position on the menu—well below the meat in nutritional importance.

For most of us contemporary gardeners, however, the vegetables we bring to the table are often the stars of the meal. Knowing much

EATING LOWER ON THE FOOD CHAIN

Even if you have no cows in the barn or poultry in the hen house, you can raise at least some of your protein directly on the land. Protein from the garden? Yes indeed! With the right crop and a little menu planning, you can provide enough high-quality vegetable protein for one meal a week.

Most vegetable proteins, unlike those found in meats, are "incomplete," or low in one or more of the eight essential amino acids. Corn, for example, contains too little lysine to be considered a complete protein. But corn can be combined with lysine-rich vegetables like dried peas or limas to form a complete protein mix.

Our grandparents may have overcooked their vegetables, but they also came up with some inspired complementary combinations like succotash, baked beans, and cornbread, in which they hit exactly the correct combinations of foods to boost the protein value of the dish right up to the optimum level.

more about nutrition and protein sources today, we now realize that garden crops can easily constitute the backbone of any meal.

Protein-Packed Pods

The widely varied legume family, which includes clover and locust trees, contains plants such as peas, beans, and lentils, which are one of the best sources of vegetable proteins. The seeds of these pod-producing plants are packed with good nutrition.

Legumes are especially useful as garden plants because of their ability to fix nitrogen from the air, thus enriching your soil as well as your diet. Legume blossoms are self-pollinating, so you can save your own seed with little chance of cultivars crossing. Most important, many of the legumes, such as soybeans and peanuts, contain all eight of the essential amino acids, making them every bit as protein-complete as meat. Here are some of the ones I like best, all nutritious, easy to grow, and good to eat.

Adzuki Beans

These small, mahogany red beans with a rich, nutty flavor are a favorite in our family. One reason we like them so much is that they cook in just 30 minutes, without presoaking. One of our standby complete-protein meals in winter is a plate of adzukis with baked sweet potatoes, steamed kale, and buttered corn. Adzukis even make good sprouts, an especially good protein source.

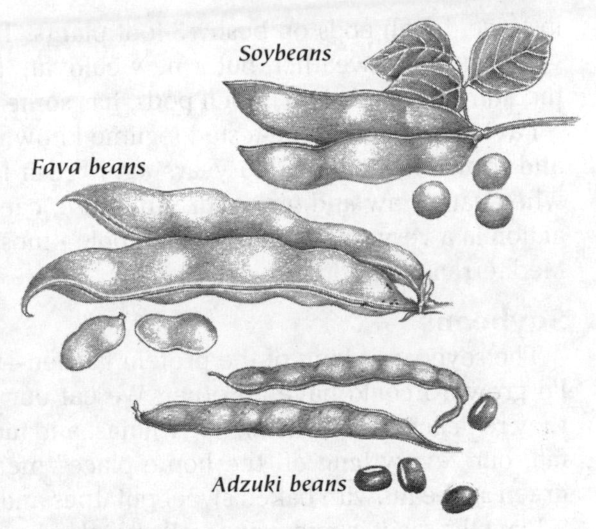

Tasty legumes are packed with protein—and flavor. Mahogany-colored adzuki beans have a nutty flavor, and large, flat fava beans taste almost like peas. Soybeans are delicious eaten fresh. Steam them until tender-crisp, then pop them from the pods into your mouth.

Although they are relatively new to American gardeners, adzuki beans have been eaten in Japan for at least 1,500 years. The earliest available cultivar, 'Adzuki Express', matures in 118 days. The plants are delicate looking when young, and the yellow blossoms appear rather late in summer, but they're soon followed by slender, 3- to 4-inch pods strung with small beans. They thrive in ordinary garden soil that is not highly alkaline. Our adzukis, growing next to a row of infested snap beans, seemed exempt from Mexican bean beetle damage.

Fava Beans

Fava beans, also called broad beans, produce the first shell beans of the season for northern gardeners. The plants survive frost well and bear best in a long, cool growing season, a quality that has made them popular in the Pacific Northwest, in England, and in parts of Canada.

Put the seeds in the ground at pea-planting time, and in 75 days or so you'll be eating the large, flat, pea-flavored shell beans. Favas grow in large, tough pods on bushy 3-foot plants. The beans usually quit growing in hot weather, but a new cultivar, 'Ipro', which produces medium-size seeds in 5½-inch pods, has some heat resistance.

Fava beans are a time-tested legume known to the early Romans and grown in China 5,000 years ago. Fresh fava beans, especially when eaten raw and green, or immature, can cause an allergic reaction in a very small minority of people—most commonly, males of Mediterranean heritage.

Soybeans

The soybean is king of the protein garden—the one protein plant I'd grow if I could have no other. We eat our soybeans green, and they're delicious—like lean, nutty limas, and much easier to grow. In fall, our "everything off the home place" meal includes a plate of green soybeans with baked sweet potatoes and sliced ripe tomatoes.

Plant the seeds in midspring well after the danger of frost has passed, spacing seeds 1½ to 2 inches apart in rows at least 15 inches apart. Soybeans aren't particular about soil. Ours have never been damaged by the Mexican bean beetle, and although a few Japanese beetles have found their way to the patch, they've done little damage. For green soybeans, pick the pods as soon as the beans swell. The green harvest generally lasts two to three weeks. Any beans remaining on the plants may be left on to dry completely and used as seeds or for soup.

Our favorite cultivar for fresh green shell beans is 'Butterbeans', which matures in 90 days. 'Envy', at 75 days, may be a good choice for gardens with a short growing season, but the beans are smaller and the yield is limited. Both 'Fiskeby V', a 91-day variety, and 'Altona', at 100 days, have yellow beans when dried, which are good for soup and baking. Their beans are also perfectly fine for eating green.

For longer growing seasons, 'Panther', at 120 days, is a black soy that has an especially fine flavor when dried.

An Easy Alternative to Meat

Without trying too hard you can consume as much as one-fourth of your daily minimum protein requirement from fresh garden produce alone. Have some cornbread, hot whole-grain cereal, soybeans

EAT YOUR BROCCOLI, TOO

Surprising as it may seem, some garden foods we thought we were eating just for vitamins, minerals, fiber, or flavor turn out to be respectable sources of small amounts of protein. So give yourself credit for the broccoli and brussels sprouts you eat.

VEGETABLE	GRAMS OF PROTEIN*
Adzuki beans (raw)	20.0
Asparagus (cooked)	2.2
Beet greens (raw)	2.2
Broccoli (cooked)	3.1
Brussels sprouts (cooked)	4.2
Cabbage (raw)	1.3
Cauliflower (raw)	2.7
Chard (cooked, drained)	1.8
Chervil (raw)	3.4
Collards (cooked, stems removed)	3.6
Corn, sweet, white and yellow (cooked)	3.2
Dandelion greens (raw)	2.7
Fava beans (green, raw)	8.5
Green beans (cooked)	1.6
Kale (cooked, without stems or midribs)	4.5
Peanuts (raw, no skins)	26.3
Peas (green, cooked)	5.4
Pumpkin seeds (dried)	29.0
Soybeans (dried, cooked)	11.0
Soybeans (green, cooked)	9.8
Spinach (raw)	3.2
Sunflower seeds (dried)	24.0

SOURCE: Based on tables in *Handbook of the Nutritional Contents of Foods.* Washington, D.C.: United States Department of Agriculture, 1975.

*Per 100-gram portion.

in soup, and sunflower seeds and peanuts for snacking, and you won't need much milk, cheese, or meat to bring your protein intake up to the recommended level.

Give your vegetables a starring role from time to time. Garden proteins have been playing bit parts at the dinner table for far too long.

A SERVING OF SOYBEANS

Fresh soybeans, cooked until tender-crisp, are so good they don't need butter or sauces. I like to pile a mound of steamed pods on my plate, as the Japanese do, and squeeze the pods and pop the beans right into my mouth.

To prepare green soybeans for a meal, steam the pods no longer than 5 to 8 minutes in a covered kettle. If soybeans are steamed too long, the stiff membrane that lines the pod separates and complicates the shelling process. Spread the steamed soys on a cookie sheet to cool. Squeeze the pods to pop the beans out into a dish. After the soys have been steamed and shelled, simmer them for another 20 to 30 minutes before serving. Or freeze them at this point, and cook again just before serving. They never get mushy.

Dried soybeans contain as much as 40 percent protein, are easy to store, and are exceptionally versatile. I've included them in baked beans and chili, using about one-fourth soybeans. They're good in soups and stews, too. Soak the dried beans overnight, then simmer over low heat for a few hours until tender.

CHAPTER EIGHT

Zip Through Hedge Trimming

While driving through area neighborhoods recently, I noticed that overgrown hedges are quite common. Perhaps there's one in your yard. Probably you inherited it from a former owner who wasn't sure how to tame it either. Reshaping an overgrown hedge can add a lot to the attractiveness of your home grounds, and perhaps even inspire your neighbors to keep their hedges under control.

When we were new homeowners, our gardening mentor—a neighbor whose privet hedges were similar to ours—advised us to prune three times a year: Memorial Day, Fourth of July, and Labor Day. His rule of thumb turned out to be just right. We found that if we followed approximately this schedule, the hedges stayed in good shape.

Most species of privet (*Ligustrum* spp.) respond well to this pruning schedule. Some other kinds of popular shrubs prefer less frequent shearing. In general, aim for two to three trimmings a year for yews (*Taxus* spp.); one to two trimmings for barberry (*Berberis* spp.), arborvitae (*Thuja* spp.), and hemlock (*Tsuga* spp.); and a single clipping for boxwood (*Buxus* spp.).

Avoid drastic shearing of flowering shrubs such as forsythia, flowering quince (*Chaenomeles* spp.), and azalea (*Rhododendron* spp.). If you are lucky enough to have a flowering hedge, maintain it in a natural shape. Keep these shrubs in bounds with judicious thinning and an occasional pruning of top growth.

The Hedge Barber's Tools

The classic tool for trimming is the hedge shears, with 8-inch blades set in 10- to 12-inch handles. Keep them sharpened. Even people who use electric or cordless trimmers to cut their hedges sometimes revert to the hand-powered tool for accurate shaping of corners. If the hedge is badly overgrown and you must cut branches thicker than 1 inch in diameter, use a pruning

Taper your hedges so they're wider at bottom than at top. This allows sunlight to reach lower branches, keeping them leafy and vigorous. Trim the top first, then work down. Eyeball the slant of the sides as you go.

SAVE AN OVERGROWN HEDGE

The secret of renovating a neglected hedge is to proceed gradually, improving the hedge's form a bit more each time you clip it. Pruning the branches will keep the shrubbery within bounds and encourage thicker growth.

To reshape an out-of-bounds hedge, you may need to cut back some woody old growth. For shrubs like privet, follow the Memorial Day–Fourth of July–Labor Day schedule and add a fourth clipping during the growing season, or even a fifth if you live in the South. If you must trim back some of the top of the hedge, make the first cut of the season in early spring, before new growth appears. Check a pruning manual or your local nursery for recommendations on renovating other shrubs.

saw. It will make a cleaner cut that heals more readily than one made by lopping shears or carpenter's saw.

Take a few extra minutes to be sure you're operating your equipment safely. If you use a ladder, place it on firm, even ground. If your clipper is electric, plan your work so that the cord won't be in your way. More than one unfortunate homeowner has been known to slice the cord while concentrating on the hedge.

Four Steps to a Neat Hedge

Most of the branches you clip in maintenance pruning will be tender, green new growth. Just how short a haircut does your hedge need? It depends on how fast your hedge species regrows. Remove most of the new growth on a privet hedge, leaving ½ to 1 inch of new growth, just enough to make a lush, green surface. Cut slower-growing evergreens with a lighter hand than the fast-recovering privet. On a hemlock hedge, for example, leave about 2 inches of new growth. Once you begin a regular maintenance schedule, you'll soon get a feel for how much is enough.

For a neatly clipped hedge, follow these four easy steps.

1. Shape the top of the hedge first. Always start clipping at the top

and work down, so you can more easily keep the top surface a uniform width. If your area receives a lot of snow, consider rounding the top of the hedge, rather than cutting it straight across, to distribute the weight of the snow more evenly.

2. Taper the hedge so that it's wider at the bottom than on the top. A narrow top surface, flaring down to a wider base, will permit sun to reach the lower part of the hedge. A wider-bottomed hedge will be more stable, too, and less likely to be broken by a heavy load of snow.
3. Keep the sides flat and even, smoothly widening to the base. Try to avoid making gouges or wavy cuts. Start cutting at one end of the hedge rather than in the middle, and eyeball the slant of the sides as you go. Some gardeners make a slightly more pronounced slant on the north side of the hedge, tapering to a slightly wider base on that side, so that more sun will reach the lower branches, but this is an optional nicety.
4. Bases of top-heavy hedges are usually scraggly and often bare of leaves because they receive too little light. To stimulate the growth of new side branches, shear the bottom branches very lightly—by ½ inch or so. Just nip off the tips. If the hedge is very skimpy, it will take several seasons to develop the bushy shape you're aiming for, but gradually, as the bottom branches are allowed to form twiglets, the hedge will begin to green up near the ground.

Repeat cutting at intervals throughout the growing season. Shape the hedge with each trimming, keeping that ideal hedge shape—narrow on top, wide at the bottom—in your mind's eye. Maintaining a regular cutting schedule will keep the hedge under control and make your pruning job easier. And, if you follow our neighbor's rule of thumb, cutting on Memorial Day, Fourth of July, and Labor Day, you'll always have a good appetite for those summer holiday picnics!

CHAPTER NINE

Treat Yourself to Shallots

Back in the Middle Ages, shallots so impressed the Crusaders that they hauled bags of the bulbs back to Europe from the Middle East. The explorer Hernando de Soto loved the little alliums' piquant taste so much, he introduced them to the New World. Today, gourmet cooks spend up to four dollars a pound for them.

But gardeners don't have to go to great lengths for the special taste of shallots. If you can raise onions or garlic, you can grow shallots.

In fact, some gardeners have found that shallots and other multiplier onions give a more consistent crop than seed-grown onions. The sets cost more than garlic or onion sets, but you can save and replant your bulbs, so future crops cost no more than your time.

Success with Shallots

Shallots are more than little onions, and growing them requires some special techniques. Like garlic, they produce a cluster of bulbs from each "set," or single bulb, you plant. Each shallot set produces 10 to 20 mature bulbs.

Elegant little shallots cook to melting tenderness in just a few minutes, adding a sweet oniony flavor to soups, sauces, and other dishes. A single bulb can form 12 to 15 new offsets in a season, so planting 20 bulbs will give you plenty for cooking and enough for keeping for next year's crop.

Shallots are hardier than onions and produce the largest bulbs when planted in fall and overwintered. But early spring planting is a good way to start your first crop of sweet, tender shallots. They'll be ready for picking in July or August.

Plant shallots in well-drained loam high in organic matter, in full sun. Space the sets about 6 to 8 inches apart, and poke them about an inch into the ground.

Selecting Shallots

Dutch shallots are prolific, easy to grow, and good keepers. The yellow-fleshed bulbs have been known to form 12 to 15 new offsets for each bulb planted. If you buy graded bulbs, you'll get 18 to 20 sets in a 10-ounce order. This is a good type for spring planting.

'Pear', 'Frog's Legs', or 'Brittany' shallots are elongated and extra

SUN-KISSED SKIN

Shallots like to feel the sun on their skins. Firm the soil around the sets well, but don't bury them. Just settle them into the soil. As the bulbs develop, keep the soil pulled away. By the time the bulbs mature, they should be fully exposed. Shallots that are too deeply covered form thick necks, and the bulbs fail to keep well.

large. These good keepers should be planted only in the fall. Spring-planted bulbs don't grow as large. In fertile soil, these shallots can produce 15 bulbs for each one planted, though a 5-to-1 ratio is more common.

French shallots are the type most people think of as gourmet shallots. Their skin is a rather dull brown, sometimes with a rosy cast. They are known for their distinctive flavor and are usually more expensive than other kinds. But they are very poor keepers that tend to dry out in storage. Such bulbs are usually adequate for planting even if they're not firm enough for eating. French shallots are good for spring planting. 'French Red' shallots are similar except for their reddish pink skin.

'Odetta's White' shallots are a recently rediscovered heirloom strain that had been kept in the same family for three generations. The pure white bulbs are only about ⅞ inch in diameter. They have a delicate flavor and are good pickled as well as cooked. 'Odetta's White' keeps well enough to replant, but the bulbs tend to dry out when stored for a longer time, probably because they are so small.

Harvesting and Using Tender Shallots

When most of the tops have dried and bent over, dig the bulb clusters, keeping them intact. To cure the bulbs, shake excess soil from the roots and spread the shallot clusters on a screen in a warm, dry, well-ventilated place for about two weeks. Then package the bulbs in paper bags and keep them in a cool, dry place (35 to 40°F and 60 to 70 percent relative humidity) for winter use. Avoid damp basements; too much moisture will promote spoilage.

Eat the largest bulbs and use the smaller ones for replanting. Plan to set aside about one-seventh of the crop as sets for the next year. Plant about two-thirds of your sets in the early fall, to give the bulbs time to establish roots before the ground freezes. Save the rest for spring planting, in case a hard winter kills off the fall-planted ones. Where winter temperatures fall as low as 0°F, or where the ground repeatedly thaws and refreezes, hill up 6 to 8 inches of loose soil over fall-planted shallots after the ground freezes. Remove the extra soil early in the spring.

Shallots are valued for their subtle, delicate onion flavor and for their ability to cook to a melting tenderness in only a few minutes. They meld readily with other ingredients in a quickly assembled sauce. Their present-day reputation as a subtle flavor enhancer and an elegant little vegetable fits the long, noble history of these palate-pleasing bulbs. Sometimes it seems to me that only the gardener knows how accessible such elegance can be.

CHAPTER TEN

Plan a Pumpkin Patch

Once grown primarily for food, pumpkins have become a fun crop. These days, garden-raised pumpkins are more likely to end up as jack-o'-lanterns than as pies. Fortunately, you can easily have it both ways: Carving pumpkins and eating pumpkins grow on the same vine. Good multipurpose cultivars are plentiful. You can also buy seed for tiny, palm-size decorative pumpkins or for huge specimens that can grow too heavy to lift. Some pumpkins contain hull-less seeds that need no shelling. All pumpkin seeds are edible.

Most pumpkin vines are galloping plants that by midsummer can cover a 12- to 25-square-foot area with their hollow-stemmed, thick vines and large leaves. If you're short of space, plant your pumpkins around the compost pile, at the edge of your corn patch, or in the corner of the garden. Or try one of the bush or semibush cultivars, such as 'Funny Face' or 'Spirit', which produce fine pumpkins on compact vines.

Pumpkins come in all sizes, from a jumbo type too heavy to lift to a mini-pumpkin that fits in your hand. If you're short of space, plant the vigorous vines around the compost pile or at the edge of the corn patch. Or try a semibush cultivar, with good-size pumpkins on compact vines.

Pumpkin Pointers

In addition to space, pumpkins need good soil, full sun, and adequate drainage. Well-aerated soil with a good supply of humus will encourage the strong roots necessary to support all those long vines, large leaves, and heavy fruits—so pile on the compost!

Pumpkin plants are tender and sappy, easily killed by frost. Most cultivars need 90 to 110 days of mild weather. Fortunately for northern gardeners, pumpkins don't require warm nights as their cousins the melons do. If you live in a short-season area, plant seeds indoors and set the seedlings out in the garden when the danger of frost is past. Use cell packs or small individual pots so their roots won't be disturbed when they're planted out. Keep young transplants cozy by covering them with a floating row cover until they blossom. (Once blossoms form, remove the cover so bees can pollinate the flowers.)

Here in south-central Pennsylvania, USDA Zone 6, I plant pumpkin seeds in late May I presprout the seeds in damp paper towels, kept warm on top of the electric water heater, before putting them in the ground. Hull-less seeds are prone to rotting in cool soil so use this method to give your seeds a better chance to sprout.

Pumpkin Pests

Pumpkin plants are satisfying to grow because they're so vigorous. They can be laid low by insect pests, though. Two of their worst enemies are the squash bug and the squash-vine borer.

GROW A GIANT

Start with seed with the genetic potential to grow large pumpkins. 'Atlantic Giant' and 'Big Max' are two good cultivars. The current world record is over 800 pounds. The thick-fleshed fruits grow huge if you pamper them and have good weather. Here are some tips for growing a big one.

- Encourage healthy root growth by digging deeply, adding compost, and mulching.
- Space plants 20 feet apart. They'll need lots of room to roam.
- Protect young plants from wind and frost.
- Pick off all blossoms until mid-July so the vine can grow large before setting fruit.
- Try to avoid pruning. Leaves are food producers; each plant leaf can nourish up to 4 pounds of fruit.
- Allow no more than one pumpkin to remain on each of the plant's vines.
- Feed the plant manure tea or other liquid fertilizer every ten days during late August and September.
- Forget about the myth that feeding pumpkin plants milk by inserting a wick into a slit in the stem yields giant fruit. Howard Dill, a champion pumpkin grower in Canada, maintains that milk feeding is not an effective way to increase pumpkin size, especially as the wound may promote disease.
- After the fruit reaches basketball size, water generously—at least once a week.

Squash bugs—flat, shield-shaped, ½-inch-long insects that may be gray or brown to black—swarm over the undersides of the leaves, sucking out vital juices. Use handpicking and insecticidal soap to deter squash bugs, or in severe infestations, try rotenone or sabadilla dust. Thoroughly cultivate around the garden edges and destroy vines at the end of the season.

If a vigorous runner or vine suddenly wilts, suspect the squash-vine borer. Borers, the white, 1-inch-long larvae of small moths that laid their eggs on the stems, can cause a vine to wilt overnight. Use floating row covers to protect young plants. When you see the telltale wilting vine, check the stem carefully for the entrance hole of the borer. Poke a flexible wire into the hole to kill the borer. Some gardeners have success with injecting parasitic nematodes into the stem to kill borers before they can damage plants.

A Pumpkin Sampler

Pumpkin growers can choose from dozens of cultivars, including these favorites. All are good for eating, and most, except those that are too flat or too small, are suitable for carving.

'Atlantic Giant'. 120 days. Developed by Howard Dill of Windsor, Nova Scotia, a grower of record-breaking pumpkins that have reached almost 500 pounds.

'Big Max'. 120 days. May grow to 100 pounds or more, with 3- to 4-inch-thick flesh, pinkish orange skin.

'Big Moon'. 110 days. Pumpkins too heavy to lift; may reach 200 pounds or more.

'Connecticut Field'. 105 days. Good for both pies and lanterns. Average 15 to 25 pounds but can weigh up to 50 pounds. An heirloom cultivar.

'Funny Face'. 100 days. Semibush vine (half the size of standard vines) produces 10- to 15-pound fruit with uniform shape and color.

'Jack Be Little'. 85 days. Ornamental, deeply grooved, 3 to 4 inches in diameter, edible flesh (but not much of it!).

'Rouge Vif D'Etampes'. 110 days. Flattened, deeply ribbed fruit can grow to 18 inches in diameter but stays 6 inches high. Fine flavor and good for storage. An heirloom cultivar, more than 100 years old.

'Small Sugar'. 95 to 100 days. Round 4- to 5-pound fruit keeps well, makes good pies. Good yield. An heirloom cultivar.

PICKING DO'S AND DON'TS

Follow these guidelines when it's time to harvest.

- Do cut pumpkins from the vine. Pulling may break the stem.
- Do pick fruit before temperature goes below 30°F.
- Do handle gently to prevent bruising.
- Do gather green-streaked pumpkins along with the orange ones. Green pumpkins will turn orange after harvest.
- Don't carry a pumpkin by the stem. It may break, and damaged flesh invites spoilage.
- Don't leave fruit exposed to a hard freeze. A light frost won't hurt it, though.
- Don't store immature or broken-skinned fruit. Use it soon after picking.

'Spirit'. 90 days. Hybrid, compact vine produces medium-size oval fruit.
'Spookie'. 110 days. Smooth, uniform, hard flesh. Good yield. 6- to 7-inch fruit.
'Trick-or-Treat'. 105 days. Semibush vine covers 12 to 15 square feet of ground, produces 12-pound fruit, taller than it is wide, with hull-less seeds.

One legend has it that, after midnight on Halloween, pumpkins become airborne and dance in the dark over the fields. I've never seen that ritual display of high spirits, but I do know that pumpkins on the porch and pies on the table make fine sights, too.

CHAPTER ELEVEN

Save Space with Bush Vegetables

One of my favorite stories as a child was "The Quick-Running Squash," by Alicia Aspinwall. It was about a small boy who plants a special squash seed given him by an odd and raggedy-looking stranger. The squash germinates immediately after the boy plants it and grows by leaps and bounds across the countryside. No animated film could have made that squash bump along as lustily as it did in my imagination, growing larger, wartier, and deeper orange as its vine stretched for miles, impossibly straddled, the whole time, by the boy who is determined not to let his special squash get away from him. Of course, the vine gallops back to the boy's own garden, where its huge fruit comes to rest by the garden wall. Finally, the squash, victim of its own exuberant vitality, bursts into pieces, and the neighborhood feasts on squash pie for a week.

Much later, when I began to plant a garden of my own, I decided that the author of that story must have been a gardener, too. Anyone who has planted a melon and watched it appropriate half of the vegetable patch will attest to the vine's remarkable ability to spread. Squash, pumpkin, cucumber, cantaloupe, and watermelon—all members of the Cucurbitaceae—are roamers, often considered too space hungry for the small garden.

These rampant vines have recently been tamed through the development of bush cultivars. Even if you have plenty of ground, perhaps you'd like to grow several different kinds of cucumbers in the space formerly occupied by a single plant. Or you might want to raise cantaloupes on the patio. Bush vegetables are worth a try.

Modern Science at Work

How does a bush vegetable plant differ from one that stretches its full length across the garden? The vine is both truncated and telescoped. By crossbreeding and selection, scientists have produced plants with what they call shorter internodes—less space between the leaves.

Some (but not all) bush plants have a more "determinate" habit than their rangier cousins; that is, they tend to grow, blossom, and fruit for a limited time. Indeterminate plants, on the other hand, keep bearing until killed by frost. Some bush cultivars start to bear earlier, and most produce full-size fruits, although there are a few cultivars that yield somewhat smaller than average fruits.

Pros—and a Few Cons

Although a few bush vegetables do produce quite early, the main reason for growing them is to save garden space. Those that form

Bush cultivars of cucumbers, squash, and melons are a good choice for smaller gardens or containers. The 'Salad Bush' cucumber shown here bears a good crop of full-size crunchy cukes in only a fraction of the space you'd need for long-vine forms.

true bushes, with no wandering vines at all, may be somewhat easier to cultivate. And container gardeners, who would not have known where to drape a 40-foot vine, can now raise a melon or two in a pot on a sunny patio.

Production per plant is usually less than that of full-size vines. But bush cultivars can be planted closer together, bringing the average production per square foot of garden space of many bush vegetables close or even equal to that of their long-vined counterparts. (Some commercial growers find the bush squash sufficiently productive and easy to cultivate that they plant them by the acre.)

Some gardeners feel that bush vegetables are inferior in flavor, a problem that some vegetable specialists blame on the smaller amount of leaf surface the plants possess. Other researchers think genetics has more to do with fruit flavor than total leaf area does. Cucumbers seem to suffer less flavor loss when grown in bush form than larger fruits like squash and watermelon. Look for catalog descriptions of cultivars, like the 'Musketeer' melon, that emphasize good flavor. Soil that's high in organic matter tends to encourage better flavor, so dig in mulch, manure, or compost, or use cover crops to add more humus to your soil.

Best of the Crop

Plant breeders are still working on bush cultivars, so check your seed catalogs for the latest offerings. Here are some time-tested bush vegetables.

Cantaloupes

'Honeybush'. 82 days. Plants cover 5 to 7 square feet, produce 2- to 3-pound, good-quality fruit with small seed cavities.
'Minnesota Midget'. 75 days. 4-inch fruit grows on short, 3-foot vines.
'Musketeer'. 90 days. Short, bushy vines spread 2 to 3 feet, produce 5- to 6-inch fruit. Yield is on the low side but flavor is good.

Cucumbers

'Bush Champion'. 60 days. Short vines produce well-formed fruit. Mosaic resistant, but susceptible to powdery mildew, so grow it as an early crop.

A MATTER OF SEMANTICS

Bushiness is a relative term; some bush plants are more compact than others. In test plantings at the University of Idaho, 'Jersey Golden Acorn' squash covered 25 square feet of ground while 'Table Queen Bush' occupied only 16 square feet. Both are space savers, though, compared with 'Hubbard', which spread across 100 square feet of garden space. 'Hubbard' is a fine old squash and a better keeper than either of these bush cultivars. For those who have room, 'Hubbard' may be a very good choice. But for gardeners who till a small- to medium-size patch, bush cultivars might mean the difference between some squash and no squash.

'Bush Pickle'. 46 days. Good fruit quality on a short plant.
'Patio Pick'. 58 days. Pickle young cukes and slice larger ones. Plant is very compact.
'Pot Luck'. 60 days. 6- to 7-inch cukes on 18-inch vines. Mosaic tolerant. Good for containers or borders.
'Salad Bush'. 57 days. Vines grow only 2 to 3 feet long, produce 8-inch cukes.

Watermelons

'Baby Fun'. 82 days. Semibush vines (about half the size of standard vines) produce medium-size, somewhat oval, sweet melons.
'Bush Baby II'. 80 days. Dwarf plants produce round, juicy melons up to 10 pounds each.
'Garden Baby'. 70 days. Earlier than 'Sugar Baby' but has similar fruit, shorter vines.

Winter Squash

'Burpee's Butterbush'. 75 days. An early butternut-type squash. Needs 3 square feet of ground and produces 1½-pound fruit with short necks.
'Cream of the Crop'. 85 days. Plants are bushy and compact, producing acorn-type squash with creamy pale flesh.
'Gold Nugget'. 85 days. Small 1- to 2-pound orange fruit on 2½-foot vines. The slightly flattened squash keep well.
'Table King'. 75 days. Bush plants bear full-size, acorn-type squash.

PLANTS IN A POT

Bush cultivars are well suited to container planting. How else could the city gardener raise cucumbers or cantaloupes on the patio or balcony? Container-grown plants, however, demand extra care. Water them daily or every other day in hot summer sun, and feed weekly with a liquid fertilizer such as fish emulsion or liquid kelp.

Tips for Bush Leaguers

A little attention to details will help you get the most out of bush cultivars. Here are some innovative ideas.

- Preventing fruit set until the plant is more mature may lead to a bigger harvest, according to Dr. John Scarchuk of the University of Connecticut. He suggests removing the first female flowers (look for a swollen area, an actual tiny fruit, at the base of the blossom) to slow down fruit set by two to four weeks. "Although the fruit will mature later, the total yield will be greater from the resulting larger and more mature plant than from the younger, less mature plant," says Dr. Scarchuk.
- For top-quality bush vegetables, pinch off excess blossoms. In tests at Cornell University, flavor was better from vines bearing three squash than from those allowed to form six. This makes sense when you remember that leaves make sugars for the fruit.
- Warm soil is critical for good flavor in melons. Mulch your bush cantaloupes and watermelons with black plastic.
- Set ripening fruits on upended cans in the garden, to warm them a bit more—a trick I learned from gardener Dick Raymond, who grows melons in Vermont.
- Remove all blossoms and even some tiny fruits from winter squash and cantaloupes at the end of August to allow the vine to concentrate on the fruits that have a chance to ripen before frost.

CHAPTER TWELVE

Plant Some Blueberries

More than 30 years ago, we planted three blueberry bushes in the yard of our old house in Philadelphia. Those same bushes, transplanted to a neighbor's yard when we moved away, are still producing fruit. They've borne hundreds of quarts of berries, and they're still going strong. And you know what a wonderful fruit the blueberry is: dusky blue, juicy, sweet . . . associated with such delectable treats as pancakes, pie, and jam, but never better than when eaten fresh, swimming in milk.

Wild blueberries have been around for eons. American Indians depended on them and made a food they called "sauta thig" from dried pulverized blueberries mixed with parched meal (probably cornmeal). Cultivated blueberries are newcomers, the result of an early twentieth century collaboration between cranberry grower Elizabeth White and USDA botanist Frederick Coville. White, after observing natural variations in size, productivity, and flavor in wild highbush blueberries near her New Jersey home, offered Coville her help and the use of some of her land for his experiments in selecting and breeding improved varieties and cultivars of blueberries. Coville released his first selected variety in 1908, and 12 years later offered his first hybrids.

Today's cultivated highbush blueberries have marble-size fruit (and some even larger) and are more productive than their wild ancestors. While wild blueberries may have a more intense flavor than most cultivated ones, they're not nearly as accessible to most of us. I grew up picking wild blueberries on summer vacations in Maine, and they were wonderful, but the cultivated berries still taste mighty good to me.

Keeping Blueberries Happy

Cultivated highbush blueberries range in height from 4 to 8 feet, with an average of 5 to 6 feet. Dwarf cultivars, as short as 15 inches, are also available. Blueberries are beautiful in fruit, with dusky blue clusters of berries hanging heavy on fine twiggy branches. The blossoms, resembling the bells of lily-of-the-valley, are lovely, too, and the glossy pointed leaves are even more beautiful when they turn deep scarlet in the fall.

Blueberries have more exacting soil requirements than most garden vegetables and tree fruits, but the conditions they need are not difficult to provide. First, they must have acid soil, with a pH of 4.0 to 5.0. If mountain laurels (*Kalmia latifolia*), rhododendrons, and azaleas (*Rhododendron* spp.) thrive in your area, your soil should be acid enough for blueberries.

If you're not sure, use a soil test to check pH. To acidify soil with a pH of 6.0 to 7.0, add powdered sulfur at the rate of 1 pound to 100 square feet for sandy loam, or ¼ pound per plant. Use up to twice as much sulfur for heavy soil. Double the application rate for soil with a pH of 7.0 to 7.5.

Highbush blueberries make a good hedge or ornamental shrub—with a delicious bonus. They're beautiful in spring, with dainty white blossoms; in summer, with clusters of dusky blue berries; and in fall, with their glossy, scarlet leaves.

Blueberry bushes like moist, well-drained soil with a high humus content. Because their roots are thready and fibrous, they don't do as well in heavy clay soil. If your soil is dense clay, build a raised bed for your blueberry bushes.

To produce fruit, highbush blueberries need at least 6 hours of sun a day during the growing season, and at least 700 hours of cold below 40 °F during the winter. Check with your local extension service to find out which cultivars are best adapted to your area.

Spacing Plants

You could plant highbush blueberries at the edge of a backyard garden, as a hedge, along a wall, or even as a foundation planting near the house. Although blueberry blossoms are self-fertile, you'll get more berries, and they'll be larger and earlier to ripen, if you plant at least two different cultivars for cross-pollination.

Space the bushes about 5 feet apart. If you opt for a whole plantation of blueberries, make the rows 8 to 10 feet apart. Plant dwarf cultivars 3 to 4 feet apart.

Ready to Plant?

Follow these steps to get your blueberries off to a good start.

1. Dig a hole 10 to 12 inches deep. Mix the soil from the hole with

BEST OF THE BLUES

There are many good cultivars of blueberries. To extend the season, choose early, midseason, and late cultivars. Here are some that frequently appear in mail-order nursery catalogs.

'Berkeley'. 5 to 6 feet high. Midseason, vigorous, productive, good keeper, very large berries.
'Bluecrop'. 4 to 6 feet high. Midseason, very hardy, very productive.
'Blueray'. 4 to 6 feet high. Early to midseason, very hardy, vigorous, tart/sweet.
'Earliblue'. 5 feet high. Early, vigorous, large sweet berries.
'Herbert'. 4 to 6 feet high. Late, vigorous, large berries, excellent flavor.
'Ivanhoe'. 4 to 5 feet high. Early, vigorous, productive, sweet berries.
'Jersey'. 5 to 8 feet high. Late, vigorous, productive, very hardy. Tart at first, sweet when allowed to ripen fully on bush.
'Northblue'. 2 to 3 feet high. Large leaves, productive, a good landscape plant. Hardy to −30°F.
'Northsky'. 15 inches high. Very hardy, to −40°F. Good for container growing and foundation planting.
'Ornablue'. 4 feet high. Very productive, dark blue berries, thick growth, symmetrical form. Good for ornamental planting.
'Rubel'. 5 to 7 feet high. Late, very hardy, vigorous, small berries, excellent flavor. The only one of White's original selections from the wild that is still offered commercially.

damp peat moss and compost, and fill the hole three-fourths full with this amended soil.

2. Set the bush in the hole and spread the roots. If you buy potted blueberry plants, loosen the roots and soil with your fingers or a fork to encourage the roots to grow outward. Set the plant out at the same level as it was grown in the nursery. (If you look closely at the stem of a bareroot plant, you'll be able to tell where the soil

level was.) Blueberry roots are so fine that they don't like to be deeply buried.

3. Water the bushes well at planting time, two to three times a week for the first two weeks, and weekly after that if rain is scanty. You don't need to prune at planting time, unless the bushes have broken or bruised branches that need to be removed.

Caring for blueberries is easy. Mulch the plants with aged sawdust, pine needles, straw, wood chips, or leaves to control weeds, retain moisture, and keep the roots cool. Because the bushes have such fine roots growing so close to the soil surface, cultivating close to the bushes can damage them—another good reason for mulching. To keep the soil rich and light textured, spread some compost around the bushes each year. Reapply sulfur or another acidifying agent every three years or so.

Remove fruit buds from the bushes for the first year or two after planting, to permit the bush to gather strength for abundant fruiting

FOR SOUTHERN GARDENS

If you live in the South or the West where winters aren't cold enough to encourage fruiting in the cultivated highbush blueberry, you can plant rabbiteye blueberries. Rabbiteyes, which need a shorter cold period, are good choices for the Gulf Coast, Georgia, northern Florida, west to Texas and Arkansas, north to Tennessee, and in southern California. They're less fussy about soil acidity than regular highbush blueberries. And as you might expect, they're not as hardy.

Rabbiteye blueberry bushes can grow to 15 feet high, so you might need to cut them back to encourage bushy growth that is within arm's reach. Plant the bushes 6 feet apart, and if you're ambitious enough to set out rows of them, space the rows 12 feet apart. Plant at least two different cultivars of rabbiteyes for cross-pollination because they are not self-fertile. 'Premier', 'Powderblue', and 'Tifblue' are just some of the cultivars available.

later on. (Fruit buds, which grow at the tips of the previous year's growth, are plump, in contrast to the more pointed leaf buds.)

Light pruning keeps blueberry bushes productive. The best time for pruning is late winter, before new growth begins. Starting about three years after planting, cut back the two or three weakest or least productive branches on each bush every year. If you're like me, you won't always get around to pruning every year. It's also fine to prune every other year, removing three to four branches each time.

Blueberries don't have much trouble with insects or diseases. If you do notice berries shriveling before they ripen, or new growth dying back, the problem may be mummyberry, caused by a fungus. Remove and burn infected berries. Prevention is best: Clear up debris under the bush and provide for good air circulation, that low-tech defense against fungal diseases.

Picking Time

A mature blueberry bush can yield 3 to 6 quarts of fresh fruit a year. Picking highbush blueberries is easy and fun—no thorns, no stooping. Some cultivars turn blue a few days before they are fully ripe, so try to let them hang on a bit to get the best flavor. You might need to protect your bushes from birds, who also know what's good. Cover them with netting as soon as the berries start to color up.

No one needs to be told what to do with a quart of blueberries: Of course you ate some as you picked. What's left can make a meal memorable, appearing as blueberry pie, cobbler, coffee cake, muffins, or breads. I even have a recipe for chicken salad that includes blueberries. The berries keep for several weeks in the refrigerator, in wide-mouth jars or other covered containers. Blueberries are a carefree fruit—no peeling, no pitting. Enjoy them!

CHAPTER THIRTEEN

Color Eggs with Natural Dyes

In ancient times, Egyptians dyed eggs as a rite of spring, and people in Persia gave each other gift eggs to celebrate spring. The custom of dyeing eggs, probably brought back to Europe by the Crusaders, was expanded in Germany to involve a generous rabbit and hidden surprises for children and was brought to the United States by German immigrants. All those years, until commercial dyes were developed in the nineteenth century, people colored eggs with whatever roots, berries, leaves, and flowers they could find around them. When my husband was a boy in eastern Poland, his family would use onion skins and beet juice to color Easter eggs.

It seems to be especially appropriate to color eggs, the symbols of renewal and new life, with plant materials rather than with chemical dyes. The bright, clear colors of commercial food color dyes are attractive, but they often penetrate the eggshell and tint the egg white, too. Natural dyes, on the other hand, can come from foods we eat every day. Their subtle colors blend well with a variety of settings. Eggs dyed in these muted hues look lovely in a nest or basket of natural vines, on pottery plates, or in wooden bowls. Sometimes the egg takes on a coloring or mottling that resembles a real bird's egg.

Natural Dye Materials

You probably have on hand some of the foods that produce good egg colors, and you can find the rest at your grocery store. Try some of these.

Blackberry shoots (growing tip and young leaves): light gray
Blueberries, frozen: light grayish blue
Red cabbage: blue
Red onion skins: light blue to purplish
Beets: raspberry color
Sassafras root, dried: orange
Paprika: light reddish brown
Coffee, instant: dark brown
Turmeric: yellow
Curly dock (*Rumex crispus*) roots: gold, yellow
Yellow onion skins: gold
Comfrey leaves: olive green

Sassafras root is often sold as tea. The trees are readily found in the wild. You can use freshly dug roots, too. While you might not have dock roots in your kitchen, the plant is a common perennial weed that sprouts in early spring in gardens and along roadsides. Curly dock has narrow leaves with crimped edges. Consult a field guide to be sure you've found the right plants.

Dyeing Naturally

You can dip already cooked eggs in the dyebath, steeping them until they reach the desired shade. For a deeper color, simmer uncooked eggs in the dyebath. If you plan to dip more than just a few eggs, double the recipe. Double or triple the recipe when simmering uncooked eggs, to be sure that each egg is covered with colored liquid.

Natural materials vary in the strength of color they produce. You may want to test-dye an egg or two, and then adjust the recipe accordingly. Allow the egg to dry before judging the color; hues may lighten when dried.

If your trial egg is slow to accept color, rub the remaining eggs with a solution of 1 tablespoon of vinegar in 1 cup of water. Also, to help the dye "take" better, you might try adding ½ teaspoon of white vinegar to each 2 cups of solution, especially for turmeric, beets, and sassafras. Alum, found on your supermarket spice shelves, will also enhance color. For good red cabbage dye, combine leaves with ½ teaspoon of alum in 2 cups of water.

Safe, natural plant dyes give pretty subtle hues and interesting marbled effects to colored eggs. Try paprika for a light reddish brown, young blackberry leaves for soft gray, or yellow onion skins for golden tones. Red cabbage yields a subtle blue. For deeper color, simmer uncooked eggs in the dyebath.

ANTIQUED EGGS

You can achieve a richly marbled, antiqued effect by wrapping eggs in onion skins or other plant materials. Tie each egg individually in a small piece of cheesecloth or nylon netting to keep the onion skins in place. Simmer as usual, turning frequently for more-even coloring. My favorites, I think, are the marbled old-gold eggs that result from dyeing with yellow onion skins.

This basic recipe will color about six eggs.

Ingredients

½ cup fresh plant material, chopped, or 1 heaping tablespoon dried or powdered plant material

2 cups water

6 eggs

1. To prepare the coloring solution, simmer the plant material in the water for about 30 minutes. Use non-reactive cookware like enamel, glass, or ceramic, rather than aluminum.
2. Strain out the cooked foodstuff and keep the solution hot.
3. For a light tint, dip hot, freshly boiled eggs in the solution and allow them to steep until they're colored to your satisfaction. Turn them several times while they're steeping so they'll color evenly. For deeper shades, use uncooked eggs and simmer them gently in the hot dyebath for 10 to 20 minutes, turning them every few minutes.

Experiment with different concentrations and cooking times and try other highly colored foods, too, to see what happens. Happy egging!

PART TWO

Now is the heyday of summer; everything voluptuously in growth. It is the full, warm, robust middle age of the year. . . .

—David Grayson (1870–1946)

SUMMER

CHAPTER FOURTEEN

Gather Garden Herbs to Dry

Harvesting herbs is one of the gentle delights of midsummer. We take pleasure in the spicy fragrance of the sun-warmed plants and appreciate their varying textures as we move among them, snipping and plucking. Whether you gather herbs by the handful or the armload, you'll be glad next winter that you saved some of this summer's abundance. Rosemary on the roast, thyme in the stuffing, savory in the stew, oregano for spaghetti sauce—what would we do without them? Dried herbs make fine gifts, too.

An even more compelling reason to maintain a year-round supply of homegrown herbs is that storebought herbs may contain residues of toxic pesticides. Many herbs sold in stores, even health food stores, are imported from nations with fewer pesticide restrictions than the United States has. Consequently, foreign-grown herbs may have been treated with pesticides now banned in the United States because of safety concerns.

Gathering In

It doesn't take much time to dry herbs, and you won't need any special equipment. Timing is important, though. Most herbs contain the highest content of volatile oils, their flavorful essence, before their flowers open.

Harvesting herbs is a fragrant summer pleasure. Gather yours by the handful or the armload while they're still in bud, on a sunny, dry day. Use sharp scissors or pruners to avoid disturbing roots. Separate baskets make it easier to dry and store herbs after harvest.

When to Pick

Perennial herbs —sage, rosemary, sweet cicely, and others—may be cut as many as three times in one season. Most annual herbs, such as basil and dill, yield two cuttings in a season, unless the first is made late. The general rule is to remove up to two-thirds of the plant's top growth during the spring and summer. As fall approaches, cut perennials less severely, to about half their height, so they will remain strong enough to weather the winter. Cut annuals to the ground in the last fall harvest.

A few tips will help you make the most of your herb collection.

- For best flavor, gather herbs while they're still in bud.
- Choose a sunny, dry day. Wait until the dew has disappeared from the herbs and the sun's warmth has started to bring out the volatile oils, but gather your herbs before the afternoon heat has a chance to evaporate the oils.
- Cut herb stems with sharp scissors or pruning shears to avoid disturbing the roots.
- Keep different types of harvested herbs in separate baskets so they won't get mixed together.
- Taller herbs tend to stay fairly clean in the garden, but low-growing types like tarragon and thyme are often gritty or muddy. Wash these herbs before drying them. Rinse muddy leaves gently under running water, or in the morning spray plants with the hose the day before or the day of picking.
- Clean dusty leaves by swishing them briefly in a tub of clean water. Shake or whirl the sprigs to get rid of excess moisture and spread them on paper towels. Cover them with another layer of towels, lightly pressed down, to blot the last bit of water before the drying process begins in earnest.

Preparing and Drying

Three conditions encourage good herb drying: heat, dry air, and good air circulation. Look for a spot that provides all three—an attic, shed, garage, or covered porch.

Darkness is a fourth factor that will help produce high-quality dried herbs. Exposure to sunlight fades the leaves to an unappetizing (and often less flavorful) gray or tan. If your herb-drying room isn't dark enough, enclose bunches of herbs in paper bags, perforated for ventilation, or tie cone-shaped shields of newspaper around them. An uninsulated attic, where it's usually dark, hot, and dry, makes an ideal drying spot. Open a window to provide ventilation. (Make sure you hang herbs away from direct sunlight coming through attic windows.) In an attic, festooning the rafters with drying herbs won't interfere with other uses of the space.

If your herbs have stems long enough to gather in bunches, you can hang them in bundles to dry. Tie 10 to 20 stalks together near the cut ends of the stems, making a small, loose bundle. Suspend the bunched herbs from string or wire strung across the room, or from hooks in the ceiling.

SPECIAL TREATMENT

Herbs with big leaves, such as large-leaved basil or comfrey, and those with juicy stems, such as lovage, need some special handling to prevent mold. Cut the leaves from the stalk to dry them. Arrange the leaves on a clean fiberglass or stainless steel screen, or try cardboard for leaves that are big but not fleshy. I've had excellent results drying comfrey leaves in the attic by spreading them on large sheets of corrugated cardboard covered with paper towels. Avoid using galvanized screens, which could react with the plant juices to produce toxic substances. Prop the screens so air can circulate under them.

Air circulates more freely around herbs if they're not touching a wall. I have dried small nosegays of herbs by hanging them from coat hooks on a small wall rack, but even then the herbs were about 3 inches from the wall and the room maintained excellent cross ventilation.

It's satisfying to use summer's own heat to preserve part of her bounty. I sometimes dry fall-harvested herbs on stainless steel screens propped close to my wood stove. You can even dry herbs in your microwave oven, although getting the timing just right takes some experimenting. It's a good idea to let thick-leaved herbs air-dry for several days before placing them in the microwave. If you'd like to try microwave drying, follow these steps.

1. Start with some fresh snippings and leaves of your garden herbs. Spread a single layer of herbs on a paper towel on the bottom of the oven, and cover the herbs with a second paper towel.
2. To protect your microwave, place a cupful of water in the oven along with your herbs.

3. Microwave at low power for 3 minutes, stirring and checking for dryness several times. When dried, the herbs will feel brittle and crisp. If necessary, return the herbs to the oven for another 30 to 60 seconds. Keep a record of successes so you'll know how long to microwave the next batch.
4. Let herbs cool, then store in airtight containers.

Storing Dried Herbs

Be sure that herbs are thoroughly dried before you store them. Dried herbs crumble easily when rubbed between thumb and fore-finger. Once they're dried, find a comfortable outdoor spot in the shade and strip the dried leaves from the stalks onto a cookie sheet in your lap. If it's dusk and someone is playing the harmonica and the fireflies are just lighting up and the cat comes to sit at your feet, so much the better.

Some leaves will break apart when you strip them, of course, but try to keep the dried leaves as whole as possible. When crumbled or pulverized, they lose flavor more quickly. It's fine to break leaves apart to distribute the flavor when you add them to food, however. Remember that dried herbs have a more concentrated flavor than fresh ones.

Store the dried herbs in tightly closed, labeled jars and keep them in a cool, dark place. Although bunches of herbs hanging from the ceiling can give a kitchen that much-admired country look, cooking herbs will stay dust-free and retain their color and flavor better if protected from light, moisture, and dust.

CHAPTER FIFTEEN

Start a Mint Sampler

The virtues of mints were discovered early. Egyptian papyrus records dating from 2800 B.C. mention mint as a medicinal herb. Later, ancient Greeks scoured their dining tables with mint and steeped the aromatic leaves in their bath water, and Arabs customarily offered a cup of strong mint tea as a gesture of hospitality. More recently, Theodore Roosevelt had a patch of spearmint planted on the White House lawn for use in beverages. During Prohibition, mint beds were ripped out in Virginia and several neighboring states because the herb was an ingredient in mint juleps. Today, the popularity of herb teas has brought mint back to the store and the pantry shelf, this time in packages. But no gardener needs packaged mint when it is so easy to grow your own.

Square Stems, Strong Scent

Mints are found worldwide—in Europe, Asia, Africa, Australia, and North America. Botanists agree—more or less—that there are about 25 species of mint, of which 8 or so are commonly grown. Mints tend to hybridize, so beyond the fringes of the 8 to 10 well-recognized plants (and even, sometimes, among them) there are intermediate forms that challenge the logic of the classifier. However, mints as a group are easy to recognize. These aromatic perennial plants have square stems and paired leaves, which are usually shallow toothed but without lobes or deep indentations. Stems rise to a height of 1½ to 3 feet, and the flowers, which may be white, pink, or lavender, appear as spikes at the tops of stems or in clusters rising from the leaf axils.

Mints hybridize readily, so even mint seed offered through catalogs may not grow true to type. However, it's easy to beg or buy a start of the kind of mint you want, because established plantings produce vigorous stolons. These underground runners eagerly send up new shoots in all directions. Most gardeners who grow mint have more than enough to give away.

Stitching a Sampler

A mint sampler makes a good casual landscaping improvement. Because of its rambling nature, mint is suited to an informal bed or a handy spot near the kitchen door, rather than to a mannered, tightly designed knot garden. It is lovely planted around a small pond. I like to tuck a few plants near the outside water faucet, where they will receive extra moisture. Keep the planting well away from vegetable garden or flower beds, though. Mint deserves its reputation as a fast spreader.

Aromatic mints make welcome iced teas for summer sipping. Give peppermint, spearmint, apple mint, and other favorites their own bed, where the fast-spreading plants can weave together into a fragrant sampler.

Mints thrive in a variety of soils and need no coddling, although I once inadvertently killed a healthy bed of mint by spreading a too-liberal dose of wood ashes over it. Moderately fertile soil without special amendments will satisfy any of the species described here. With few exceptions, mints do best in moist ground. Most tolerate at least some shade. However, the oil of plants grown in deep shade will be less aromatic than that of plants grown in full sun.

Dig a small rectangle or oval of ground. Prepare the ground as you

CURBING WANDERLUST

Mint is easy to start but hard to confine. Select a separate spot for your mint bed where it will not invade more "timid" plants. Various gimmicks are often suggested to keep mint in its place. You can drive a slate shingle or a sheet of metal in at the edge of the clump, or plant the mint in a bottomless barrel or bucket placed in the garden. Such devices work for a while, but sooner or later mint's wanderlust wins out and the stolons jump (or burrow under) their bounds. Keep a sharp eye out for straying plants and uproot them mercilessly. If you'd rather not take a chance, plant your sampler in a wooden half-barrel or other large container.

would for a new flower bed, removing sod and loosening the soil. Divide the bed into four or five parts, depending on how many types you want to plant. Set rooted mint stems every 4 to 8 inches in the bed. They'll fill in by season's end. The borders of the various mints will blend as they spread and interlace, giving a pleasing, softly fuzzy effect.

Although mint is generally trouble-free, it is occasionally attacked by mint rust, a fungal disease that shows up as speckled orange spots, usually appearing first on the lower parts of the plant and then progressing upward. If you want to be completely rid of the rust, which is merely disfiguring but not fatal to the plants, you can start a new bed with a handful of healthy stolons. If mint rust is a problem in your area, avoid putting manure around your plants, because it may contain mint rust spores. You can still pick uninfected parts of the plants.

A Sampling of Mints

Many mints are available for your sampler. The following are the most useful and widely planted mints. Unless otherwise noted, these mints are hardy to Zone 5.

Some nurseries offer varieties and cultivars for the mint fancier, including 'Blue Balsam' mint, a pungent type with shiny, dark green leaves; 'Emerald and Gold', a variegated spearmint; and 'Silver' mint, one with silvery foliage but less aroma than most other mints. Whether you plant a mint sampler for variety or a single clump for easy picking, mint will reward you with its eager growth, its refreshing aroma, and, perhaps, a cup of tea.

Apple Mint

A favorite of dooryard gardens, apple mint (*Mentha suaveolens*) is also known as woolly mint for the downy quality of its rounded leaves. Apple mint has a pleasingly mild but unmistakably minty flavor and, like spearmint, is a wonderful garden resource for an impromptu pot of tea or a special sauce to serve with lamb.

Corsican Mint

Corsican mint (*Mentha requienii*), also called Spanish mint, is a minute creeping plant with leaves that are only 1/16 to 1/8 inch across. Plants grow no more than 1 inch high with flat foliage and tiny lavender flowers.

Corsican mint is often planted between stepping stones or in a rock garden. It is not reliably winter-hardy but will often survive moderately cold winters if well mulched and grown in a sheltered place. One of the most charming plantings of Corsican mint that I've seen was at Well-Sweep Herb Farm in Port Murray, New Jersey, where a 5-inch mat of the diminutive herb grew comfortably in a tree notch.

European Pennyroyal

Like most other mints, European pennyroyal (*Mentha pulegium*) thrives in damp places. It does especially well in sandy soil well supplied with nutrients. This mint grows about 4 to 8 inches high, with a creeping habit. It bears round or oval, ½-inch-wide, dark green leaves, usually with plain margins. In bloom, the flowering stems can reach 1 foot tall.

The specific epithet, *pulegium,* refers to its effectiveness as a flea repellent, and that is probably the best way to use it—in an ointment or an oil. Pennyroyal leaves often have an irritating effect on the genitourinary tract when ingested, so don't be tempted to drink a cup of pennyroyal tea. Use it to shampoo the dog instead. It certainly must be avoided by pregnant women because in large doses it is reported

CAT'S CUP OF TEA

The strong, rather musky aroma of catnip (*Nepeta cataria*) is not always agreeable to people, but cats—even large cats, like lions—love it. Oddly enough, cats are uninterested in catnip unless the leaves have been bruised to release the essential oils. Hence the old saying, "If you sow it, the cats won't know it; if you set it, the cats will get it." When you transplant catnip plants ("set" them) into your garden, the handling of the leaves is enough to release that aroma that cats can't resist.

If you want to make your favorite cat happy, catnip is very easy to raise from seed, started six to eight weeks before your last spring frost. Another square-stem mint in the Labiatae, or mint family, catnip is a perennial with highly aromatic, serrated oval leaves and white flowers dotted with purple. Catnip forms a bushy plant 2 to 3 feet high and does well in fairly dry soil, even in partial shade. Catnip reseeds freely but may die back in winter if cut too severely in fall.

to be an abortifacient. (Doses large enough to have this effect usually cause irreversible kidney damage, too.)

Field or Corn Mint

Field mint (*Mentha arvensis*) is a wild mint with lance-shaped, often hairy leaves, possessing a strong mint aroma and coarse flavor. Stems often remain unbranched, and flowers are borne in small, dense clusters in the leaf axils. Field mint thrives in drier ground than most other mints.

Orange Mint

Orange mint (*Mentha* × *piperita* var. *citrata;* sometimes listed as *M. citrata*), also called bergamot mint or eau-de-cologne mint, has a penetrating citrus aroma. The stems are often purplish, and the toothed, smooth-surfaced leaves are bluntly rounded at the base. Orange mint is good for an occasional cup of tea, but, to my taste, the distinctive flavor palls sooner than that of apple mint or spearmint.

A few leaves of orange mint are a fine addition to a potpourri. Some herbalists contend that the fragrance of other aromatic plants is enhanced by the influence of orange mint growing nearby.

Peppermint

Thought to be a cross between spearmint and water mint, peppermint (*Mentha* × *piperita*) has lance-shaped leaves on short stems. Some herbalists recognize two strains of peppermint: black, with purple-tinged stems; and white, with leaves of lighter green, a more slender stem, and a milder aroma and flavor.

Peppermint has been listed as an official drug plant since the mid-nineteenth century. Its marked pungency comes from menthol, a recognized antiseptic and topical analgesic. Recent studies tend to support peppermint's antiseptic reputation. According to biochemist James Morris, reports from India's Gorakhpur University describe peppermint oil as an effective antifungal agent. Oil of peppermint has many uses in toothpaste, candy, and liqueurs. And, of course, an infusion of the leaves—good old peppermint tea—has long been used to aid digestion.

Spearmint

Spearmint (*Mentha spicata*), also called lamb mint, has a milder, sweeter, less-breathtaking aroma than peppermint. Its leaves are also lance shaped but more sharply pointed, and they are virtually stemless. Spearmint is an excellent choice for mint sauce, tea, or jelly. Curly-leaved mint, *M. spicata* 'Crispata', is a spearmint cultivar with wavy edges. (Some sources list it as a cultivar of water mint, *M. aquatica*.) American Indians used spearmint to treat indigestion and diarrhea and to disinfect wounds. It is usually propagated by stolons or cuttings because the seed does not always come true to type.

Using Mint

A well-established clump of garden mint will give you two or three cuttings a year. You can use it fresh, or dry it for later use. Cut the stems 2 to 3 inches above the ground. For the best flavor, pick when flower buds are well formed but not quite open. The plant's aromatic oil content is then at its peak. To dry any mint, harvest the leafy stalks on a sunny day in mid- or late morning, as soon as the dew has evaporated. Avoid bruising the leaves, and let them remain on the stalk until they are dried.

Mild-flavored mints make wonderful teas, sauces, jellies, and garnishes. You can also use any mint, mild or pungent, as an ant chaser. I tried this folk remedy in an old house where the ants had at least a hundred routes into my kitchen. Simply strewing fresh mint sprigs on counters and floors really did help keep the ants away.

When making summer bouquets, I almost always tuck in cuttings of apple mint with the flowers. Often these root, and then I have a supply of started plants to send home with friends.

CHAPTER SIXTEEN

Plant Flowers for Evening Pleasure

What do you think of when you hear the words "summer evening"? Soft air, late-falling dusk, shelling peas on the porch, resting after a busy day? Perhaps, in your fantasy, you are sitting on the deck with friends, watching as the green garden slowly fades from sight. As dusk falls over the yard, flowery fragrances rise in the gentle evening air.

With the fading of the light, fragrant delights come into their own. The evening-scented and night-blooming plants you dotted strategically around your homescape are in bloom, perfuming the air with their haunting aromas. The white and pale-colored flowers that might have seemed unremarkable (or might still have been in bud) by day stand out against the deepening night. Night-flying moths, drawn by the easily visible pale flowers, hover about, adding another dimension of interest to the quiet evening scene.

The Night Garden

Here are some easy-growing flowers to enjoy at the end of the day. Add them to beds and borders, and try some in pots. A window box of night-scented flowers will bring a sweet perfume through open windows when the breeze stirs.

PLANNING FOR PLEASURE

With a few simple plantings, you can extend garden-grown pleasures into the evening hours. Of course you'll want to plant fragrant and night-blooming flowers near your outdoor sitting area. Fill containers for the porch or patio to enjoy the pleasure of night flowers up close. If your deck is high above ground level, arrange plants in containers around the edge of the area. Remember to put a few night flowers near the garage for a sweet-scented welcome when you return home in the evenings, and add a few more beside the path you take to reach the house. The flowering tobacco (*Nicotiana alata*) I plant at the edge of the flower border delights us with its romantic jasmine scent when we pass it on our way to the house.

Evening Bloom

These flowers wait quietly in the garden until early evening. Then they put on a show, unfolding delicate blossoms that make the night garden a delight. Sometimes you can even watch them open!

Ipomoea alba (Moonflower)

This member of the morning glory family, sometimes listed in catalogs as *Calonyction aculeatum,* produces saucer-size white flowers on 10- to 15-foot-tall vining plants with large, attractive heart-shaped leaves. If you plant them to climb an arbor, they'll give you shade by day and flowers by night.

Seeds of the morning glory family have a hard seed coat. Nick them with a file or rub them between two sheets of sandpaper to abrade the seed coat so the seeds can absorb water more readily. Plant seeds of this tender annual directly in the ground after the last spring frost, when the soil is warm. Moonflowers like loose soil with good drainage. Don't overwater the plants. Thin seedlings to 1 foot apart. Moonflowers can make a breathtaking sight if you plant them where you can see them highlighted by moonlight.

Datura inoxia subsp. *inoxia* 'Evening Fragrance' is another plant that is called moonflower. It has grayish blue leaves, up to 8-inch white flowers with pale purple margins, and prickly egg-shaped seed pods. This moonflower has a shorter stem—3 to 4 feet—and doesn't vine. It makes an attractive bushy plant for containers. All of its parts, however, are poisonous, so keep it away from children. Like the moonflower *Ipomoea alba, D. inoxia* subsp. *inoxia* 'Evening Fragrance' blooms in the evening and droops the next day.

Mirabilis jalapa (Four-O'Clock)

The funnel-shaped flowers of four-o'clocks open in late afternoon and last until morning of the following day. If it's cloudy, they'll usually stay open all day. They come in happy colors—yellow, orange, purple, rose, crimson, pink, and white and, amazingly, can have different colors and marbled color mixtures on a single plant. They're delicately fragrant.

Plant seeds directly in the garden after frost. Four-o'clocks are very adaptable plants that tolerate poor soil and summer heat. They bloom from summer till frost. Give them full sun and thin plants to stand 12 to 15 inches apart. They often self-sow.

Four-o'clocks are a tender perennial, treated as an annual where winters are cold. You can dig up and save their tuberous roots just after frost in the fall, as you would with dahlias. Keep them in a dry, cool (but not freezing) place over winter and replant them in spring, after danger of frost is past. Or pot up the roots in early spring and let them leaf out indoors until safe planting-out time.

Oenothera glazioviana (Evening Primrose)

This showy evening primrose puts on a real performance. Invite some friends for an informal primrose-blooming party. Children love to watch the pinwheellike flowers spin open just at dusk. At dusk, the tightly wrapped flower buds swell and then unfurl like small umbrellas. As the sepals snap backward, the four yellow petals of the flower spiral open. Within 10 seconds or less, the 3-inch flower opens two-thirds of the way, becoming fully open within a minute or two.

The flowers of this hardy biennial have a delightful light lemon fragrance that seems to match their lemon yellow color, and they last until noon of the following day. Watch for the clear-winged hawk or sphinx moth—it looks like a hummingbird—that visits the flowers in the evening.

Start seeds in flats and transplant to the garden when they have their true leaves, spacing them 2 feet apart. Seedlings you set out this summer will bloom next summer. The sturdy, branching plants grow 3 to 4 feet tall. In composted soil, some of mine have attained the size of small shrubs. They have a long blooming period—six weeks or more. You'll probably have to plant them only once: These evening primroses produce large amounts of seed and self-sow readily.

Evening Fragrance

The flowers of these plants stay open day and night. But they smell sweetest after the sun goes down. Plant these where summer night breezes will carry the scent to your favorite sitting spot.

Hesperis matronalis (Sweet Rocket)

Loose clusters of lilac or white blossoms top these 2- to 3-foot-tall perennial plants in May and June. The plant is an old-fashioned favorite, sometimes known as dame's rocket. Its flowers, open day and night, are especially fragrant in the evening. Keep faded flowers clipped off to encourage continued bloom. Sweet rocket makes a nice low hedge near a patio or wall.

Plant seeds either directly in the ground or start them in pots or flats indoors. Seedlings started early indoors will bloom the first year.

Set plants 15 to 18 inches apart. They tolerate poor soil. Sweet rocket self-sows generously, but the extra plants are always welcome.

Matthiola longipetala subsp. *bicornis* (Evening Stock)

With its single flowers in soft tones of lavender and pink, evening stock, sometimes listed as *Matthiola bicornis* in catalogs, is less ornamental than the double-flowered bedding stock, *M. incana.* You won't mind the understated flowers, though, when smelling them is such a delight. The flowers open in the evening.

Plant evening stock in the garden where it is to grow, or start indoors in late winter for early summer bloom. You can even sow directly into pots or window boxes. Cover the seeds very lightly or not at all; light improves their germination. Set out started plants of this hardy annual about two weeks before your final spring frost date, spacing them 12 inches apart. Stock appreciates rich soil and must have good drainage. Evening stock grows 12 to 18 inches tall.

Stock blooms best in cool weather. Plants that I've dug in fall and kept over winter in a cool greenhouse have bloomed in the greenhouse and again in the garden the second year.

Nicotiana alata (Flowering Tobacco)

The trumpet-shaped flowers of nicotiana, especially the older, white, night-blooming forms, release a haunting fragrance after dark. Be sure to search out the old-fashioned type for best fragrance. (You'll probably need to grow the plants yourself from seed. Newer hybrids, sometimes sold as bedding plants, have more flowers in a range of colors and a bushier, more compact shape, but keep them for a daytime display. For best fragrance, plant the tall, white, evening-blooming species.)

Scatter seeds of this annual on the soil surface or start them indoors in pots. Avoid covering the seeds, which need light to germinate. Nicotiana thrives in good soil with good drainage and doesn't mind partial shade. Thin the seedlings to 12 to 15 inches apart to give them plenty of room. They'll reach 2 to 4 feet tall. Blooming time begins in June and continues until frost. Mulch to keep the roots cool in summer's heat. Once started, the plants volunteer generously.

Petunia × *hybrida* (Petunia)

Old-fashioned, smaller-flowered petunias, often listed in catalogs as

Petunia multiflora, are more fragrant than large-flowered double hybrids, and they look less bedraggled in wet weather. These sprawling 10- to 15-inch-tall plants bear showy funnel-shaped flowers in pastels, white, and deep reds and purples. Whites are the most fragrant of all.

For earlier bloom, start seeds indoors 2½ to 3 months before the last spring frost date. Scatter the tiny seeds, uncovered, on the surface of a planting flat or individual pots. Light promotes germination. Plant out started seedlings after the soil warms, spacing plants about 10 to 12 inches apart. For the patio, crowd a dozen plants in a large clay pot filled with a mixture of potting soil and compost. Petunias like full sun and very good drainage.

Special pleasures are yours in the evening garden. Fragrances intensify, and light-colored flowers stand out against the darkening night. Sweetly perfumed petunias, like this old-fashioned multiflora type, are a favorite of night-flying sphinx moths.

CHAPTER SEVENTEEN

Discover Grandmother's Vegetables

Behind the picket fences and boxwood hedges of yesterday's gardens, there were vegetables to be found that might not be recognizable to the average contemporary gardener. Some of these were staples in Grandmother's garden. Others were, even then, heirloom cultivars, like the special strain of beans handed down in Grandfather's family for several generations, maintained by faithful replanting and family legend. Still others were grown out of habit or because they were dependable, rather than for any special flavor qualities.

Keeping Old Favorites Alive

To keep a vegetable's heritage alive, plants must be grown to renew the seed and the crop must be harvested and cooked to be appreciated. Perhaps you'd like to grow some of these old reliables in your garden. You'll never know until you try what you might have been missing! Here are some popular old favorites and directions for growing and serving them.

Root Vegetables

In the days before supermarkets and cross-country trucking, our families depended on root vegetables to get them through the fall and winter. Today, root vegetables make a filling, nourishing addition to our dinner plates, and they're still just as good in savory stews as they were a generation or two ago.

Black Salsify

Although they resemble one another in form and even in flavor, salsify (*Tragopogon porrifolius*) and black salsify (*Scorzonera hispanica*) are unrelated. Many people who have tried both prefer black salsify, or scorzonera as it's also known, for its delicate flavor. Scrub the roots, then cut into strips and sauté in butter, or simmer whole roots until tender and serve with a spinach souffle.

The white-fleshed, black-skinned roots are long and thin and quite frost-hardy. Although the plant is technically a perennial, it is treated like an annual, harvested in fall and winter after spring planting. It requires about 120 days to mature. Plant the seeds in spring, as early as the ground can be worked, and thin the seedlings to stand 4 inches apart. Insects are seldom a problem. In fact, scorzonera is frequently planted near carrots in European gardens since it has an apparently well-deserved reputation for repelling the destructive carrot rust fly.

Overwintered roots send up new tender shoots in spring. These furled leaves make a good spring vegetable, cooked and served as you would asparagus.

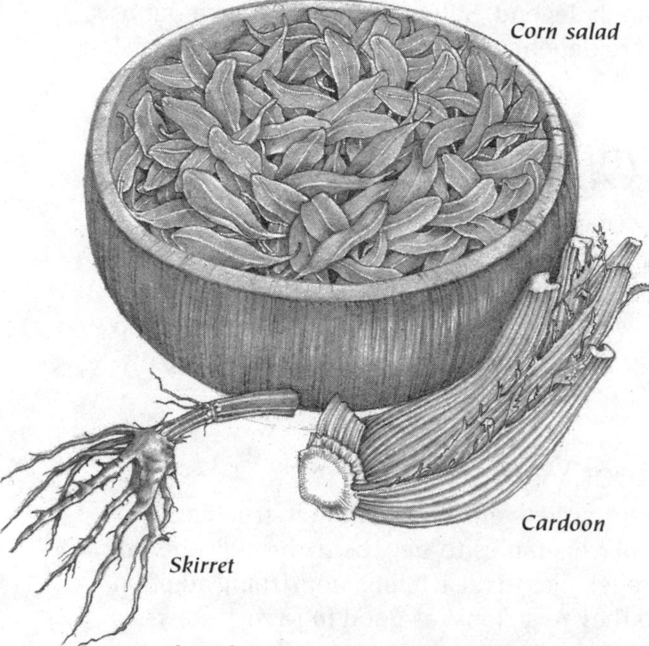

Grandmother's garden held many vegetables that are still worth growing today. Try mild and agreeable skirret, like a small parsnip with finger-size roots; cardoon, an older cousin of the artichoke, grown for its tender heart; or cold-hardy corn salad, which provides welcome, mild-flavored greens in early spring and late fall.

Cardoon

Back in the 1890s, cardoon (*Cynara carduncùlus*) had enough commercial importance to appear in a book written for market gardeners. This member of the large thistle family is an older cousin of the more highly refined globe artichoke. It resembles a large celery plant with deeply cut, slightly woolly or hairy gray-green leaves and spiny ribs along the stalks. A perennial in the warm Mediterranean area where it originated, cardoon is treated like an annual in the North, where it often has the last word, nevertheless, since it self-sows readily.

Sow seeds indoors six to eight weeks before your first frost-free date, and set out plants about 2 feet apart in rows spaced 3 feet apart. In the rich, deeply dug soil it prefers, cardoon grows to 4 feet tall and nearly that wide from leaf-tip to leaf-tip. It will grow in part shade, so you can plant it next to your tall corn. In a dry season, the stalks may turn woody and hollow-centered unless irrigated.

Cardoon is grown for the tender heart stalks and leaves that form in its center when the plant is "blanched." The naturally bitter flavor of the cardoon is tempered by the blanching process. To prepare for fall eating, start in September by bunching the stalks of each clump together and wrapping newspaper around them. Handle the plant carefully—it can be prickly. Fasten the paper with string or rubber bands. Then bank soil around the stalks, almost up to the coarse top leaves of the plant. Take care not to let soil sift down into the heart of the plant.

Blanching takes four to five weeks. Sometime in October, unwrap the plant and cut the stalks at soil level. Wash the stalks, peel the spiny strings from each stalk, and chop the stalk into 1-inch pieces. Simmer the vegetable until tender—about 20 minutes. Serve with cheese sauce, spaghetti, or butternut squash. You can include a cup of cooked cardoon cubes in your favorite casserole, or cook them in chicken broth until tender and then marinate them in Italian dressing.

Cardoon survives the first few light frosts of fall and will last even longer if well banked with earth. True devotees go so far as to gently bend the stalks down into foot-deep trenches and mound soil over them to gain a few more weeks of the delicacy.

Skirret

Skirret (*Sium sisarum*) is a perennial root vegetable, much like a small parsnip with multiple finger-size roots. The flavor is mild and agreeable—akin to that of parsnips but less sweet.

The tangle of slim roots probably accounts for skirret's fall from favor. It does take time to clean and prepare the roots. But the vegetable is easy to grow, fairly hardy, and not attractive to insects. Hose off the roots right in the garden and rinse them again in the kitchen after you've separated them from the crown. Because of its hard-to-clean root surface, skirret is often cooked whole until tender and then peeled and sliced for soups, stews, or side dishes. Sometimes the core is tough. In that case, simply slice off the tender outer meat of the vegetable in long strips and discard the core.

Skirret seeds share the parsnip's rather exasperating habit of germinating slowly and quite unevenly. Start the seeds indoors, so you don't lose them in the garden. You can sow them in late summer or early fall, transplanting the seedlings to a bed of well-limed, rich soil. Plants started in early spring may be harvested in fall. Space the plants 10 inches apart in rows 2 feet apart. Skirret needs a good supply of moisture. Water deeply if a week or so passes without an inch of rain.

When you harvest the roots in the fall, you'll notice that small side roots have formed. To increase your planting or share with neighbors, simply cut off these roots and replant them. Hardy skirret will live through winter and come back next year.

Great Greens

If you're looking to round out summer salads or cook up a mess of tender greens, consider these heritage vegetables.

Corn Salad

Also known as lamb's lettuce or mâche, corn salad (*Valerianella locusta,* sometimes listed as *V. olitoria*) has been grown in European kitchen gardens since its domestication from the wild in Elizabethan times. It was dubbed "corn salad" because the plant was a well-known weed in European grain fields, and at that time any grain was called "corn." In America, corn salad has been included in gardens since at least the beginning of the eighteenth century, and possibly earlier.

There's good reason for its continued popularity. Corn salad is a hardy, insect-resistant, mild-flavored green that fills in the menu in the early spring and late fall when other tender salad materials have shriveled under the influence of frost. Indeed, it will often survive the winter if planted in a relatively sheltered spot and mulched well with some airy, nonpacking material like loose straw.

Corn salad loves cool nights. In warm weather, it rapidly goes to seed. Once the seed stalk forms, the leaves turn bitter. Plant seeds outdoors in very early spring, or at summer's end (late August or early September) for a fall crop. Full rosettes of delicate, light green leaves will go on bearing well past the first frost if not subjected to heat. Thin the seedlings to about 6 inches apart in rows 14 to 18 inches apart. Or plant the seeds in wide rows convenient to the back door, for quick picking trips in frigid weather. Corn salad is not particular as to soil but responds well to a good humus-rich loam well supplied with lime.

The leaves are very mild—quite bland in flavor. Most gardeners consider this a virtue, since there are usually enough pungent or peppery wild and tame greens around to give a salad character. Use corn salad in tossed salads along with escarole, cress, and dandelion greens, or in a dish of mixed, cooked leafy vegetables. It combines well with the more authoritative flavor of turnip or mustard greens.

Rocket

An old, old salad plant that dates back to Roman times, rocket is a fast-growing, 10-inch-high, hardy leafy annual that will provide picking greens within two months after planting. Historical documents show that Puritan John Winthrop brought rocket seeds with him when he sailed to New England from London in 1631. In recent years, rocket has become better known as arugula, a staple of the salad bowl in trendy restaurants, where its pungency adds a piquant accent to a mixture of blander greens. Its botanical name is *Eruca vesicaria* subsp. *sativa.*

Plant rocket seeds in late August for fall eating. Start again in spring, sowing as soon as the soil is dry enough to work. You can plant them out a good four to six weeks before your final frost. Because the plants can rapidly pass the point of perfection, make repeated plantings several weeks apart for a continuous supply. Space plants 6 to 9 inches apart.

Rocket that is grown quickly in cool weather, in rich soil with plenty of moisture, has the best flavor. Even rapidly grown rocket has a pungent flavor, akin to that of horseradish—but that is its special contribution to the soup or salad. Pick the leaves while they're still small, about 3 to 6 inches long. (The fully developed leaves, which can be as much as 2 feet long, develop a strong, unpleasant flavor.)

An Oddity for Eating—Or for Fun

Unicorn flower, proboscis flower, ram's-horn—the common names for *Proboscidea louisianica* are a clue that this plant is something different.

Unicorn flower is sometimes listed in catalogs as martynia, or *Martynia proboscidea.* By any name, it's worth growing just for the fun of it. The description of it in T. Greiner's 1895 book, *How to Make the Garden Pay,* as "an annual of the easiest culture—large, strong growing, rather coarse, yet decidedly interesting" still holds true. The plant reaches an average height of 2 feet, with leaves as much as 10 inches across and a rather viny, trailing habit. Bell-shaped, catalpa-like flowers in shades of yellow, purple, and white appear in early summer, followed by 3-inch-long, curved, pod-like fruit with long, slender curved hooks.

The unusual curved pods of unicorn flower (*Proboscidea louisianica*) make tasty pickles, or you can dry them for arrangements or crafts.

If you'd like to follow in Grandmother's footsteps, collect a hatful of the young, tender pods and pickle them, using either your favorite sweet/sour mixture or a vinegar-brine preservative like that used for dilled cucumbers. Be sure to catch the pods while they're still young and tender if you want them for pickles.

After you've admired the flowers and eaten the pickles, let some fruit mature into the hard-shelled claw form that makes it so tempting to hobbyists. Shake out the seeds to plant next year, and use the fantastically shaped dried pods for Christmas tree ornaments, in pod and nut wreaths, in mobiles, and in other decorative arrangements.

To grow the unicorn flower in most northern gardens, start seeds early indoors in pots and set them out in the garden row after danger of frost. In mild climates, you can simply sow the seeds right in the garden row. Thin the plants to stand 2 feet apart in rows 3 feet wide. Seeds shed from this year's plants will often volunteer new plants the following year. In the warm regions of the Southwest and Mexico, where unicorn flower originated, it is a perennial.

CHAPTER EIGHTEEN

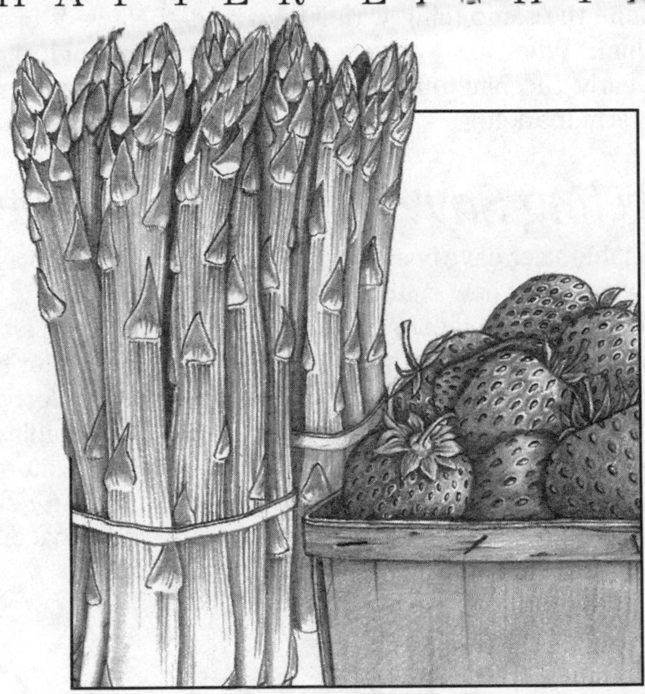

Sell Your Garden Produce

Selling surplus vegetables is a satisfying sideline. Last year, extra cuttings from our 30-foot spinach row paid for enough seed to plant 20 garden rows. On a whim, I called the produce manager of a local supermarket one day when our spinach was outdoing itself and I happened to be heading for town. I wouldn't have made the six-mile trip to town just to sell the spinach, but it was an easy way to reap an additional return from our garden.

We've done the same thing with lettuce and—believe it or not—with zucchini. (When he was seven, our son, Greg, sold over 50 pounds of early zucchini to a local grocery store, and we later sold some to a farm market.)

Marketing Savvy for Small Growers

Our vegetable sales have been incidental to the operation of a large garden in which I try new cultivars, experiment with growing techniques, and produce enough to freeze and give away. If you want to devote part of your garden to income-producing vegetables or fruits, give some thought to which foods you'll want to market. Select crops that grow well and sell well in your area, and choose vegetables that seldom are bothered by insects or diseases; they'll look more appealing, and your growing costs will be lower. If you aim for supermarket or farm market sales, you'll want to produce crops that buyers want and those that will bring in the highest return.

At the beginning of the season, early strawberries, asparagus, peas, lettuce, and beans often command premium prices. Stores are most likely to buy zucchini early in the season, so if you want to sell it, aim for an early crop and sell only your freshest and best. Raspberries, which are so perishable that they're virtually unshippable, are usually in great demand, and they're easy to grow.

Selling your vegetables takes some thought and effort, but the results pay off. Choose healthy, high-yielding crops that sell well in your area. Some gardeners have good luck with specialties like early strawberries and asparagus, which often bring premium prices.

THINKING CORN? THINK AGAIN

Sweet corn is an obvious and popular cash crop, and you might make a profit on an especially early sweet corn or perhaps a planting of 'Silver Queen', a cultivar that is widely known. But in terms of productivity for the space and the growing time it takes, corn is at the bottom of a list of 11 popular vegetables. What tops the list? Lettuce! Cherry tomatoes, cucumbers, Swiss chard, radishes, snap beans, tomatoes, carrots, peppers, and eggplants all yield more dollar value per foot of garden space than corn.

Cash Crop Basics

Spend some time developing markets. Take samples and be prepared to let produce buyers know how much and how often you can deliver. Try local markets, restaurants, and supermarkets, and don't be afraid to ask a decent price for your wonderful garden-fresh produce.

Large chain stores often must commit to season-long contracts with wholesale produce suppliers, but independent grocers are often willing to buy. Some stores prefer to feature locally grown produce when it's available. Health food stores pay 30 to 40 percent more than general food markets, but they usually sell less produce. Smaller stores sometimes lack storage and display cases, which can limit the shelf life of your vegetables.

Restaurants make excellent markets for homegrown produce because they have a steady demand for quality food, and they pay higher prices—often retail or 10 to 20 percent below retail price for vegetables washed and delivered. A friend of mine developed a market for her homegrown herbs at several specialty restaurants in a nearby city.

In his book *Cash from Square Foot Gardening,* Mel Bartholomew comes out strongly in favor of restaurants as the best market for the gardener who wants regular, rather than incidental, sales—and who is willing to devote the necessary time to both gardening and dealing with restaurants. Bartholomew's enthusiasm for the restaurant market is based on his evident success in selling his own produce. He's found that he can make arrangements with chefs or restaurant owners to buy all his surplus produce each week. He washes, bags, and delivers the goods two or three times a week. He's firm about requesting cash on the spot, he's scrupulous about keeping to his promised delivery schedule, and he brings only first-rate, fresh-picked food.

Setting Prices

One important decision you'll have to make as a market gardener is how much to charge customers for your produce. When you sell surplus vegetables and fruits to the produce manager of your local food store, you should receive market price: the going rate for that vegetable for that day. (Most managers will have a printed price list that they can show you.) If you sell produce at your own stand, you can set your own prices, of course, keeping them low enough to en-

YE OLDE ROADSIDE STAND

The vegetable stand is a traditional selling method, though it's not always the best for the average gardener. But if your location is good and you don't mind being available to tend the stand, you could do well. Use signs and newspaper ads to help steer customers in your direction. Set your prices slightly higher than those charged by the local supermarket, and offer menu and recipe suggestions to educate your customers.

If your roadside stand is near a city or a summer resort, your high-quality produce will command good prices. Shepherd Ogden, of Londonderry, Vermont, built up an enthusiastic following of regular customers for his gourmet lettuces, tomatoes, seedlings, bulbs, cut flowers, and dried flower wreaths. "The urbanites who summer here are desperate for stuff," Ogden says. "Some even drive up from Connecticut in spring to buy seedlings of our special lettuce varieties at our stand."

courage sales but high enough to make a profit. Many growers of organic food price their wares just a bit above the prices charged in chain stores for the same food that is not organically grown and not as fresh.

Bartholomew maintains that a growing area of 1,064 feet, containing 15 intensively planted beds 4 feet wide and 16 feet long, can produce as much as $5 per square foot, or $5,320 in a season. The raised beds he recommends are based on square-foot grids, which break down the planting areas into manageable units, help to avoid overplanting, and aid in estimating harvest amounts.

Dave Marchant, of the New Alchemy Institute in Falmouth, Massachusetts, has experimented with marketing the produce grown in an intensively planted acre on the institute's grounds. "It's really pretty easy to tap into the restaurant trade," Marchant says. "Lettuce, cut flowers, and cut herbs were our biggest restaurant sellers. Basil is an incredible seller. On a backyard basis, limit yourself to one or two restaurants. When dealing with the better restaurants, you get almost retail price. We sell in farmers' markets and at a roadside stand, too. People are very interested in fresh lettuce and herbs."

If you really get into the business of selling garden produce, whether to stores or restaurants or at your own stand, you'll need to set up a bookkeeping system that charges the business for your time as well as for expenses like advertising, packaging supplies, and seed and fertilizer.

Penny Pinchers

If you're considering selling your produce, you'll want to devote as much garden space as possible to salable crops. Most gardeners overplant a few vegetables out of habit. If these are easily sold, fine, but if they're not, substitute some cherry tomatoes or lettuce or whatever crops are in demand in your area.

When planning your cash crops, consider how long a particular crop takes to grow and how much preparation it needs after picking. Radishes, for example, are ready in a month but need to be washed before they're salable. Tomatoes grow more slowly, but they produce fruit for weeks once they mature. Plus, if you stake and don't spray tomatoes, they needn't be washed.

Cut gardening costs in order to boost your profit margin. You can economize by sowing seed more sparingly, making compost rather than purchasing fertilizer, and using soap sprays or wood ashes rather than packaged products to deter insects.

Supplying your local markets with good, fresh food grown nearby is a service to your fellow townspeople, who might not have space or time for gardens. And ultimately the whole food distribution system, which is now cockeyed enough to truck broccoli from California to Long Island, where broccoli can grow perfectly well for much of the year, can only be improved by an increased reliance on locally grown food. While you're reaping dollars from your home ground, you'll be helping, in a small but significant way, to bring food production closer to the consumer.

CHAPTER NINETEEN

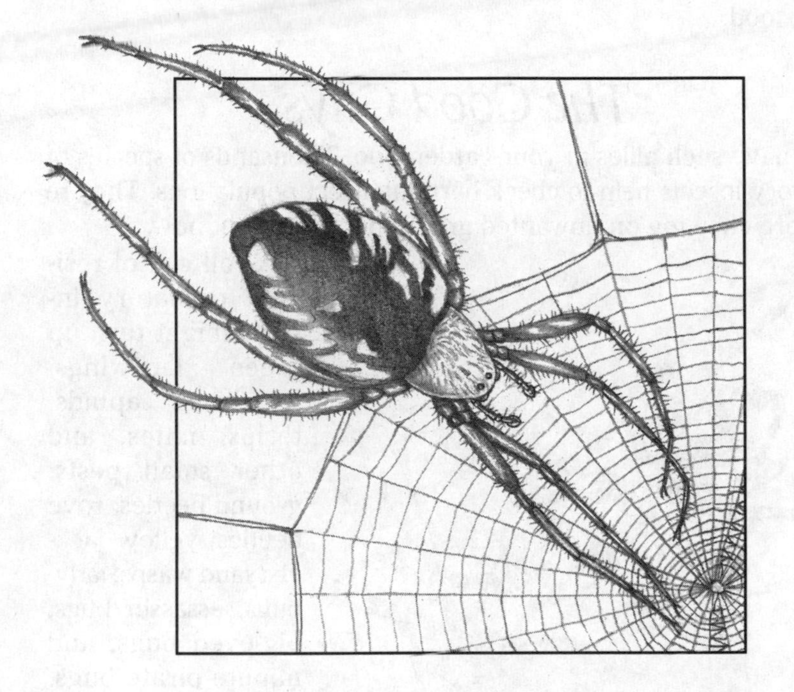

Welcome Beneficial Insects

Some summer evenings we like to sit on the east patio and look out over the garden. We often think, as we survey the greening rows, how much effort is going on out there under the leaves, under the mulch, unseen. There's a whole world of insect life humming in our garden. Some, it is true, eat holes in the cabbage, but others—many others—gobble the leafhoppers and sting the caterpillars that would otherwise damage much more of our good home-grown food.

The Good Guys

You have such allies in your garden, too. Thousands of species of predatory insects help to check harmful insect populations. They're out there chewing on unwanted grubs and mites right now.

A whole world of insect life keeps your garden safe from harm. Green lacewings, ground beetles, ladybugs, and wasps spend their lives trapping and eating harmful insects. Arachnids like this striking *Argiope* spider, a common sight in many gardens, are welcome, too.

A roll call of resident predatory insects might turn up green lacewings, which eat aphids, thrips, mites, and other small pests; ground beetles; rove beetles; yellow jackets; sand wasps; ladybugs; assassin bugs; big-eyed bugs; and minute pirate bugs. Syrphid or hover flies eat leafhoppers and other damaging insects and also pollinate fruit and vegetable flowers.

Spiders of all sizes spend their lives trapping and consuming harmful insects. (Just to keep the record straight, these eight-legged predators are not insects but arachnids. True insects have only six legs.)

Some predatory wasps paralyze their prey with a sting and then carry it off for their larvae to eat. A single wasp can kill hundreds of harmful insects in a season. Parasitic wasps lay their eggs in the insect, in its larvae, or in its eggs, and the wasp larvae then hatch to a ready meal. There are thousands of species of ichneumon and braconid wasps in North America, many of them tiny. *Trichogramma* wasps and tachinid flies also parasitize insect pests. Most wasps are solitary, unlike the social paper wasp, which lives in colonies, and in most cases their appetites are highly specialized.

Extending Hospitality

You can multiply the effectiveness of these and other resident beneficials by taking a few simple measures to encourage them and to attract others to come and forage in your garden. If you've purchased nonnative beneficials like the *Trichogramma* wasp or larvae of helpful natives like the green lacewing, some of these measures can also help to maintain and increase their populations.

The simplest gesture of hospitality you can extend to your resident insect allies is to provide a supply of water, especially for lacewings, which need water in both the larval and adult stages. Set 1- to 2-inch-deep containers of water in your garden, using about four containers for a 40 × 50-foot garden. Place a stone in the middle of each container for the insects to land on.

After water comes food. You can provide this, too, by allowing certain herbs and weeds to bloom and by planting sources of nectar to attract many helpful predatory and parasitic insects. A garden containing many different kinds of plants attracts helpful insects because it provides alternative sources of food, shelter, and prey—another good reason, if you need one, for spicing your vegetable garden with some flowers and herbs. Damsel bugs, which eat mites, thrips, and other such pests, like to curl up in nasturtiums and other roomy flowers, and other insects and spiders do, too. Spiders take refuge in low-growing, dense clusters of flowers.

Favorite Foods

Wasps have short tongues and can't reach the nectar in larger flowers. Flowers of the Umbelliferae, or carrot family, which bear heads of tiny blossoms in clusters called umbels, are especially attractive to these wasps. Anise, caraway, coriander, cumin, dill, fennel, lovage, and parsley are excellent sources of nectar for many tiny helpful wasps. You might also try letting some overwintered carrots and parsnips go to seed. A well-nourished female wasp may live longer and thus have a chance to lay more of her eggs. Wild Queen-Anne's-lace also produces umbels of wasp-nourishing flowers.

THE DOOMED

The tomato hornworm is a light green caterpillar the size of your little finger. It's a common sight in many tomato patches to see this caterpillar hosting larvae of the ichneumon or braconid wasp, which look like grains of rice standing on end on the caterpillar's back. The wasp larvae are using the caterpillar for food. But let it crawl on its doomed way undisturbed. Any further damage it might do will be more than offset by the newly spawned parasites its body supports.

Many other weeds, including cocklebur, knotweed, lamb's-quarters, nettle, and pigweed, produce nectar accessible to beneficial insects. Plants in the Compositae, or daisy family, provide less nectar than the Umbelliferae, but they produce it for a longer time. Useful nectar-producing members of the daisy family include black-eyed Susan (*Rudbeckia hirta*), coreopsis (*Coreopsis* spp.), goldenrods (*Solidago* spp.), lavender cotton (*Santolina* spp.), strawflower (*Helichrysum bracteatum*), sunflowers (*Helianthus* spp.), and yarrows (*Achillea* spp.). Other plants that provide nectar that beneficials can use are buckwheat, buttercups (*Ranunculus* spp.), sage, and strawberry. Some plants, like the Jerusalem artichoke, have nectaries on their leaves and stems and can feed hungry bug helpers even when not in bloom.

Ladybugs, lacewings, and some other predators, both native and introduced, thrive on Wheast, a commercial insect food that provides the protein necessary for egg laying. Mix the Wheast with water until it is the consistency of molasses and then dot droplets of the food on plant leaves where you want beneficial insects to help control crop-damaging insects.

If you order beneficial insects by mail, time your order so that it arrives after their prey comes on the scene, not before. (Your county agent should know these dates for your area, and often the companies that ship these insects nationwide do, too.) In many cases, eggs or larvae are shipped, rather than adults, and they need a ready supply of food as soon as they hatch.

Don't Poison Your Pals

If insect infestation threatens your garden, first try control measures like handpicking to spare the lives of many helpful insects. Cover susceptible crops, such as cukes, squash, and melons, with lightweight row covers to exclude harmful insects like cucumber beetles from your plantings. Introduce juvenile predatory nematodes to control soil-dwelling larvae.

If you have a severe pest problem and decide you must use a botanical insecticide like rotenone or pyrethrin, be sure to wear protective clothing, including a mask, and to apply any product you use according to label instructions. Rotenone kills bees and other flying beneficial insects, and it may persist for seven days (not one or two as commonly supposed) before it breaks down. Pyrethrin is less toxic than rotenone and breaks down more rapidly, but it will destroy some of your beneficial allies, such as lady beetles.

And finally, learn who your friends are. A few minutes spent with a good insect identification guide will show you what assassin bugs, green lacewings, rove beetles, and some syrphid flies look like, so you'll be less likely to swat or squash them when you're handpicking harmful bugs. When you're relaxing on the deck watching your garden grow, picture a few of the thousands of busy insects that help to tip the balance in your part of the green growing world toward more lettuce, fewer leafhoppers. And be glad.

CHAPTER TWENTY

Feast on Cantaloupes

Muskmelons and cantaloupes are some of the most delicious garden foods you can grow. If the weather cooperates, if the soil is right, and if the bugs don't bite too hard, you can enjoy an eight-week picking season of luscious, juicy, sweet fruits. I've grown wonderful melons here on our farm, but I've also had years of slim harvests. I hope you can gain enough help from my experience to be able to feast on your own homegrown melons.

When we first moved to the farm and expanded the old kitchen garden next to the house, there were summers when I picked muskmelons by the basketful. Then I had an off year with them, skipped a few years, planted them again in a summer of record cool weather (melons need heat to do well), and then waited a bit before trying again. My melon-growing efforts were interrupted, too, by the three years we spent building our house and by the year both children, bless them, married within three months. So I didn't get to do what I'd advise others to do: Keep trying, and work at correcting the conditions that caused problems in the previous year.

Learning from Experience

Last year I planted a row of muskmelons again, in the garden plot we've developed next to the new house. I'd gotten a few good fruits from several plants the previous year and wanted to try for more. The seeds I planted the first week of June got off to a good start and the plants looked healthy for six weeks or so. I dusted them with rotenone to keep down the striped and spotted cucumber beetles, which spread disease. The weather was pretty good—warm but not sweltering, with plenty of evenly spaced rain (perhaps a bit too much at times).

But I didn't pick a single ripe melon from that row. Some of the vines died of disease before the fruit they carried could ripen, and others were pulled up by a foraging deer. A simple rope strung across the path at the edge of the woods seemed to be effective in redirecting the deer, because damage stopped after we put it up, but that didn't bring back our vines.

Still determined to repeat the successes of my "beginner's luck" years when I could slice into a ripe, aromatic, meaty 'Ambrosia' with such great satisfaction, I decided to take another look at what I'd been doing and to review more about what muskmelons need. You know: If all else fails, read the directions.

I remembered, then, that I had mulched my earlier, productive melons with black plastic to keep the soil warm around them, a step I had omitted in my new raised-bed garden. And I realized that, because watering the garden is easier in my present setup, I might have overwatered them during one dry spell after fruit had formed.

Start melon seeds indoors, and use black plastic to warm the soil after planting out. For sweeter taste, avoid overwatering after fruits have formed, and protect them from pests and diseases. Then slice into a ripe, aromatic melon with satisfaction: You've earned it.

I was reminded, too, as I read up on them again, that muskmelons and cantaloupes often do better when started early indoors and set out as strong transplants. It's important, though, to keep the seedlings growing steadily, both in pots and later, when they're in the ground. I had slipped up here some years by allowing the seedlings to stay too long in small pots where they got rootbound, which checked their growth. I recalled, also, that the plants I raised for the old garden were kept warmer under lights than those I grew more recently in my cooler, shadier greenhouse. And this year I'd made the mistake of repositioning the vines rather more drastically than muskmelons like, lifting and draping them back over the bed because I hadn't left enough room between the melon bed and the adjacent row.

It's All in the Flavor

Not all of my years of melon disappointment were as fruitless as this last one. Sometimes I'd get fruits, but not very sweet ones—fruit-salad quality, we call them.

Several factors influence melon flavor—the boron content of the soil, the weather, and, most important, the total amount of leaf surface the plant develops. The leaves, which manufacture carbohydrates, can zoom the sugar content of melons as high as 15 percent if they're abundant and functioning well. But leaves that are shriveled from disease or coated with mildew are less effective, so the fruit is not as sweet. Low boron can cause bland flavor. Well-composted soil

CANTALOUPE OR MUSKMELON?

We call them cantaloupes, they're listed as cantaloupes in some seed catalogs, and they're labeled 'lopes in the food market. But most of the orange-fleshed, netted-skin fruits we grow and eat in North America are really muskmelons.

Along with their cousin the honeydew melon, cantaloupes and muskmelons are classified as groups of the species *Cucumis melo.* Botanically speaking, cantaloupes are *C. melo,* Cantalupensis group; muskmelons are *C. melo,* Reticulatus group; and honeydews are *C. melo,* Inodorus group. All three subgroups, being members of the same species, cross readily with one another, making identifying specific types very confusing if you're saving seed.

True cantaloupes, represented by the European 'Charentais' and 'Vedrantais' cultivars that can be found in some American seed catalogs, lack the musky aroma of the muskmelon. Unlike muskmelons, true cantaloupes don't slip from the vine when ripe.

is generally not lacking in this mineral. Heavy rain and poor drainage result in higher water content, which dilutes flavor. Warm nights can make the plant use more of its sugars in metabolism and store less in the fruit.

Muskmelon Basics

Muskmelons like warm weather. Depending on the melon species or cultivar you choose, fruit may be ripe in about 65 to 85 days. Start them indoors to get a jump on the season. Starting early indoors can help your plants fend off insect pests, too, because the plants will be big and strong before cucumber beetles hatch.

Start seeds indoors in individual pots around the time of your last frost. If you're using black plastic mulch to warm the soil, you can start two to three weeks earlier. As they grow, slip them into larger pots, without disturbing their roots, so they won't get rootbound. Transplant to the garden, again working carefully so as not to disturb the roots, when soil is warm, about two to three weeks after the time of the last spring frost. If you prefer to sow seeds directly in open ground, wait until two weeks after your last frost.

Muskmelons do best in soil with a pH of 6.0 to 6.8. Dig some compost into the row to buffer the soil pH so it's not too acid. Make sure the bed has good drainage and full sun and is in a spot protected from the wind. Melons need plenty of room to ramble. Set plants 18 inches apart in a wide bed, or plant in hills of two to three seedlings, or six to eight seeds, spacing hills 3 to 5 feet apart in rows 5 to 6 feet apart.

Mulch the rows with black plastic to warm the soil. If temperatures dip to near 50 °F, cover the plants with Hotkaps (or homemade equivalents) or Reemay (or other spun-bonded row covers) to keep them comfortable until the weather returns to 70 °F or warmer. Fertilize seedlings weekly to keep them growing rapidly. You may want to use diluted fish emulsion or compost tea for this purpose.

Pay attention to preventing disease so the plants have a chance to live long enough to ripen fruit. Choose cultivars with some disease resistance or tolerance. I don't know of any muskmelon or cantaloupe that is resistant to all or even most of the diseases that affect melons, so all you can hope for here is some improvement, not a total solution to the problem of disease. Handpick striped and spotted cucumber beetles. Use rotenone to control severe infestations. Keep nearby perennial weeds under control to discourage aphids that spread mosaic disease. You may also want to set developing fruits on overturned tin cans or margarine tubs to prevent bottom rot.

Fruit set is best when temperatures are in the range of 68° to 70°F. Avoid overwatering after the fruit forms for best flavor, and hope for sunny days and cool nights. Harvest muskmelons at "full slip"—when slight thumb pressure easily parts the stem from the fruit, leaving an indented scar. Sniff for a fruity aroma and look for orange skin showing between netting, two other signs of ripeness in muskmelons.

I'm going to follow my own advice this year and do all I can to keep my melon patch happy. Then—I'm counting on it—I'll need that big basket to gather my muskmelons again!

CHAPTER TWENTY-ONE

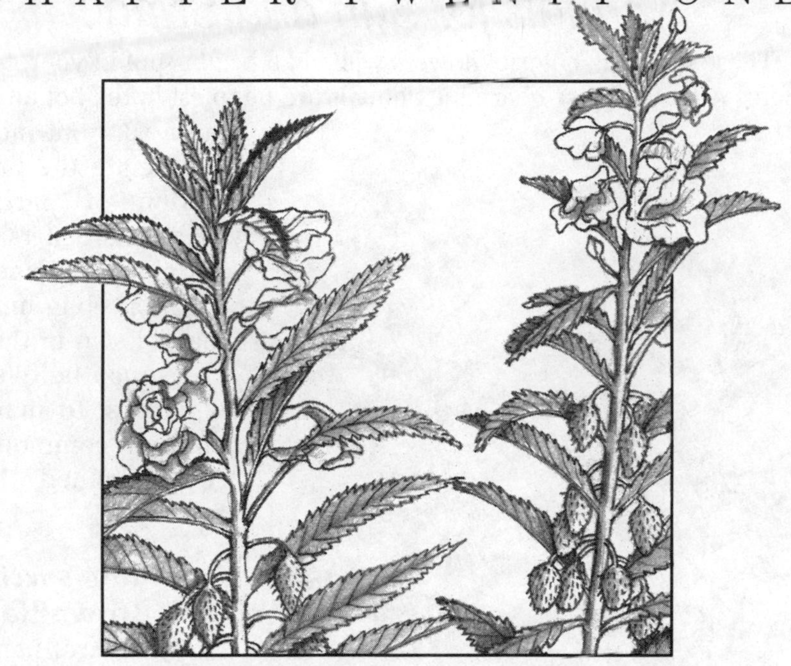

Add Uncommon Annuals to Your Garden

Do your well-thumbed seed catalogs flop open automatically at the marigold and zinnia pages? These dependable favorites are a must for most flower gardeners, but they're only part of the picture. Your garden will be more interesting if you spice it up with some of the lovely, less widely used annuals. And you'll have the fun of discovering new flower friends, some of which will probably become regular features in your garden.

Annuals for Sun and Shade

These graceful, colorful flowers will add a bright spot in your gardens. A few of these charming annuals are happiest in the hot afternoon sun, but most appreciate the protection of partial shade. Gardeners in warmer climates should keep in mind that full sun in their areas may be overwhelming to many annuals commonly recommended for sun.

Old-fashioned garden balsam is easy and fast growing. The sturdy plants keep flowering till frost, with blossoms like little camellias in shades of rose, salmon, lavender, and white. Collect seeds for next year from the fat, fuzzy seedpods, or let them pop open and scatter for surprises next summer.

Browallia speciosa **(Browallia)**

Try several hanging baskets of crisp white or blue browallia to cool your porch or balcony. The 1- to 1½-foot plants become a mass of bloom.

Start seeds indoors two months before your last spring frost. Keep the seeds uncovered, because they need light to germinate. Browallia likes rich soil and cool conditions. Give it light shade unless your summers are cool.

Impatiens balsamina (Garden Balsam)

These easy growers have blossoms that look like tiny camellias. They range from 1 to 2 feet tall, depending on the cultivar, and bear pink, rose, purple, or white flowers on bushy plants. Garden balsam does well in sun or partial shade.

Balsam likes well-drained, ordinary garden soil. Plant seeds directly in the garden after frost, or start early in pots a month before the frost-free date. Scatter a few pinches of fine soil over the planted seeds but don't bury them; they germinate more completely if they receive some light. Thin or transplant to 1 foot apart. Keep well watered in hot summers. The fat seed capsules pop open when ripe, scattering seed for more balsam next year.

Lobelia erinus (Edging Lobelia)

Masses of intense blue, ¾-inch flowers on creeping or cascading plants make lobelia a stunning foil for bright annuals. You can also get seed for white, pale blue, lavender, and rose-colored lobelia.

Start seeds indoors 2½ to 3 months before your last spring frost. Scatter seeds on the surface of the flat or pots, and leave uncovered. Seedlings are very tiny and grow slowly. If you transplant from a flat, keep the little plants in groups. Space clumps 8 inches apart. Plant in full sun with afternoon shade or in partial shade. Mine do well on an east patio.

Lobelia blooms especially well in cool weather. Like many annuals, it often comes on strong again in early fall. Try trailing varieties in hanging baskets.

Nemophila menziesii (Baby-Blue-Eyes)

Try a border of baby-blue-eyes instead of ageratum for a change. The fragrant, gently cupped, 1½-inch flowers in pure sky blue with white centers grow on 6- to 12-inch plants with interesting notched leaves.

Start seeds indoors in early spring, or sow directly in the garden in midspring, when soil warms up a bit. Baby-blue-eyes isn't fussy about soil but needs good drainage and cool conditions. Space plants about 6 inches apart. Look for volunteer seedlings in the garden next spring. Baby-blue-eyes prefers partial shade, but with adequate moisture it can grow in full sun.

Nigella damascena (Love-in-a-Mist)

The "mist"—the delicate soft foliage—forms a pleasing background for the pretty blue, white, or rose flowers. Plants grow 1 to 2 feet tall. The 1½-inch flowers are long lasting in bouquets or on the plant, and the seedpods make interesting additions to dried arrangements.

Plant seeds directly in the garden where they are to grow; the seedlings suffer from transplanting. Sow seeds about the time of your last frost, and thin to 10 inches apart. Love-in-a-mist thrives in ordinary soil but needs good drainage. If you leave some pods on the plant, it will self-sow for next summer's flowers.

Papaver rhoeas (Corn Poppy)

White and warm shades of red, salmon, or pink may tint the crepey petals on these 2- to 3-inch poppies. Also known as Shirley poppies, the plants grow 2 to 3 feet tall. Collect seeds from your corn poppies as the pods mature, and scatter the extra in your wildflower meadow.

It's easy to plant these beauties. Just remember not to disturb the seedbed after you plant the seeds. Scatter seeds on the surface of well-drained soil a month or so before the final frost. No need to cover; just press them lightly into the surface. Thin the plants to 10 to 12 inches apart.

Schizanthus × *wisetonensis* (Butterfly Flower)

Sometimes called poor man's orchid, butterfly flower does resemble those exotic blossoms in miniature. It comes in shades of lavender, purple, rose, pink, and white, with throat specks and shading. Plants grow about 1 foot high and make effective mass plantings for beds. They're nice in window boxes or hanging baskets because they have a tendency to sprawl. Pot up some plants for a cool patio, too. They flower well when potbound, so you can crowd them a bit.

Start seeds indoors in late winter or early spring. Just press the fine seeds into the soil surface. Avoid covering the seeds with soil, but do cover the planting flat or pots with a sheet of opaque plastic or damp newspaper because the seeds need darkness to germinate. Keep germinating seeds at about 60° to 70°F. Plant out seedlings after frost, spaced 1 foot apart, in rich, well-drained soil. Butterfly flower will grow in full sun, but in warmer climates partial shade is best.

Thunbergia alata (Black-Eyed Susan Vine)

Dark throats give the 1½-inch yellow or orange tubular flowers of this fast-growing vine a black-eyed Susan look. Some seed mixtures contain white flowers, too. Provide a trellis, netting, or fence to support the plants. The vines can grow to 6 feet long. Hot summers will slow down flower production, but in the cooler days of early fall the now-mature vines will be covered with dark-eyed flowers.

Plant seeds outdoors where you want them to bloom, or start indoors one to two months before your last spring frost. Keep planted seeds good and warm—75° to 80°F. Space plants 1 foot apart in good soil, in either sun or part shade.

Like its namesake, black-eyed Susan vine (*Thunbergia alata*) has a cheery, dark-centered flower. But this Susie is a climber, perfect for a trellis and graceful in hanging baskets or window boxes.

Trachymene coerulea (Blue Lace Flower)

Picture a head of Queen Anne's-lace dipped in blue watercolor. All summer long, 3-inch umbels of soft blue flowers top the 20-inch plants of blue lace flower. The flowers are lovely in bouquets, and dry well for fall arrangements.

Plant seeds directly in the ground in sun or partial shade. They don't transplant well. Avoid disturbing their roots. Thin seedlings to stand 9 to 12 inches apart.

CHAPTER TWENTY-TWO

Shade Summer Crops for Better Yields

One day last summer my husband asked, "What are those patio chairs doing in the garden?" "Oh, they're shading the lettuce," I replied. The determined gardener sometimes needs to explain odd features in the landscape. It was the hottest, driest summer in years, but we were able to pick lettuce to go with our tomatoes by shading the seedlings and watering the plants regularly.

Protection from the Sun

It's true that shade is usually an unwelcome intruder in the vegetable garden. Most vegetables need at least 8 hours of sun each day in order to produce well. But there are certain times and circumstances when a bit of shade can make the difference between success and failure of certain vegetable crops, especially in hot high-summer weather. Knowing how and when to offer a touch of shade is one of the arts of gardening.

Newly transplanted seedlings need some protection from the full force of the sun's rays for the first few days after they've been planted. Even well-hardened-off seedlings that have been popped directly from cell packs or pots into the ground will benefit from a day or two of shade if the weather is hot and dry.

Fruiting vegetables require more light than leafy ones do, so there aren't many times when you'll have to shade them. Here are some ideas on when to offer your summer garden a respite from the sun.

- Lettuce will be sweeter and crisper, and less likely to bolt to seed, if given some light shade in summer. Because lettuce starts to form a seed stalk if it receives 14 hours or more of light, judicious application of shade, and the use of bolt-resistant cultivars like 'Anuenue' (my favorite), will help to lengthen the lettuce harvest. Lettuce is probably the crop most frequently shaded by gardeners who want to keep the harvest coming all summer long.
- Certain leafy crops like chard, parsley, and sorrel can tolerate and even benefit from light shade in midsummer.
- In the herb garden, chervil, mint, sweet cicely, sweet woodruff, and tarragon thrive in part shade.
- Certain tomato cultivars, like 'Moira', tend to be subject to sunscald because of scant leaf cover. They'll be less likely to suffer scald if planted in the center of the row, where they receive some shade from adjacent plants, rather than on the end, where they are more exposed.
- Strawberry plants need all the sun they can get while fruiting. But where summers are hot, they often benefit from a bit of light shade after bearing, either from taller neighboring plants or from leafy brush stuck in the ground between the rows.
- Security lights or porch lights that burn all night can simulate long days. If such a light shines on your garden, you might want to cover

light-sensitive greens like lettuce and spinach for a few hours in the evening to give the plants a longer period of complete darkness.

A Dozen Ways to Make Shade

Shading arrangements can range from the impromptu to the elegant. Here are some homemade options for supplying shade. Be sure your constructions are sturdy: A shade frame that topples and crushes the lettuce is worse than no shade at all. You might want to experiment with the following options to see which works best for you.

Protecting the garden from hot summer sun means better yields of lettuce, spinach, chard, and certain tomatoes. Newly planted-out seedlings and strawberries that have finished fruiting appreciate cool shelter from the heat, too. Use your ingenuity to fashion sun shades like these.

- Poke clippings of shrub or tree branches into the ground around plants to offer quick, temporary shade.
- Shade seedlings with an upturned berry basket: the plastic grid kind for light shade, and the wood or cardboard kind for deeper shade.
- Toss a light covering of dry grass clippings or straw over plants—best used for newly set out transplants or seedlings—to protect plants for a few days.

- Grow short plants in the shade of nearby tall plants—pole beans, corn, sunflowers. Remember, though, that shadows are short in summer.
- Bend a length of wire fencing in an upside-down U-shape, cover with tied-on strips of cloth, and set over rows.
- Use slatted crates to cover small plantings.
- Drive sticks in the ground along both sides of the row or around the bed and drape old sheets, cheesecloth, or other light, loose fabric over them.
- Plant lettuce in a cold frame and cover the frame with a length of slatted wood snow fencing instead of glass. Or plant lettuce in a wide bed rather than a long single row, to make it easier to cover. Fashion a mesh awning or slatted cover to cut down on light intensity.
- Improvise a stick or board frame around a garden bed to support a large window screen or a section of snow fence.
- Construct a box of lath—like an orange crate, only larger—and set the box over plants that need shade. (Lath—inexpensive thin, narrow strips of wood—is sold by the bundle at lumberyards.)
- Try woven polypropylene or knitted polyethylene shade fabric to provide relief from the summer sun. Woven polypropylene fabric is available in a range of shade densities. The 55 percent shade density is useful for cacti and flowering tropicals; 63 percent for general foliage plant growth; and 73 percent for rejuvenating plants and helping them adjust to new conditions. Knitted polyethylene fabric is available in similar shade percentages.
- In a pinch, you can always pop a few aluminum-frame lawn chairs with slatted or woven webbed seats over the plants until you can come up with something more stable. Be prepared to do some explaining, though!

CHAPTER TWENTY-THREE

Cut Garden Greens All Season

126

Leafy garden greens may be a less dramatic crop than soaring stalks of corn or spreading pumpkin vines, but, comparing row space inch for inch, they'll probably contribute more food value to your meals. Greens are "in" these days (if that matters), and it's about time.

You're probably already growing early spring greens like lettuce and spinach, and perhaps some kale and Chinese cabbage for fall.

The big greens-gap tends to be in the summer, but that needn't be so. Enough good greens, like Malabar spinach and Swiss chard, thrive in summer to give you a different one for each day in the week and twice on Sunday.

Long-Yielding Greens

A continuous harvest until frost (and in some cases, even later) is yours with one planting of these greens, if you keep them well weeded, watered, and fertilized. Because these vegetables are available fresh for much of the season, it's not necessary to freeze large quantities. This steady yield takes some pressure off the gardener who does lots of home preserving.

HIGH VALUE

Any way you look at it, greens are a remarkable value. Seed is inexpensive, and a healthy patch of greens takes up only a little room in the garden, compared with space gobblers like squash and melons. They're easy to care for, and most garden greens have few insect pests. These leafy vegetables are rich sources of vitamins A and C and folic acid, at low caloric cost. Greens also contain a good balance of calcium and phosphorus, which helps our systems retain more bone-strengthening calcium.

Summer Greens Strategy

To help your plants produce tastier leaves, and more of them, follow these growing tips.

- Grow greens in rich, well-drained soil and fertilize them at least once during the growing season.
- Add limestone to highly acid soil; greens prefer neutral or slightly acid soil.
- Mulch lettuce and chard to keep soil cooler.
- Keep plants well watered for best production and flavor.
- Pick often to encourage production of tender new leaves.

Add variety and flavor to salads, stir-fries, and casseroles with tender shoots of cut-and-come-again summer greens. Malabar spinach, Swiss chard, and vegetable amaranth, shown here left to right, thrive in summer heat and keep up a steady yield until frost.

A Selection of Tasty Greens

These summer greens have more substantial leaves than delicate spring lettuce. Use the smallest new leaves and tender shoots in salads. Steam or stir-fry greens, or wilt them in a bit of oil or butter. Try them instead of spinach in Italian or Mediterranean dishes like lasagna or spanakopeta. Here are some reliable cut-and-come-again greens for summer picking.

Beet Greens

Beet greens (*Beta vulgaris*) actually contain more vitamins than the roots we consider our primary crop. They're usually mild flavored and quick growing and seem little affected by summer's heat. We cage our rows to fend off the local rabbits and woodchucks, who seem to appreciate the flavor, too. The 'Perpetual Spinach Beet', a promising new cultivar, produces leaves that resemble those of chard but taste more like spinach. This one can be eaten raw in salads.

Unlike spinach, an annual that is ever eager to go to seed, 'Perpetual Spinach Beet' is a biennial, so it won't run to seed during its first growing season. You can pick it well past the first frost. As with chard, it's best to take outer leaves from young plants and to treat yourself to inner leaves when the clump is well established.

Malabar Spinach

Malabar spinach (*Basella alba*) produces large, glossy, thick leaves on long vines. This warm-weather native is very frost-tender, so wait to plant seeds until frost is past, or start seedlings early indoors in individual pots. Give the vines a fence, string, or trellis for support.

Malabar spinach leaves have a mild flavor and lose less volume when cooked than spinach. Avoid overcooking, which gives the stalks a gelatinous texture. Plants mature in about 70 days. Let them branch a bit before you start picking. Harvest the newer growth at the tips of the vines. You can root slips of Malabar spinach in the fall and keep the plant alive inside as a house plant, then reroot new cuttings in spring.

New Zealand Spinach

Useful New Zealand spinach (*Tetragonia tetragonioides*) is a spreading, low-growing plant that endures heat and even dry weather without losing quality. Its medium-size, thick, triangular leaves provide mild-flavored cooked greens in summer and fall.

New Zealand spinach seeds germinate best in cool soil. In fact, this plant is a reliable producer of volunteer seedlings the following season. To speed germination, soak the hard seeds in water for several hours, nick them with a file, or abrade them by rubbing with sandpaper. The plants don't start to spread until the weather warms up, so they're good candidates for interplanting. Space them 1 foot apart in rows 2 to 3 feet apart and plant leaf lettuce or radishes between for a quick crop. Once they take off, the plants are self-mulching. Harvest young leaves, which are the most tender. This will also encourage the plant to branch and produce more tender young growth.

Swiss Chard

Swiss chard (*Beta vulgaris,* Cicla group) is an "old reliable" for many gardeners, but it must be admitted that it sometimes has a strong flavor in summer's heat. For best summer chard flavor, choose tender young leaves and steam them briefly. Overcooking in water ruins flavor. Try chard sautéed or in soups, and use it in place of spinach in lasagna.

You can begin cutting Swiss chard as soon as the leaves grow about 8 inches tall. A spring planting, as early as two weeks before your last spring frost, will continue through heat, cold, and moderate

GREENS FROM THE POTATO PATCH

The leaves of sweet potato plants are a traditional food in Africa and the Orient. We tried eating the stir-fried young leaves of a sweet potato vine in our garden and found them mild flavored and well worth including in the menu. Most sweet potato plants put forth a prodigious amount of leafy greens, and a few snipped-off young shoots will never be missed during the active growing season.

drought. A summer planting will be ready for picking in fall. Cut off flower stalks to prolong the harvest. Some gardeners prefer to cut the 2-foot plant back in midsummer so it can sprout more tender new leaves for fall. Chard has an exceptionally deep, strong root, and I've had plants that survived winter here in south-central Pennsylvania.

Vegetable Amaranth

Vegetable amaranth (*Amaranthus tricolor*), also called tampala and sometimes Hinn Choy, is a remarkably adaptable, efficient, and nutritious plant. Its raw leaves contain more calcium than kale, chard, or spinach. The attractive, branching 1- to 3-foot-tall plants, related to both ornamental cockscomb and weedy pigweed, are often tinged with a deep, rich burgundy shade—"coleus-like," as one catalog so aptly puts it.

Unlike spinach, vegetable amaranth likes warm weather and will produce well even in soil that is on the lean side. Young leaves may be served raw in salads, but amaranth is probably most often eaten as a cooked vegetable. When young and tender, the leaves need only brief steaming or stir-frying. If your crop is large, you can harvest and dry the leaves on airy screens. Dried amaranth leaves contain an excellent quality of high-lysine protein.

Sow vegetable amaranth seeds directly in the garden after frost, ¼ inch deep in rows 18 inches apart. Thin the plants to stand 8 to 10 inches apart. Leaves will be ready to pick in six to eight weeks. If you pick only the side shoots and top growth, the plant will continue to branch out until frost kills it.

CHAPTER TWENTY-FOUR

Make a Garlic Braid

A garlic braid hanging in the kitchen is a wonderful symbol of abundance and good cookery. The plump bulbs with their tight satin-paper skins are pleasant to look at, even for those who don't actually eat a lot of garlic. (But do they know what they're missing?) Garlic's reputation for protecting the household from vampires can make your garlic braid an amusing conversation piece, too.

Garlic braids are fun to make. For such an attractive room accent, they require hardly any effort and no skill beyond the ability to make a pigtail. Start by drying your summer harvest of garlic, with tops attached, on screens for a week or two.

Making the Braid

Select 16 well-rounded, shapely bulbs of garlic with strong tops. Snip off the roots as close as possible to the base of the bulb, leaving only a short tuft of root threads. Then rub the root stub with your thumb to dislodge any remaining soil. There's no need to wash the bulbs; they last longer if they're kept dry. Simply peel off the loose, dirty outer skin to reveal the clean, white wrapper underneath.

The kitchen table makes a good place to work. Put your 16 bulbs in easy reach. The only other equipment you'll need for this project is a few feet of strong white string. Ready to begin?

1. Choose three bulbs with tops of different lengths, so they won't all end at the same place in the braid. Arrange the garlic on the table side by side, with the bulb ends closest to you and the tops pointing away from you. Line them up so that the tops are even across the top and the bulbs are staggered.
2. Cut a piece of strong white string about 6 inches longer than the garlic tops (about 30 inches, depending on the length of your tops). Lay it next to one of the dried garlic tops, leaving the extra 6 inches of string extending at the upper end for a hanger.
3. Cut a short piece of string, about 6 inches long. Use it to tie the three garlic tops and the long piece of string together, almost at the very top. The short piece of string will not be used in braiding.
4. Begin braiding the garlic tops together, starting at the ends farthest from the bulbs. Always include the long string as though it were part of one of the garlic tops, to strengthen the braid. You may want to secure the upper end of the braid before you proceed, such as by hanging it on a nail or placing a few books over it.

   To braid, lap the tops of the right bulb over the tops of the middle bulb. Then lap the tops of the left bulb over the middle tops (which used to be the right bulb tops). Try to braid with even tension on the tops, so the "links" are the same size and fit snugly next to each other. Continue alternating right and left until you get near the first bulb.

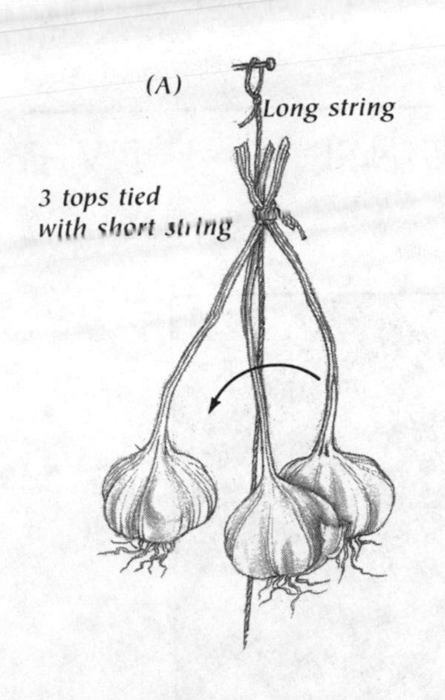

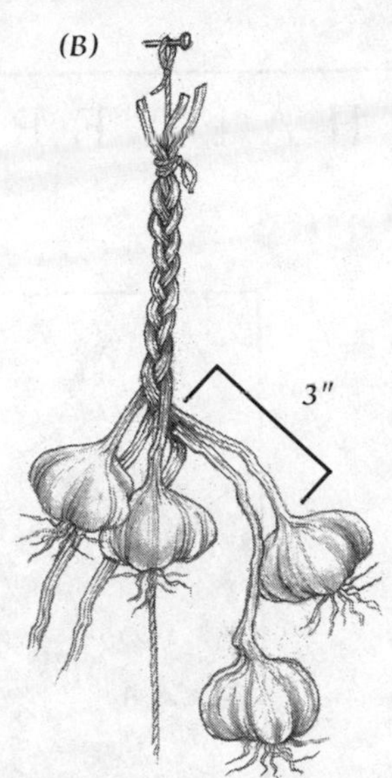

Attractive braids of garlic are easy to make and long keeping. Set aside bulbs, with tops still attached, after harvest and curing.
(A) If you can braid a pigtail, you'll have no trouble making a simple garlic braid. Lap the tops of the bulbs, alternating right and left, and always include the long string as part of the braid.
(B) To make sure there are no bare spots in your braid, work in a new bulb as you need it, overlapping the old and new tops by about 3 inches. You'll need about 16 bulbs for a good-size braid.

5. As you get close to the bottom (bulb) end of each strand of garlic tops, add another strand of garlic tops (with a bulb on the other end of it), overlapping the two strands (old and new) by about 3 inches.
6. Continue to braid until you have used up all the bulbs. Then tie the braid together at the bottom with string. Make a loop in the string at the top, cut off any extra string, and hang.

I hung my creation on the wall near the kitchen bookcase. It's been there for eight years now, and it looks as good as the day I hung it. The bulbs have dried so much that they're not solid any more. You could dent them by pressing on their sides. But I don't squeeze them, so they still look great.

You can, of course, use your garlic braid as a handy dispenser of those wonderful flavorful bulbs, peeling off cloves as you need them, and then make another braid next year. My friend Kate, who makes beautiful garlic braids for sale, tucks colorful dried flowers into her braids as she plaits them, a lovely touch that makes the garlic braid worthy of hanging on the front door.

CHAPTER TWENTY-FIVE

Practice Creative Plant Staking

Plants need help sometimes—to climb, to stand upright, to bear the weight of their heavy fruit or large flowers. You don't need to invest in a lot of high-tech gadgetry to support those flowers and vegetables in your garden that happen to be top-heavy. Instead of plastic poles, metal cages, and prefab teepees, you can use found items from your garden, household, or workshop to prop up plants that need support.

Helping Plants Stand Up

Plants that receive less than an ideal amount of sun, or that grow in poor soil, may produce spindly, weak stems in need of support. I have noticed this in my own garden with hollyhocks: Those that grow in full sun can stand up by themselves, but hollyhocks in partial shade lean forward and need to be tied to keep their stems upright. Overfertilizing, too, can cause sappy, floppy growth. You can encourage some plants, like chrysanthemums, to be more self-supporting by pinching them back several times during the growing season to promote more bushy growth. Still, if you have a garden, chances are you'll need to do a certain amount of plant staking.

Plant supports require an investment in preparation time and storage space, but they'll help you to grow more and better flowers and fruit on whatever amount of ground you have.

Floppy Flowers

Let's start in the flower garden, where such beauties as delphiniums, Canterbury bells, lilies, and carnations often need something to lean on to keep flowers upright and visible. Added strains from rain and wind can send tall, single-stemmed flowers sprawling, spoiling their blossoms and, even worse, breaking their stems. Plants that flop over can crush and smother their smaller neighbors.

Stick Figures

The good news is that it's easy to do. And here's even better news: The staking method many professional gardeners recommend as best of all is the least expensive. Twiggy branches pruned from shrubs or trees will do the trick. These versatile freebies make excellent flower supports because they blend into the scenery. As the plant grows, it hides much of the support, and what does show looks natural, not intrusive like a metal pole.

Select twiggy sticks that branch in three dimensions so they'll mesh with the plant and help to hold plant branches away from the main stem for better air circulation. Use only green sticks. Old, brittle ones may break under the weight of the plant and the force of the wind.

Choose sticks that are about 6 inches shorter than the mature height of the plant. If some protrude above the flowers later, you can prune

It's gratifying to find a low-tech, inexpensive solution that works as well as these stick supports do. Twiggy branches give asters, baby's-breath, Canterbury bells, and other floppy flowers something to lean on. The woody sticks are unobtrusive and soon hidden by leafy foliage.

them off. Put the sticks in place before the plants have grown quite tall enough to need them—when they're about one-half to two-thirds their mature height. Sharpen the ends of thick sticks (1 inch or more in diameter) with a hatchet so they'll be easier to push deeply into the ground. If you push the sticks into the ground when it is soft after a rain, they will go deeper and be better anchored. In a carefully tended flower bed, you may want to strip off leaves from your support sticks before inserting them.

Twiggy plant supports work best when used with plants that are arranged in groups. They're also suitable for "clumpy" plants with heavy-headed flowers. Try them with artemisia, asters, baby's-breath, chrysanthemums, daisies, nasturtiums, and phlox. Bee balms (*Monarda* spp.), Canterbury bells (*Campanula medium*), coreopsis (*Coreopsis* spp.), sweet William (*Dianthus barbatus*), and sweet pea (*Lathyrus odoratus*) also do well with these supports.

Tall, single-stemmed plants like delphiniums, lilies, and foxgloves (*Digitalis* spp.) call for a different strategy. You can tie them to a single strong stake, ½ to 1 inch in diameter. Cloth strips, discarded pantyhose, and twist-ties make good plant ties. Tie the twine loosely around the plant stem, then tie a loose knot between the plant stem and the stake so the stem won't be injured by rubbing, and, finally, tie the twine securely around the stake. For a plant that needs more support than a single stake, surround the stalk with three or four slender unbranched sticks or lengths of bamboo, looping them together with twine.

Vining Vegetables

Over in the vegetable garden, supports for vining plants can increase yields, improve fruit shape, and prevent fungal disease by allowing for better air circulation. Here are some suggested vegetable plant supports that you can make from materials you probably have on hand.

Bean Supports

Pole beans start bearing a bit later than bush beans, but they stay in production for a longer time so they're well worth the trouble of staking. A popular way to support them is by bean teepees. Make yours of three poles, each about 8 feet long. (Cut saplings are fine.) Sharpen the thick end of each pole and thrust the sharpened end into the ground, leaning the three poles together and tying them together at the top. I like this method because our soil is rocky; the poles sup-

PICK UP STICKS

Trees and bushes with branches that make good plant supports include alders (*Alnus* spp.), birches (*Betula* spp.), butterfly bushes (*Buddleia* spp.), hornbeams (*Carpinus* spp.), pin oak (*Quercus palustris*), poplars (*Populus* spp.), and *Vitex* species. See what you can find in your area. (And look over the fence to see what kind of prunings your neighbor is discarding.) But be sure you know what kind of sticks you're picking up. I once made the mistake of collecting an upright section of leafless "brush" that turned out to be poison ivy. (The hairiness of the stems *should* have given me a clue, but it was a balmy April day and I wasn't looking for trouble!)

port each other and therefore need to be inserted only a few inches into the ground.

In rock-free soil, you can drape your bean vines on strings suspended from a top pole supported by two side posts. Sink these free-standing posts 15 to 18 inches into the ground. Beans climb string readily, and this bean "wall" is easy to pick from both sides.

If you're trying to cram a generous selection of vegetables in a small space, try this suggestion: Plant a dozen pole bean plants in a 10-gallon tub. (Be sure to punch some drainage holes in the tub.) Insert a 6- to 8-foot pole in the center of the tub. Stretch strings between the top of the pole and soil level, anchoring them with wooden pegs or wire "hairpins." A maypole on your deck!

Tomato Cages

You don't *have* to support tomatoes. If you have plenty of space and mulch, you can let them sprawl. But if it's important to use your garden space as efficiently as possible, or if you have slug problems, you'll want to consider supporting your tomato plants. Yields of usable fruit are higher when the tomatoes don't rest on the ground.

The easiest tomato support system is a cylinder of concrete reinforcing wire. You can form the cylinder by tying the edges of a section of reinforcing wire mesh together with extra wire. Or use wire cutters to cut a vertical wire on the other edge to hook the cylinder together. Remove the horizontal wires on the bottom so the vertical wires anchor the cage in the earth surrounding the plant. The plant leans on the cage as it grows. Picking is easy, too—just reach over the cage. The only drawback is that cages are bulky to store.

Wood cages and fences are two alternatives that you can make from scrap wood and fencing. Use scrap lumber to make wood cages, usually 3 to 4 feet tall, with four upright posts and eight short horizontal braces. Set them right over the plants. These also take storage space, but they stack more compactly than the ungainly wire cylinders and you can make them from scraps. Or corral your plants between parallel lengths of 3- to 4-foot-tall wire fencing nailed to sturdy stakes. Drive the stakes into the soil, keeping the two sections of wire fencing about 2 feet apart, with the tomato plants between them. To brace the plants, poke slats (or sticks) through the wire at intervals, with the ends of the slats resting on the opposite wire fence.

Cucumber Frame

Cuke vines yield more fruit, with better shape and less rot, if they grow up and out rather than sprawl on the ground. Here's a cucumber frame that will be especially worth your while if you like to grow those long oriental or burpless cucumbers, because it will allow them to grow straight. The increased amount of leaf area exposed to the sun makes for a larger yield with this support method—as much as a 50 percent increase, in some studies. To make this cucumber support, nail scrap wood together to form two rectangular frames. Now nail or staple a section of wire fencing to each frame. Screw two hinges on one of the long sides to attach the frames and permit them to be folded flat for storage. In the garden, position the frames to form a triangle, or an upside-down V, with the hinged side at the top.

Vegetables will be better shaped and less prone to rot if you keep them off the ground. Parallel walls constructed of sturdy stakes and wire fencing, with slats inserted to brace the plants, hold tomatoes in reach for easy picking.

Pea Brush

You know that ad that features a progression of items, starting with the original classic, followed by a series of fads of the decade and returning, finally, to the classic? Well, twiggy brush is the classic support for peas. There's nothing better. For midsize pea and sugar pea cultivars that grow 3 to 4 feet tall, you can use sturdy brush alone (taller, stronger, and more widely branched than what you'd use for flowers). For sugar-snap peas, which grow 6-foot vines and even then don't know when to quit, I add 5-foot-tall metal stakes spaced 10 feet apart, with twiggy brush poked into the soil between them and twine stretched between the posts at 1-foot intervals.

CHAPTER TWENTY-SIX

Brighten Shady Corners with Perennials

What grows on the shady side of your house, in that nook by the garage, or in the corner of the yard where the neighbor's trees overhang your fence? Shady spots are often left to grow weeds or grass, but you can make them into assets instead. A good selection of flowering plants will not only grow but even bloom in shady places. Choose a few of these shade brighteners for your home place and see what a difference they can make in a formerly drab corner.

Each of the following perennials will bloom in light to medium shade—conditions you would find, for example, on the east side of a building or wall, under high branches of overhanging trees where light shifts as the sun moves, or even on the north side of a building where there is plenty of light but no direct sun. Deep shade, such as that found in the woods or under evergreens, is too dense for the plants mentioned here.

EVALUATING SHADE

In many spots, the pattern and depth of the shade shifts throughout the year as the sun changes its path and tree leaves appear and then fall. The terms used to describe shady conditions often vary from one source to another, making things even more confusing. To sort things out, use your own eyes to evaluate your spot of shade.

- Is the shade constant, all day long, as sometimes occurs on the north side of a house (deep shade)?
- Do the shadows shift, making dappled shade, when leaves on overhead trees are stirred by wind (partial shade)?
- Is the shade deep and dark, as it often is under a group of evergreens (deep shade)?
- Is the shade created by deciduous trees that don't leaf out until late spring and drop their leaves in fall (partial shade)?
- Is the shade created by a stationary object, such as a garden shed or tree, whose shadow moves with the sun (partial shade)?
- Are the leaves that create the shade small and open, like those of a birch tree (light shade), or large and dense, like those of a maple (deep shade)?

Shade Brighteners

If you're not sure how shady your shady spot is, experiment with some tolerant plants. If bloom is sparse or the plant looks weak, move it to a brighter place and try something else. Some plants that will grow in full sun in the North do better in partial shade in the South where summers are hotter.

Try these shade-flowering plants to spark up your home grounds.

Aruncus dioicus (Goat's Beard)

These are large, almost shrublike perennials that can reach up to 6 feet across when they're happy. In early summer, plumes of creamy white flowers rise 4 to 6 feet above the light green leaves.

Goat's beard likes dappled shade and appreciates humus-rich soil. Give it extra water in a dry summer. It does best north of Zone 7 and is hardy to Zone 3. Goat's beard is dioecious: Individual plants bear either all-male or all-female flowers. The male plumes are more feathery and upright. Goat's beard needs a lot of room.

Astilbe spp. (Astilbes)

Feathery plumes of flowers in shades of pink, rose, magenta, and cream rise gracefully over ferny foliage. Several species and many cultivars of astilbe (sometimes called false spirea) are available, ranging in height from 1 to 4 feet. Bloom times range from early to late summer, depending on species and cultivar.

Astilbe likes rich, moist soil and thrives in shade. In northern gardens, you can also try it in full sun, but shield it from the full brunt of hot summer sun. The plant is sensitive to dry soil. Mulch to preserve water, and provide protection from wind. Divide astilbe plants every three years to keep them flowering well. Astilbes are hardy to Zone 4.

Begonia grandis (Hardy Begonia)

This easy-to-care-for hardy begonia has pointed "angel-wing" leaves with attractive red veining and small pink or white flowers. Blossoms appear in late summer but the attractive leaves make the plant decorative all season long.

Hardy begonias thrive in moist soil with humus and grow 1 to 2 feet tall. Give them light, dappled shade or an eastern exposure. They're hardy to Zone 6, surviving winter unmulched here in my south-central Pennsylvania garden. Farther north, protect them with mulch over winter. To increase your plantings, collect and plant the small bulbils that develop in the leaf axils.

Cimicifuga racemosa (Black Snakeroot)

This attractive native plant can grow as tall as 6 feet, so it's a good background feature in your shady garden. Slender spires of long-

Tall black snakeroot (*Cimicifuga racemosa*) bears handsome candles of creamy white that light up those often-neglected shady corners. The aromatic flowers, said to repel insects, bloom in midsummer.

lasting, creamy white flowers bloom summer into fall.

Give black snakeroot a moist, shady spot with rich, acid soil, like its natural home at the edge of the woods. The slightly rank odor of the flowers has a reputation for repelling insects, which gives the plant the nickname "bugbane." The odor doesn't carry far, so it's not objectionable. Hardy to Zone 3.

Dicentra eximia (Fringed Bleeding Heart)

This bleeding heart, with finely cut grayish green leaves, is a native wildflower of the eastern United States. The spring blossoms of rosy pink are slender and elongated in contrast to the plump, heart-shaped flowers of the common bleeding heart (*Dicentra spectabilis*). White-flowering cultivars are also available. The plant forms a ferny clump 1 to 1½ feet tall.

Plant fringed bleeding heart in light shade or dappled shade, like that of the open woodlands floor where it grows naturally. Eastern exposures are fine, and even a sunny spot will do in northern gardens, where summers aren't long and hot. It's hardy to Zone 3. Fringed bleeding heart does well in average garden soil but needs good drainage. To increase your planting, divide the plants in early spring when the first shoots appear above the ground.

The Pacific bleeding heart (*D. formosa*) is the western form of this wildflower. It's similar in appearance but prefers cool, dry summers.

Digitalis grandiflora, D. × *mertonensis* (Foxgloves)

These perennial foxgloves tend to be somewhat shorter than the biennial common foxglove (*Digitalis purpurea*). Yellow foxglove (*D. grandiflora*), 2½ to 3 feet tall, has pale yellow flowers with brown netting within. Strawberry foxglove (*D.* × *mertonensis*), 3 to 4 feet tall, has deep pink flowers. In both species, flowers are drooping and bell shaped, with the opening less visible than in the biennial species.

Plant foxgloves in well-drained soil with a good supply of moisture, in light to medium shade. They'll form strong, healthy clumps in rich soil. Remove spent flowers from summer bloom to encourage repeat blooming later in the season. Divide *D.* × *mertonensis* every two years to keep it vigorous. *D. grandiflora* is hardy to Zone 3, and *D.* × *mertonensis* is hardy to Zone 4.

Geranium spp. (Cranesbills)

Cranesbills, or true geraniums, bear loose clusters of 1-inch open blossoms in spring or early summer in shades of pink, blue, magenta, white, and lilac. Most grow about 1½ to 2 feet tall. (The showy "geraniums" we fill our window boxes with actually belong to the genus *Pelargonium.*)

These rewarding plants come in many species and cultivars. Plant a selection of different species to extend the blooming season. Some of my favorites are *Geranium dalmaticum* (dalmatian cranesbill), a low-growing, trailing type that spreads rapidly but is never unwelcome; *G. macrorrhizum* (bigroot cranesbill), a vigorous easy grower with aromatic leaves; and *G. sanguineum* (blood-red cranesbill), an adaptable plant that does well in shade or sun.

In general, hardy geraniums like moist but well-drained soil and light or partial shade. Some species will tolerate full sun in northern gardens, and others grow best in deep shade. Most are hardy to Zone 3.

Helleborus niger, H. orientalis (Hellebores)

These long-lasting flowers, like large, nodding buttercups, add interest to the midwinter garden with their February and March blooms. Christmas rose (*Helleborus niger*), 1 foot tall with white flowers, seldom blooms as early as December—usually February or later. The Lenten rose (*H. orientalis*), 1½ feet tall with rosy purple, white, or greenish flowers, blooms about the same time. In areas where spring is cool, the flowers of hellebores may last into May. Leaves are evergreen.

Both Christmas rose and Lenten rose like rich soil and shade. Christmas rose (*H. niger*) is a little fussy about growing conditions: The soil must be slightly alkaline and consistently moist, so be sure to add plenty of compost. Mulch to keep the ground cool and retain moisture. It often takes several years to bloom after planting and should not be divided.

The beautiful but tough Lenten rose (*Helleborus orientalis*) blooms as early as February. The nodding flowers, in shades of white, green, or rosy purple, last for weeks. They self-sow freely in a shaded spot with rich, humusy soil.

Lenten rose (*H. orientalis*) is not as demanding. It will grow in most shady spots, with an occasional drink of water. It is easy to establish and self-sows. Hellebores do well under high trees or in the spaces between shrubs, and they're perfect for the north side of the house. Hellebores are hardy to Zone 4.

Lobelia cardinalis (Cardinal Flower)

Stately 2- to 4-foot spires of rich, deep red flowers make this summer-blooming perennial a breathtaking sight. This American wildflower, found from Texas to Florida and north to New Brunswick, needs moist soil. Although it is often found near streams in the wild, it will also grow in moist, humus-rich garden soil, in light to medium shade or morning sun.

Cardinal flower is a short-lived perennial, sometimes lasting only three to four years, but it does reseed itself. Be careful not to smother the basal crown when you spread mulch in the fall, and keep an eye out for young plants as they emerge. The plants are very hardy, to Zone 2.

Mertensia virginica (Virginia Bluebells)

Another beautiful blue flower, one of the loveliest of all. These early-spring–blooming bells nod above handsome oval leaves, rising to a height of 1 to 2 feet. In moist, shady areas, they form spreading colonies. You'll find these American wildflowers in both wildflower and perennial nursery catalogs.

Give Virginia bluebells rich soil with plenty of moisture. Add plenty of moisture-retaining humus to the soil, and mulch the plants. Choose a site in dappled shade or a spot with sun in early spring and shade for the remainder of the season. Virginia bluebells lose their leaves when the plants go dormant in summer. Don't worry: That's their way of escaping the stress of summer heat. They'll be back next spring, perhaps with new plants growing beside them. Hardy to Zone 3.

Myosotis scorpioides (Forget-Me-Nots)

These sprawling plants bear sky blue, scalloped flowers with a bright yellow eye. Moist soil and light to medium shade make perennial forget-me-nots happy. Plant them by a stream if you have one, or near the outdoor water faucet. They'll also do well in good, moist, well-mulched garden ground. One of the most charming plantings of forget-me-nots I've seen was a ring of the plants set around a backyard pool (a dug-into-the-ground bathtub). Plants I started from seed thrived by our pond until they were uprooted by pond repairs.

Perennial forget-me-nots, sometimes offered as *Myosotis palustris*, have narrow leaves and form sprawling clumps about 8 inches high. They bloom in spring and early summer and are hardy to Zone 3.

Polemonium reptans (Creeping Polemonium)

Creeping polemonium, sometimes called Jacob's ladder or Greek valerian, makes a pretty border for a bed of shade-loving flowers. These charmers, which grow wild in eastern woodlands and the midwestern plains, form compact, foot-high mounds of attractive paired leaves, with blue flowers appearing in spring.

Ordinary garden soil with good drainage in partial or light shade suits polemoniums. They'll also thrive in sunny spots in the North. We find them growing naturally in the woods under tall, late-leafing trees. Hardy to Zone 3.

Primula spp. (Primroses)

Primroses bloom in a rainbow of colors from yellow through rose, red, pink, purple, and blue. In most species and cultivars, the crinkled leaves form a compact basal cluster, with clusters of perky, open-faced flowers rising above the foliage in spring and early summer. Heights range from 8 to 15 inches.

Give your primroses partial or light to medium shade and consistently moist soil rich in humus. Mulch to retain soil moisture. Primroses don't like hot, dry summers. Some primroses lose their leaves and go dormant in summer. Mark the plantings so you won't accidentally dig them up. On the other hand, I've had a few primroses rebloom in fall after being watered through a summer of record heat and drought. Many species are hardy to Zone 3.

Tradescantia × *andersoniana* (Common Spiderwort)

This old dooryard favorite with grassy foliage blooms all summer. The three-petaled flowers open fresh each morning, replacing those of the previous day, which lasted only into the afternoon.

Easy to please, common spiderwort adapts to a wide variety of conditions. It grows especially well in rich, moist soil and will bloom in either light shade or full sun. Cultivars come in a wide range of colors: blue, mauve, purple, white, and near-red. Plants grow 1 to 2 feet tall. If the foliage gets straggly in midsummer, cut it off just above ground level. Cut-back plants sometimes bloom again in early fall. Hardy to Zone 3.

Veronica spp. (Speedwells)

Veronicas are available in many species and cultivars, most with graceful wands of tiny blue to lavender flowers. I have a deep pink cultivar in my garden, and other pinks and a white form are available, too. Plant heights range from 1 to 3 feet. Veronicas bloom in summer.

Veronicas do well in light or partial shade, though most species will also grow in full sun. Average garden soil suits them just fine. My plants thrive with annual applications of compost. Divide them to encourage more bloom. Some veronicas are hardy to Zone 3.

PART THREE

White
chrysanthemum . . .
before that
perfect flower
scissors hesitate.

—Yosa Buson (1716–1784)

AUTUMN

CHAPTER TWENTY-SEVEN

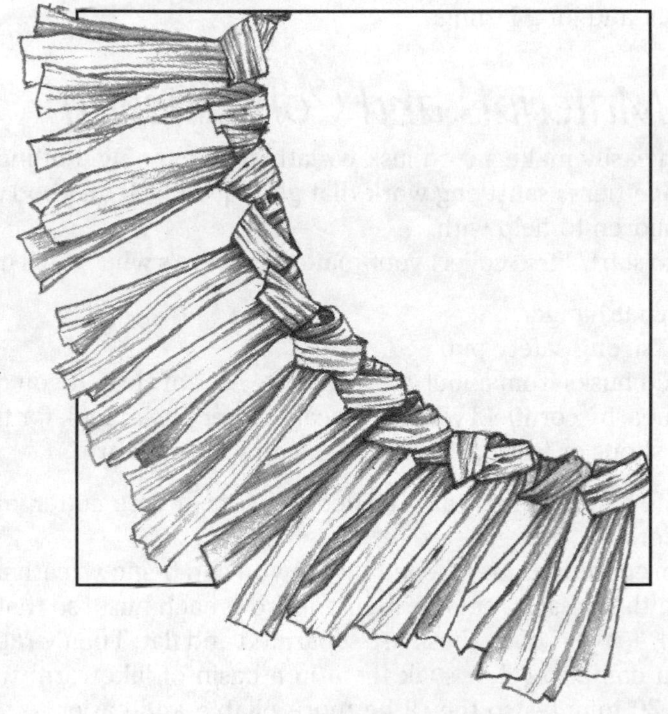

Craft a Cornhusk Wreath

Dried cornhusks are part of the mellow look of fall, along with pumpkins, gourds, autumn leaves, and Indian corn. We associate them with the bounty and ripeness of harvested fields, roadside stands overflowing with fresh produce, and friendly front-porch displays of the fruits of the season. For another decorative symbol of fall's abundance, you can make a wreath out of cornhusks. Cornhusk wreaths look great on doors or walls, either indoors or out.

A neighbor showed me how to make these wreaths some years ago. I've made a number of them, for us and for gifts, but I've never seen the wreaths sold or displayed anywhere else. The wreaths are lightweight and long lasting.

Materials and Construction

You can easily make a cornhusk wreath in an evening. Putting the wreath together is satisfying work that goes quickly. It's a good project for children to help with.

Ready to start? First, collect your materials. Here's what you'll need.

- A wire coat hanger.
- A large, strong safety pin.
- The dried husks from about 10 to 12 large ears of corn. If you don't have a nearby cornfield where you can gather husks, look for them at craft shops or in a Spanish or Mexican grocery store.

Only a few simple tools are needed: scissors, a wire cutter, and a pair of pliers.

A few preparations are needed before you can begin wreath making. Using the scissors, cut the stem end from each husk, so that the individual "leaves" of the husk are separated and flat. Then wrap the husks in a damp towel or soak them in a basin of lukewarm water for 20 to 30 minutes so they'll be more pliable and easier to work with.

From Coat Hanger to Wreath

There's something gratifying about transforming an ordinary wire coat hanger into an attractive wreath.

Pull the wire coat hanger open, and bend it into a circle. You can leave the hook on to act as a hanger, camouflaging it later with a large bow. For a neater appearance, cut off the hook and rejoin the cut ends. Crimp the joined ends with the pliers so they'll stay together.

Now you're ready to start making the wreath. The technique is simple. Here's how you do it.

1. Tear wet cornhusks into strips about ½ to ⅝ inches wide. Most cornhusks are about 8 to 9 inches long. Small variations in length don't matter.

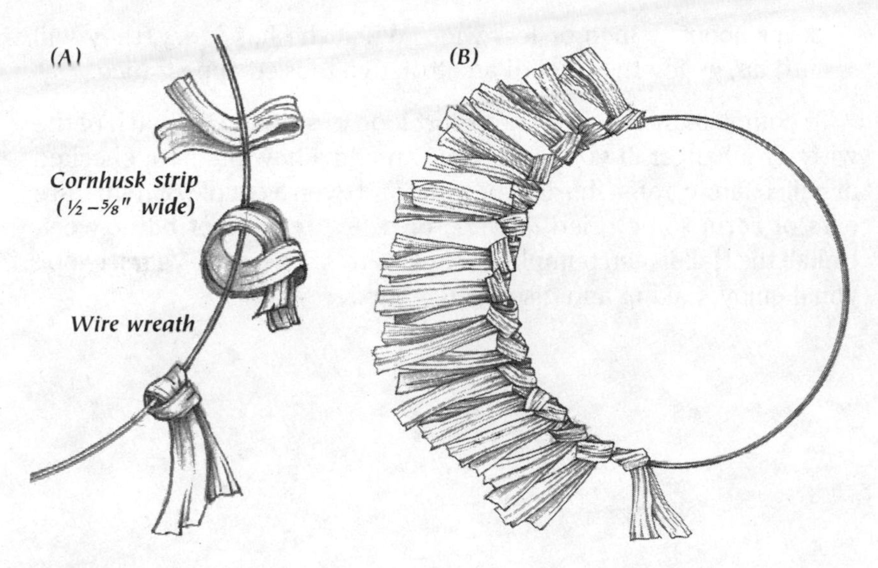

Making the wreath is an easy skill to learn, just as much fun for children as it is for grownups.
(A) Bend a thin strip of cornhusk into a U-shape and place under wire wreath form with loose ends facing wreath center and looped end outward. Bring both ends up and over the wire, inserting loose ends through loop. Pull ends outward firmly until knot is tight.
(B) Add strips, pushing them together tightly as you work. The more strips you cram in, the fuller the wreath will look.

2. Working with one strip at a time, bend the strip into a U-shape. Lay the strip under the wire hoop, so that you can see the U-shape and the two loose ends face the center of the hoop. Bring both the bent end and loose ends up and over the wire hoop, insert both loose ends through the bent end, and then pull the two loose ends tight to fasten the strip firmly to the wire.
3. Continue to add cornhusk strips until the wire circle is entirely covered with them. Push the looped husks together as you work, cramming as many husks as possible onto the wire for maximum fullness.
4. When the wire is completely covered with looped husks and you can't fit any more on, fringe the husks, one husk strip at a time. To do this, grasp the safety pin at its joint. Poke the point of the pin into each husk near the loop, and draw the pin out to the loose end of the husk. Split each husk strip once or twice, creating thin

strips about ¼ inch or less wide. When the husks dry, they will curl up, giving the wreath an attractive tousled appearance.

To complete the wreath, tie a short loop of string to the back of the wire for a hanger. If you wish, you can add a bow made of checked or calico fabric, raffia, burlap, or rope, and even a couple of miniature ears of corn, some dried flowers, or a few tendrils of bittersweet. Unlike the Halloween pumpkin, this wreath will keep for years. I hope you'll enjoy making and displaying yours.

CHAPTER TWENTY-EIGHT

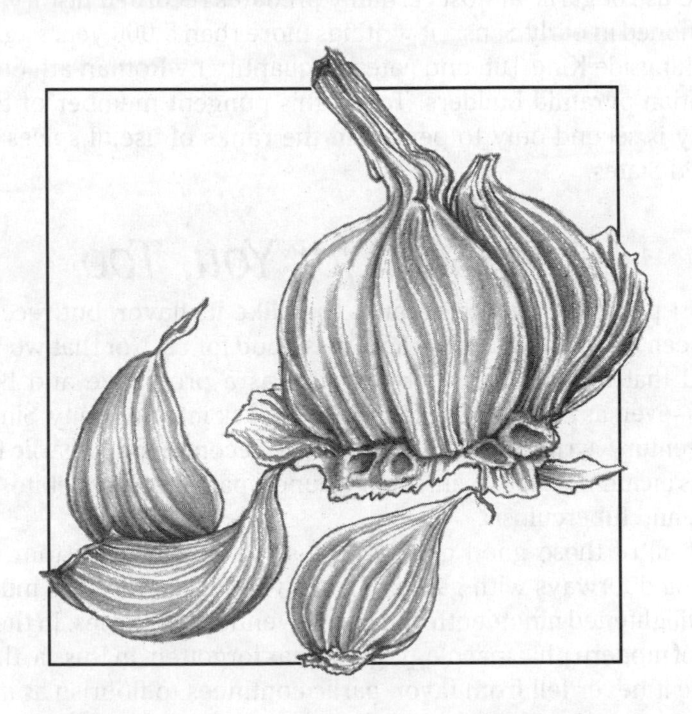

Plant Garlic Now for Bigger Bulbs

At our house we savor garlic in all its forms—a whiff in cold cucumber soup, a handful of cloves cooked in the eggplant parmesan, perhaps a breathtaking six-clove dose squeezed raw over fresh snap beans with grated cheese. A traditional Chinese saying declares "I'm glad I was not born before tea." In our family lexicon, we substitute "garlic."

The use of garlic almost certainly predates recorded history. It was mentioned in early Sanskrit writings more than 5,000 years ago, buried alongside King Tut, and eaten in quantity by Roman athletes and Egyptian pyramid builders. Today this pungent member of the lily family is second only to pepper in the ranks of useful spices in the United States.

And Good for You, Too

Most people eat garlic because they like its flavor, but recently it has been discovered that garlic also is good for us. Not that we hadn't heard that before. Garlic's reputation as a protective and healing herb—even as an aphrodisiac—extends back into antiquity. Since the first century, writers and herbalists have recommended garlic for ailments including asthma, infected wounds, parasites, snakebite, toothache, and tuberculosis.

But all of those good qualities, plus the medieval custom of festooning doorways with garlic to repel vampires, were too much for the enlightened nineteenth and early twentieth centuries. In the clear light of modern pharmacology, garlic was forgotten. In Russia, though, where it never fell from favor, garlic continues to flourish as a treatment for arteriosclerosis, colds, fatigue, and high blood pressure.

Gradually, scientists have begun to take garlic the healer as seriously as cooks take garlic the food. Louis Pasteur, in 1858, commented favorably on the antiseptic effect of garlic, but it wasn't until the 1940s that garlic's active antimicrobial compound, allicin, was identified by Swiss Nobel Prize winner Dr. Arthur Stoll. More recent reports, published in respected medical journals, indicate that garlic has been shown to inhibit pathogenic bacteria, control blood cholesterol, and discourage clot formation. A Japanese researcher has found that garlic increases the body's ability to assimilate Vitamin B_1. Although they don't concur yet on exactly how garlic's antibacterial action works, many researchers seem to agree on its value. And unlike some medications, garlic is safe, palatable, and free from side effects.

Still, as I crush a big clove into a bowl of eggplant, parsley, and olive oil dip, I reflect that we value garlic mostly for its flavor. We've grown our own for years, and since I've learned how to raise it, garlic has become one of our most satisfying crops.

Fall Gives a Fast Start

In my earlier garlic growing years, I planted in the spring. When an experienced garlic grower told me that I'd get larger bulbs with fall planting, I switched to his schedule: planting garlic cloves by the middle of October, usually around the 12th. He was right.

Fall planting produces larger bulbs for two reasons: Winter chilling promotes bulb formation, and the plants, which form roots in the fall, are mature enough to form big bulbs when long days trigger bulb growth. Spring-planted cloves, without that running start, are not as well developed when the sun says "bulb up now."

Planting and Caring for Garlic

Garlic hardly ever produces viable seeds. (But a few seed-producing plants have recently been discovered.) To plant garlic, separate the bulbs into their component cloves, each of which will produce a new bulb. I purchase only large garlic bulbs, and I plant only the largest cloves from those large bulbs. We eat or give away the smaller inner cloves.

Garlic likes rich, well-drained soil. I plant the cloves in a 20- to 24-inch-wide raised bed, four or five cloves across the bed, or about 4 inches apart. Keeping the pointed ends up, I push each clove 2 to 3 inches deep in the soft soil. To keep the soil rich and the cloves nice and plump, I rake two bucketfuls of fine compost into the 25-foot-long bed each year.

My October-planted garlic plants form good strong roots before the ground freezes over. By Thanksgiving, they have usually sprouted several inches of top growth. When the ground freezes hard later in December, I mulch the row with young cedar trees culled from our meadows,

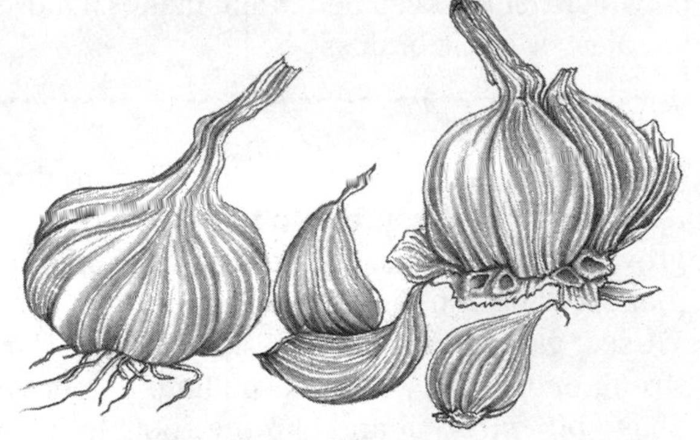

Garlic adds savory goodness to eggplant Parmesan, chicken dishes, soups, and sauces—and it may ward off colds and vampires, too. Buy large garlic bulbs, and plant only the largest cloves. Each clove of garlic will produce a new bulb.

so the soil won't heave and tear the garlic roots during winter thaws. (You could use discarded Christmas trees.) I remove the mulch in early spring, usually in mid-March.

Before April is too far gone, my garlic row is a thicket of fresh green spears. By May, weeds get a toehold. I know by now that young garlic doesn't like competition, so I never fail to hoe and hand-pull that first crop of weeds. I have to weed again in June.

I've read that garlic yields best if it receives a regular supply of moisture, so I try not to let my garlic row dry out. Generous watering during the growing season certainly seems to make a difference, but stop watering when the bulbs are within two weeks of harvest. Maturing bulbs need to dry and harden so that they'll keep well. I learned this the hard way: One year, in my zeal to keep the garlic well supplied with water, I kept watering weekly until harvest time, which caused the bulbs to rot and fall apart from too much of a good thing.

HARVEST EARLY

It's best to harvest garlic when the lower leaves turn yellow. I used to wait until the tops had fallen over, but by then the outer bulb scales have usually either decayed or pulled away from the bulb. Garlic harvested earlier has a smoother, tighter skin cover, which helps it keep better and makes it more attractive for gifts, sales, or garlic braids.

Toward the end of July, the tops start to dry and bend over. Keep up your guard if you haven't yet harvested. If you allow weeds to grow rampant in that week after the bulb tops die down, they can make it difficult to find the bulbs.

Use a garden fork to harvest your crop. Garlic tops aren't usually strong enough to withstand pulling, unless your soil is very loose. Shake off extra soil and clip the roots to a ⅜-inch stub. Spread the bulbs on a screen in a shady, well-ventilated place to cure for a week or two. Then clip the tops and store the bulbs in a cool, dry place. Avoid refrigerating the bulbs or sealing them in plastic; cold and high humidity promote spoilage. My garlic lasts the winter in a paper bag kept in a cool pantry closet.

CHAPTER TWENTY-NINE

Take Your Garden When You Move

Every year thousands of gardens change hands. People transfer to new jobs, their housing needs change, they seek a different climate, or perhaps they finally find the country place of their dreams. There's no denying that moving is often a wrenching experience. Apart from the regret at leaving friends and familiar haunts, there is the poignant question of the garden in which you have invested so much care and time.

Your first impulse, perhaps, is to cart it all—perennials, topsoil, and trees—to your new home. You wonder and worry whether the new owner will remember to thin the irises, prune the grapes, and mulch the orchard trees. You mentally recount the bushels of leaf mold and manure that you've dug into your soil. You compare the bare yard in your new place to the luxuriant landscaping you've achieved at your old home.

But then you remember that moving is an adventure, too, and that starting a new garden will be a satisfying part of that adventure. The long-term plantings you've put in were made for the future, with an acceptance of all its possibilities. Now the fruit trees you've started will feed another family, and you'll soon plant more in a new place.

Transplanting House and Garden

In the five household moves we've made, these thoughts of regret and then acceptance have been our pattern, too, as each time we left behind a lovingly tended garden and planted a new one at our new address. It made things easier when we were able to take started plants along for our new yard. We have, in fact, gone to what some might consider rather ridiculous lengths to transfer the best of the old garden to our new residence.

Our first move was from the little old Philadelphia house we had bought the year after our marriage to another old house on a tree-lined street in a small Indiana town. Our first journey to our new town was a house-hunting trip, and we loaded the back seat of our car with cans and cartons of perennial transplants—rhubarb, coral bells, columbine, lily-of-the-valley, chrysanthemums, and more. Those precious plants stayed in the motel bathroom with the lights left on while we toured prospective homes. Then, when we'd decided on a house, we asked the owner's permission to plant our flowers and vegetables in an out-of-the-way corner in the yard, so they'd be there waiting for us when we returned with children and household goods.

One of our other moves was more complicated. We sold our old residence, then spent the following four weeks camping while searching for a country place to buy. When we couldn't seem to find a property that was right for us, we decided to rent a house for a year to leave us free to buy our dream homestead when we found it. So that time, the only treasures we could bring from our former home were the few flower seeds that had ripened early, and other seeds saved from previous years.

During the month we spent between homes, I missed working with the soil. But I was surprised to find that my appreciation of others' gardens was keener when I had none of my own; their shasta daisies seemed larger, their columbines more colorful, when I was not half-consciously comparing them with my own or smugly thinking, My peas are ahead of those! Perhaps I needed this chance to appreciate beauty beyond my own yard, beauty not of my making or owning; to admit the wonder of all growth, even when I hadn't done the planting.

A Fast Summer Garden

The spades and forks weren't off the moving van long, though, before we had them in the ground. In fact, we had our garden planted before most of the cartons were unpacked. Six weeks after moving into our rented home in early July, we were eating our own zucchini, cherry tomatoes (from purchased plants), lettuce, chard, beet tops, dill greens, and radishes. Soon after that, beans were on our table, followed by full-size tomatoes, beets, carrots, cabbage, and brussels sprouts.

Planting later in the season, as we did, called for a slight modification of usual practices. We planted seeds in shallow furrows, watered well, and then pulled dry

A big pot of flowers on the front step does wonders for the morale of a transplanted gardener. Use cheerful blooming annuals and squeeze in as many as you can for instant results.

soil over the seeds. This helped to prevent crust formation. When planting the vegetables, I reserved a row for some perennial seeds: balloon flower (*Platycodon grandiflorus*), blanket flower (*Gaillardia* sp.), and shasta daisy (*Chrysanthemum* × *superbum*). The thrifty little plants made a good start for the flower border I developed the following spring.

At the greenhouse where we bought the tomato plants, we also chose an appealing array of geraniums, petunias, and ivy, and arranged them in a great big clay pot on the front step. This instant "welcome garden" was worth its weight in gold for the sense of home that it gave us. Visitors and neighbors seemed to appreciate it, too.

We now live on a farm, where we hope to stay for many years. But when we do need to pull up stakes, we'll be prepared to follow the guidelines that we've learned in our previous moves.

Before You Move

Planning for moving the garden begins even before you list your house for sale. The more time you have to plan, the better prepared you and your plants will be.

Put It in Writing

Most sales agreements include the plantings as part and parcel of the property. If you want to take some plantings with you, it's a good idea to get them ready to go before you draw up any papers. Make sure you add a special clause to your contract to exclude any plantings that won't be included in the sale, and list them specifically. (It is, of course, unfair to remove trees or shrubs that have been shown as part of the property and not specifically reserved, and illegal to do so if an agreement of sale has been signed.)

Buyers may sometimes agree to let you take along a certain tree or other plant that's important to you. For your own protection, get the whole arrangement recorded and signed, no matter how amicable your verbal agreement may seem to be.

Planning Ahead

You can't pack your garden in neat cardboard cartons, but you can take steps to make moving easier. Start with these ideas.

- Divide perennial vegetables and flowers like rhubarb, irises, daylilies, and phlox, and plant each division in a clay pot or perforated can sunk in the ground.

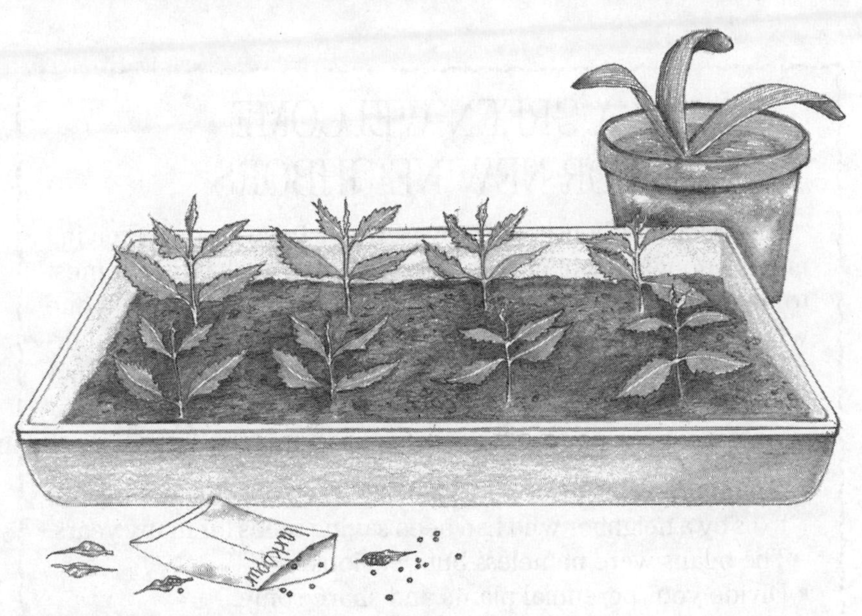

Start early to prepare your garden for the move. Root cuttings of your forsythia, collect seeds from your favorite blue larkspur, and pot up the perennials you can't live without.

- Set aside a special nursery row for plant starts and divisions you intend to take with you to your new home, making it clear to prospective buyers of your house that this group of plants is not included in the sale.
- Root cuttings of herbs, vines, houseplants, pussy willows, roses, grapevines, and other shrubby perennials either in the house or in your nursery row. Dip the cut end in rooting hormone (one that doesn't contain chemical fungicides) and insert it in damp vermiculite. Cover pot and stem with a plastic bag until roots form.
- Consider collecting scion wood for future grafting. From February through April, you can take cuttings from fruit and nut trees. You can graft these cuttings, called scion wood, to trees on your new place. Keep the cuttings cool and protect them from drying until you're ready to make the graft. To learn the technique, consult a good book on grafting at your library, or see "Resources" on page 300 for recommended reading.
- Save seeds of all flowers and vegetables that form seed before you leave.
- If you're moving cross-town, not cross-country, start flats of early spring vegetables to plant in your new garden.

A GREEN WELCOME FOR NEW NEIGHBORS

In our various household moves, we've been on the receiving end of enough neighborly kindnesses to learn what means most to newly transplanted gardeners. If you're the well-rooted one who is in a position to welcome new people to your neighborhood, here are some things you might do to help *them* to put down roots.

- Offer seeds—something most gardeners have to spare. One of our favorite housewarming gifts was a bag of bean seeds given to us by a neighbor who had been saving seeds for many years. The beans were nameless but delicious.
- Divide your perennial plants and share some.
- Give new neighbors the addresses of local nurseries and garden centers that you have found to be reliable. Share sources of manure and mulch, too.
- Be ready to answer basic, nitty-gritty questions about gardening if your new neighbors are first-time homeowners who haven't gardened before.
- Donate a bucketful of compost for some of their special plantings. (Although we moved our compost pile—two trips in a pickup truck—on our latest move, that wouldn't be a practical option for most people.)
- At the beginning of the planting season, pot up some extra seedling transplants for your neighbors.
- Consider a cooperative arrangement: Instead of both planting cherry tomatoes or other often-overproduced crops, you might plant zucchini and your neighbor might plant tomatoes and then you can both share the produce.
- If you welcome your new neighbors with a cooked meal, include a dish from the garden. If it's a regional specialty, so much the better. We have warm memories of the Indiana persimmon pudding and Lancaster County vegetable soup with homegrown lima beans that kind neighbors made for us.

WELCOME, NEW OWNERS

I've made it a practice, when we move, to leave a diagram of the garden plantings for the new owner, naming fruit trees by cultivar and showing the location of spring bulbs that wouldn't be evident in the summer. Also, I usually start a small vegetable garden, both because I can't help planting something each spring and because the food plants we've left behind have meant a great deal to the new owners.

At Your New Home

First, treat yourself to an instant garden—a big flowerpot on the front step or a ring of bright annuals around the mailbox. Such a sign of home, a declaration of intent to put down roots, will do wonders for the morale of a family still stumbling over packing boxes and eating quick meals from mismatched plates.

Concentrate the first year on long-range improvements that take time to show results. Improve the soil for your new garden space by tilling or digging, planting cover crops, and adding manure. Get a compost pile going. Plant fruit, nut, or ornamental trees, shrubs, and hedges, and put in rhubarb, asparagus, and other perennial vegetables.

Talking about gardening with your neighbors is a good way to get acquainted. Ask them which plants do especially well or poorly in your area. Find out about late freezes and summer droughts.

Moving has more than once given me a feeling of kinship with the pioneer woman who saved slips, seeds, and rooted cuttings from her old homestead to start anew in unfamiliar territory. For her it was a necessity. For us, retaining a favorite strain, an old family rose, an assortment of beloved perennials, or a scion from a good fruit tree provides the sense of continuity that has made home wherever we've been. As we plant anew and put down new roots, we begin to see that transplanting can be stimulating to gardeners, too.

C H A P T E R   T H I R T Y

Add Grace with Grasses

Grasses are spreading, and with good reason. Of the hundreds of available species and cultivars of ornamental grasses, there are some for every situation: backyards, flower borders, public buildings, seaside gardens, town parks. Heights range from several inches to over 10 feet, and plant forms run the gamut from cushion mounds to spiky bushes to arching fountains of graceful stems to towering plume-topped stems.

All-Year Interest

Most popular ornamental grasses are attractive in every season. Fresh green growth starts in spring, and by summer, the plants are fully shaped, with developing flowering heads. Grasses are lovely in fall, softly colored with striking seed heads that last all winter. The arching stems of many species provide a pleasing counterpoint of line and texture to a garden of flowers, trees, and shrubs.

Stems, seed heads, and leaves often change color with the seasons, from green to bronze to tan, for example. Some grasses have subtly colored rosy pink, lavender, and blue-green phases. Others may be wine red or deep red. The leaves and seed heads are colored in every imaginable tone of gold, russet, bronze, brown, or tan in fall and winter, adding interest to the landscape.

SOUND AND MOTION

Ornamental grasses add more than color and texture to a garden. Most also contribute two more distinctive features: Their thin, pliant stems are responsive to the slightest breeze, so they add motion to a still life of trees and flowers. They contribute delightfully relaxing sounds, too, with their soft rustling, swishing, and sighing in the breeze.

Tough, Easy-Care Plants

Ornamental grasses are as practical as they are versatile. Most will thrive in a wide variety of soil types. They don't need to be staked or deadheaded, like some of our more pampered perennials. Grasses perform best in full sun but will accept light shade. Sedges and rushes, which are similar in appearance but botanically different from grasses, can take more shade and dampness than true grasses. (They're usually lumped together with grasses in nursery catalogs. Sedges have solid stems; grasses, hollow stems. Both have narrow leaves and insignificant, wind-pollinated flowers.)

If you're designing an ornamental grass garden from scratch, include a variety of plant types for an interesting contrast in textures.

Place tall plants at the back of the border, medium-size ones in the middle, and shorter ones in front. Ornamental grasses make good accents in an already established perennial bed or foundation planting, or you can use them as specimen plants in a lawn.

When planting, allow a space between plants equal to their projected height at maturity. If you're planting a row of them for a screen, though, space them closer—about half as far apart. For best results, give them good soil, reasonably well supplied with organic matter, and good drainage.

Grasses don't need a lot of maintenance. Most grasses can compete well with weeds, but mulch improves their appearance and makes care easier. Decaying mulch will boost soil fertility, too. Apply an annual topdressing of compost, but avoid heavy doses of manure or other high-nitrogen fertilizers that will encourage weak, lank growth.

It's a good idea to shear off all dead leaves and stems in early spring. They'll look bedraggled anyway after winter, and cutting them off provides room for the new spring growth. When old top growth is left in place, some grasses will grow outward, leaving a bare space in the center of the clump. For large, heavy-stemmed clumps, use an electric hedge trimmer or lopping shears to cut old stems back to about 2 inches.

If your grasses spread a lot or begin to crowd each other, dig and divide each clump into four parts and replant. Where roots are thickly entwined, as in our large clump of eulalia grass (*Miscanthus sinensis*), you'll need to use an axe to chop them apart. A few species of ornamental grasses, such as ribbon grass (*Phalaris arundinacea* var. *picta*), are invasive. Subdue these roamers by planting them in bottomless buckets or large pots, or sink other root barriers like foot-deep strips of fiberglass or lawn edging between plants.

Choose the Best

You can pick up some good landscaping ideas by visiting botanical gardens or your local garden center, which might have a demonstration planting of ornamental grasses. Consult catalogs, too, to see how many choices you have. Here are a few widely available, especially lovely grassy plants to consider. (All are perennials. Check seed catalogs for annual ornamental grasses.)

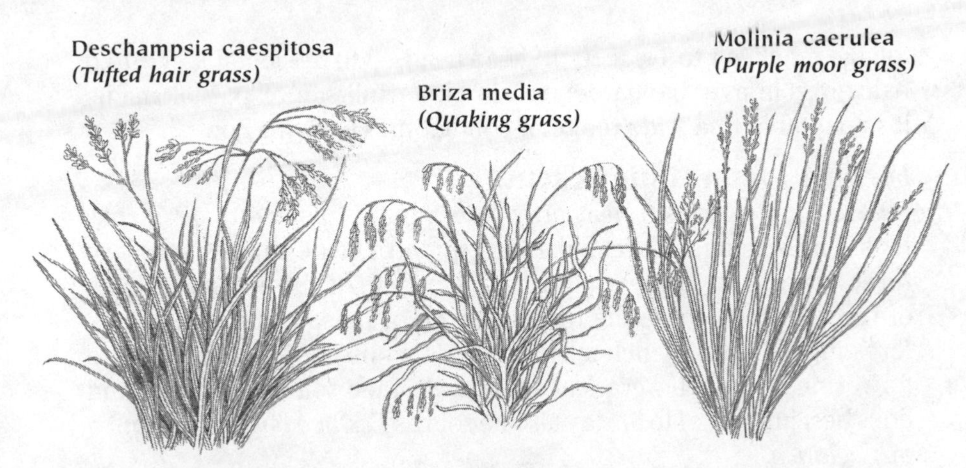

Low-growing grasses are perfect for the front or middle of your garden. Even a single tufted mound adds a new note of texture. But grasses can be habit-forming, once you take a look at their many colors and styles.

Short Grasses

The following grasses are under 2 feet tall according to the height of the foliage. Keep in mind that seed heads are often borne high above the leaves.

Briza media (Quaking Grass)

Quaking grass forms tufted, ½- to 1½-foot-tall mounds of slender leaves topped by showy seed heads with a braided appearance, much used for dried arrangements. Grow it in ordinary soil, in full sun. It tolerates heavy and even poorly drained soils. Avoid over-rich soil for best stem and seed head development. Quaking grass spreads by rhizomes and also self-sows. Hardy to Zone 4.

Carex morrowii 'Aureo-variegata' (Variegated Japanese Sedge)

Another good groundcover grass, variegated Japanese sedge forms a swirling clump of ribbonlike yellow or cream grass blades with green edges. Foliage and flowering stems are about the same height, 1½ feet. Plant this evergreen grass in shade, partial shade, or full sun, in moist, acid, humus-rich soil. Hardy to Zone 5.

Deschampsia caespitosa (Tufted Hair Grass)

Tufted hair grass, with its delicate flowering seed heads, is most effective when seen against a dark or plain background. The mounded foliage reaches 1 to 1½ feet; the seed heads, 3 to 3½ feet. Plant tufted hair grass in average garden soil in either full sun or partial shade. It's adaptable to a wide range of conditions. Hardy to Zone 5.

Festuca caesia (Blue Fescue)

Blue fescue forms a neat gray-blue mound about 8 to 12 inches high. The self-contained clumps don't spread. Divide blue fescue every three years or so to get around its tendency to die back in the middle of the clump. Because the tufted texture of these plants is more interesting than the 16-inch-tall seed heads, some gardeners clip off the flowering stems. This grass needs well-drained soil and full sun, and does best in Zones 4 to 9. May also be sold as *Festuca ovina* var. *glauca* or *F. glauca.*

Hystrix patula (Bottlebrush Grass)

This grass gets its name from the shape of its spiked seed heads, which may reach 3 feet. Bottlebrush grass grows upright, in clumps that reach about 1 foot tall. Plant it in humus-rich, well-drained soil in partial shade. It self-sows readily. Hardy to Zone 5.

Imperata cylindrica 'Red Baron' ('Red Baron' Japanese Blood Grass)

Blood grass is grown for its color, which deepens in fall and fades in winter. Upright, 20-inch grass blades, green at the base but otherwise distinct red throughout, spread by extending rhizomes but grow slowly. Blood grass seldom forms flowers. Plant this grass in soil well supplied with moisture but also well drained, in either full sun or part shade. Hardy to Zone 5; possible in Zone 4 with a winter mulch. May be sold as *Imperata cylindrica* var. *rubra.*

Luzula sylvatica (Greater Wood Rush)

Greater wood rush makes an unusual groundcover plant for shady areas, forming tussocks of evergreen foliage. The foliage reaches 1 foot tall, and the flowering stems stretch to 3 feet. Plant in humus-rich, woodsy soil, in shade or part shade. The 8-inch-tall hairy wood rush (*Luzula pilosa*) is also a good choice. Both are hardy to Zone 4.

Molinia caerulea (Purple Moor Grass)

Purple moor grass is slow growing but dramatically effective when mature. Plant it where you can see and hear it swaying in the wind. This grass grows in dense, upright clusters of arching leaves, 1 to 1½ feet tall. The purplish, sometimes brownish seed heads reach 2 to 3 feet. Purple moor grass prefers fertile soil, acid to neutral but not alkaline, with a good supply of moisture, and will grow in either full sun or partial shade. Hardy to Zone 4.

Schizachyrium scoparium (Little Bluestem)

A drought-resistant native prairie grass, little bluestem grows in an upright clump about 10 inches tall, with seed heads that reach 2 to 3 feet. Leaves turn a soft, rosy orange in fall. Grow it in ordinary, even poor soil and full sun. A good plant for naturalizing. Hardy to Zone 4. May be sold as *Andropogon scoparius.*

Sporobolus heterolepis (Prairie Dropseed)

This native grass grows slowly. It will be a handsome plant in its third season, when its foliage reaches about 1½ feet and its seed heads stretch to 4 feet. The arched foliage turns orange in fall, and the 8-inch seed heads are decorative in the fall and winter garden. Give this grass ordinary soil and full sun. Hardy to Zone 4.

Tall Grasses

The leaves of these grasses grow over 2 feet. As in the previous list, remember that seed heads often grow higher than the foliage.

Calamagrostis × acutiflora 'Stricta' (Feather Reed Grass)

This narrow, upright clump of grass, with leaves about 2½ feet tall, resembles a sheaf of wheat. The graceful, 5-foot-tall seed heads are buff-colored plumes that last all winter. Feather reed grass bends to the weather, but returns to its upright position with great resilience. Ordinary soil, even heavy clay, suits this adaptable plant, and it does well in either full sun or light shade. Hardy to Zone 5.

Helictotrichon sempervirens (Blue Oat Grass)

The cool gray-blue leaves of this grass set off the bright colors of your favorite flowers. It forms a tall, spiky clump with arching leaves and slender, feathery seed heads. The foliage reaches 2 to 2½ feet tall, and the seed heads grow to about 4 feet. Give this grass light, well-drained soil with plenty of humus, good air circulation, and full sun. Blue oat grass likes cool weather and may not perform as well in very hot, humid summers. It's hardy to Zone 4 and evergreen in mild climates.

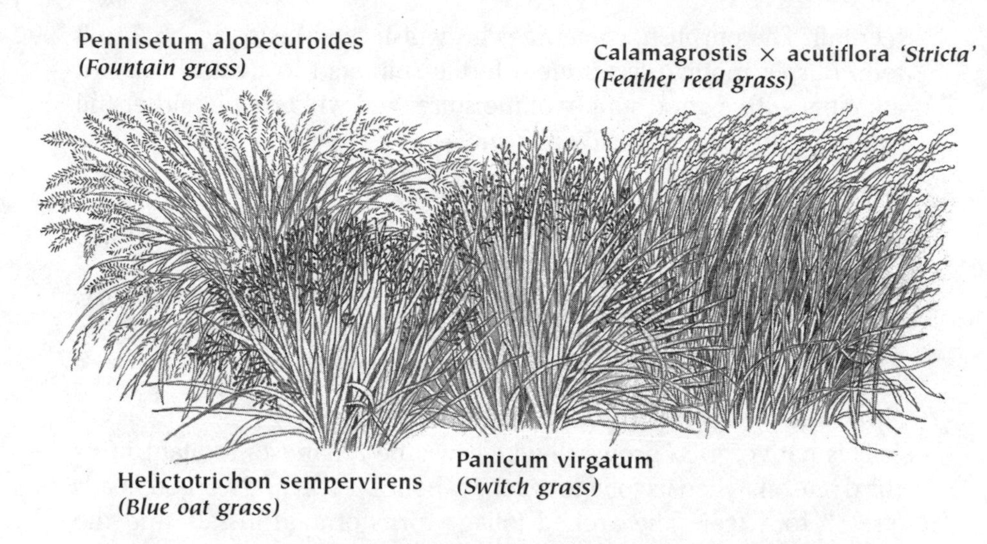

The spiky or fountainlike foliage of tall grasses makes a good foil in the garden for all sorts of flowers. In summer and fall, these attractive plants come into their own, pushing up seed heads that can reach 6 feet high or more and mellowing to autumn colors. And in winter, you'll appreciate them even more, when their bleached leaves rustle in the wind and keep the garden interesting.

Miscanthus sinensis (Eulalia Grass)

Sometimes called Japanese or Chinese silver grass, this grass forms large, upright clumps that can reach 6 to 10 feet tall. The leaves are gently arching, and the seed heads look like feathery plumes. Undemanding eulalia grass does fine in ordinary soil. Full sun is best, but part shade is tolerated. Avoid overfertilizing eulalia grass; too much nitrogen promotes overgrown stems that may fall over. Hardy to Zone 5.

Panicum virgatum (Switchgrass)

Switchgrass is a deep-rooted native prairie plant that turns yellow or orange in fall, fading to buff over winter. It forms upright clumps 3 to 5 feet tall, and its airy flower heads are attractive from midsummer bloom till fall. Plant switchgrass in ordinary garden soil in full sun or part shade. It tolerates heavy soil and both dry and wet sites. Hardy to Zone 3.

Pennisetum alopecuroides (Fountain Grass)

This is a graceful plant, with fuzzy flower heads that look like those of foxtail grass, a common roadside weed. It grows in upright mounds about 2½ feet high, with flowers that reach 4½ feet tall. (Dwarf forms are available, too.) Plant fountain grass in average garden soil in full sun. Divide plants every five to six years to keep them tall and bushy. Hardy to Zone 4.

Phalaris arundinacea var. *picta* (Ribbon Grass)

Ribbon grass, also known as gardener's garters, is grown for the striking effect of its striped green and white foliage. The variegated 2½- to 3-foot foliage grows in upright sprays, and it spreads rapidly by rhizomes. Try it as a groundcover, but be sure to use root barriers so that it won't take over. When foliage turns brown in summer, cut it back to 6 to 8 inches and fresh new leaves will grow. Ribbon grass does well in average garden soil in full sun but will tolerate a wide variety of conditions. Hardy to Zone 4.

Uniola latifolia (Northern Sea Oats)

Northern sea oats, sometimes called wild oats, form an upright, fairly loose, 3-foot clump, with inch-long seed heads that turn pleasing shades of green, purplish, and bronze as the season progresses. Northern Sea oats self-sow and also spread by rhizomes. The seed heads are pretty in dried arrangements. This grass likes fertile, well-drained soil, in either full sun or partial shade. Hardy to Zone 5. May be sold as *Chasmanthium latifolium.*

CHAPTER THIRTY-ONE

Harvest Great Squash

After canning tomatoes for six weeks, it's a relief to start harvesting squash. These beauties will keep on the shelf for months without any processing. Gathering winter squash is a mellow ritual of fall—one of those things that I like to do, when I can, on a just-right day. The sky is that clear, intense blue reserved for Indian summer days and feedstore-calendar photos. The air has warmed after a near-frosty morning, but there's still a keen edge to the breeze. The squash hills we laid out so precisely last spring are now a tangle of vines, some dry and brown, others still living. Finding the orange and green and buff squash under the thickly intertwined and prickly vines becomes a treasure hunt.

Varieties mingle. The butternuts have traveled into buttercup territory. I collect the squash and brush them off, admiring their sturdy shapes, no two alike. They are all the colors of fall: burnt orange, deep green, tan, cream, gold, slate green. Their surfaces are ribbed, ridged, warted, smooth. Using hand pruners, I nip off all but 1 to 2 inches of the stems and carefully pile the ripe fruits in the garden cart—a cornucopia on wheels.

Playing Favorites

Which kind of squash will we eat first? That's not a difficult decision to make in our house, and it probably won't be for you either, if you've ever tried 'Hokkaido'. The grayish green fruit of this medium-size Japanese squash is rounded and faintly ribbed. Yields tend to be on the low side, and neither insect resistance nor keeping quality are remarkable. We grow 'Hokkaido' because it tastes so good. The flesh is dry, sweet, and nutty flavored. For us, the brief storage life of 'Hokkaido' is irrelevant: We never get enough of them, and we feast early on all we can manage to grow.

'Buttercup' is next on our list for quality. The fine-grained flesh is sweet and drier than most other varieties. The medium-size (3 to 5 pounds), dark green, square-shouldered fruit has a "button" swelling on the blossom end. 'Buttercup' is so good that knowledgeable gardening friends at our dinner table have been able to identify it on the first bite. We never get our fill of this one either, so its relatively short storage life hasn't interfered with our enjoyment.

'Butternut', a high-yielding, long-storing, insect-resistant cultivar, is our old reliable—the one we plant to be sure of getting some squash. The smooth-skinned, cylindrical, tan fruit keeps well into the winter under good storage conditions. While neither as sweet nor as dry fleshed as either of our two top favorites, 'Butternut' tastes good in midwinter, especially after baking, which tends to concentrate its flavor.

'Spaghetti Squash' (or 'Vegetable Spaghetti'), with oval, yellow, smooth-skinned fruit, has tender flesh that forks out in long pastalike strands after cooking (bake or simmer for 45 minutes). We like it smothered in cheese and garlic, or under spaghetti sauce. Its yield and resistance to insects rate about average. For us it has been a fairly good keeper, lasting until January under good conditions. Store this squash in a dry, fairly cool area.

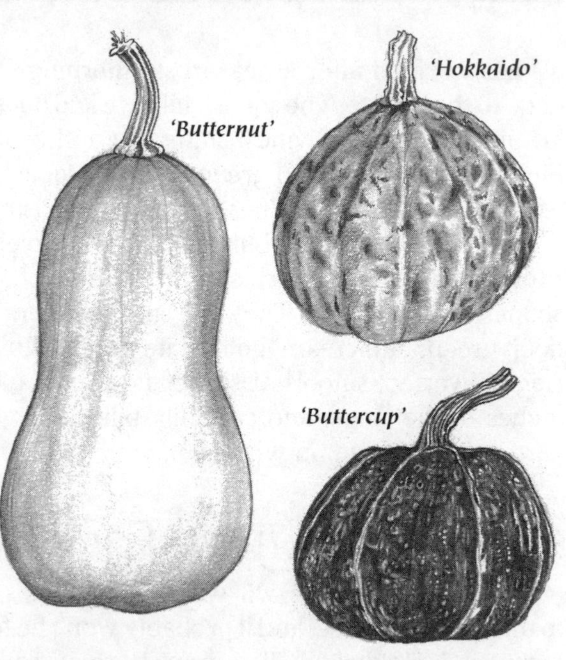

Gathering squash is one of the pleasures of the fall garden. Grayish green 'Hokkaido' is dry, sweet, and nutty flavored. Medium-size 'Buttercup' has sweet, fine-grained flesh. Old reliable 'Butternut' tastes good especially after baking.

In addition to our favorites, other good squash to add to your fall food basket include 'Hubbard', 'Delicata', and 'Acorn'. 'Hubbard' is a large, bumpy-skinned, hard-shelled squash that is well known for its long storage life. 'Delicata', a faintly ribbed, cylindrical squash, has a slightly irregular surface, cream striped with dark green. It has a good flavor and keeps well. A smaller 'Delicata' type, 'Sweet Dumpling', has similar markings on 4-inch, fist-size fruit. Both cultivars store well without curing. 'Acorn', with smooth, ridged, dark green skin, averages 2 to 3 pounds. Most squash keep better after curing in the sun, but avoid curing 'Acorn'. Well-stored 'Acorn' squash can have excellent flavor and texture, but under poor storage conditions the flesh tends to turn stringy.

Planting and Care

We plant our squash in late May, 10 to 14 days after our last frost, in composted hills 6 to 8 feet apart with five or six seeds per hill, or sometimes in rows 4 feet apart with plants placed 1 foot apart. I often presprout the seeds before planting. Eventually, I thin each hill to a population of three or four plants, but I usually pinch off the extras gradually, not all at once, in case insects kill some of the spares. If we planted in rows, I thin them so plants are 2 feet apart, again doing this gradually in case some are destroyed by insects. We mulch the squash patch after the soil warms up, just before the vines start to run.

Bugs and Borers

Squash of all kinds are susceptible to insect damage. Cucumber beetles sometimes damage young seedlings and also spread disease. Our most devastating squash pests, however, are the squash borer, a larva that burrows into the stem and kills the plant, and the squash bug, a gray, shield-shaped marauder that sucks plant juices and scars fruits.

Covering your squash bed with floating row covers provides good insurance against insect pests, but only if you put them in place shortly after your seeds sprout. Vines that wilt "overnight" are a sign of borers. Check for an entrance hole in the stem where the wilted part of the vine begins. Poke a wire into the hole or slit the stem and kill the larva. Squash I've planted on and around the compost pile have usually been free of borers, but these have been plagued by hordes of squash bugs. I intend to try dusting my next squash planting with sabadilla dust, a product made from the seed of a South American plant, which is especially effective against the adult squash bug. Insecticidal soap also deters squash bugs, and rotenone helps combat severe infestations. Some simpler pest control measures are worth trying, too. Handpick the light brown eggs of squash bugs from the undersides of the leaves. Place boards in the squash patch for adults to hide under during the day; then lift the boards and destroy the bugs. Always clear away and destroy infected vines after harvest to avoid playing host to overwintering insects and diseases.

Harvest

If insect pressure is severe, you might need to gather your squash early, but under ideal conditions you can leave them out until frost threatens. Many gardeners don't worry about a bit of frost touching their squash, but others insist that squash shouldn't be frosted at all. It is certainly true that squash subjected to heavy frost will rot sooner in storage. If you're planning to cook and eat the squash right away, you can harvest anytime. But leave squash that's intended for storage on the vine until the outer rind is too hard to puncture with a fingernail. Harvest the fruits on a dry day. Take care not to bruise them, and leave at least a 1-inch stem stub. Squash that has lost its stem usually spoils early.

Most squash will keep longer in storage if cured first to dry the flesh and toughen the skin. It's easy to cure squash: Just leave them out in the sun for a week or two after picking and cover them on frosty nights. Then, to keep the fruits until you're ready to eat them, put them on slatted shelves or in cartons in a dry spare room where the temperature stays about 50° to 60°F. Colder temperatures and dampness promote spoilage. When kept too warm—much more than 60°F—squash flesh tends to turn stringy. Changes for the better occur in stored squash, too. After one or two months on the shelf, most squash contain more vitamin A than they did when you put them away.

CHAPTER THIRTY-TWO

Grow Terrific Tulips

When I planted tulip bulbs in the front yard of our first house, I thought I had done the job once and for all. So I was surprised to see our neighbor, who had been gardening for 40 years, replanting his tulip bed. In response to my questions, he replied, "Tulip bulbs don't last as long as daffodils. They tend to lose vitality as they age." To be sure of having a nice display of tulips, he told me, "I redo this bed every five or six years, or when I notice that the tulips are declining." In the South, tulips decline even faster and are often grown as annuals.

Plant Right to Get the Most out of Your Tulips

Though some tulips seem to come up with a good show year after year, more often the investment seems to dwindle in only a few years. Here are some ways to start your tulip plantings out right and keep them growing strong.

Plan Your Planting

If you've been tucking tulip bulbs in here and there, using a trowel, you might want to try the trench planting method, which provides an impressive display. A well-prepared trench planting, like the one our neighbor was working on, will probably have a longer productive life than spot plantings in small holes dug by a dibble or trowel because soil is looser and drainage better in the trench. Also, the bulbs are more likely to be planted at the proper depth and less likely to be surrounded by air pockets, which discourage their growth. Tulips lend themselves to a formal arrangement, but a circular or free-form shape might be preferable for your site. Avoid stringing the tulips out in a single line. Planting in groups—three to five bulbs together—is more natural and showier.

If you're planting a lot of tulips at once, dig a trench and set in the bulbs in a staggered pattern. Be sure to fill the trench slowly to avoid dislodging the bulbs. If squirrels or other furry friends are a problem, line the trench on the bottom and sides with a single piece of galvanized wire mesh before planting.

Although many tulip species will bloom in light-filtered shade, most perform best in full sun. Bulbs that receive too little sun are not able to store enough energy to bloom a second year. And the flowers will last longer if the planting is sheltered from wind. Wait until the soil is cool before putting the bulbs in the ground. For most gardeners, that's sometime between mid-October and mid-November. In southern states, delay planting until mid-December. For best results in Zones 8 to 10, plant precooled bulbs or purchase tulips that don't need a cold treatment.

TWO TO THINK ABOUT

Bulb catalogs offer a generous selection of tempting tulips, from tiny species types to showy, ruffled parrots. Before you indulge yourself with your favorite kinds and colors, be aware of two tulip-buying concerns.

Species tulips grow wild in several Mediterranean and Eastern European countries. They flower early and are longer lived than many other types. Unfortunately, many of these bulbs are collected from the wild with no thought for conservation. Make sure your source supplies nursery-propagated bulbs.

Rembrandt tulips with streaked and feathered petals are lovely, but avoid planting near other tulips. Their variegated colors are caused by a virus that can harm other types of tulips.

Planting

Tulips appreciate—even demand—well-aerated, well-drained soil. They'll sulk and rot in a soggy spot. To improve drainage, shovel out the soil to a depth of 10 to 12 inches. It wouldn't hurt to thrust your digging fork into the bottom of the trench to aerate the bed a bit more. Return 2 to 3 inches of the soil you removed to the bottom of the trench so that the bulbs rest on loose, free-draining soil, with no air pockets beneath them. Smooth and level the bottom surface. Bulbs planted at the same depth bloom together.

Space larger bulbs about 6 to 8 inches apart, smaller bulbs about

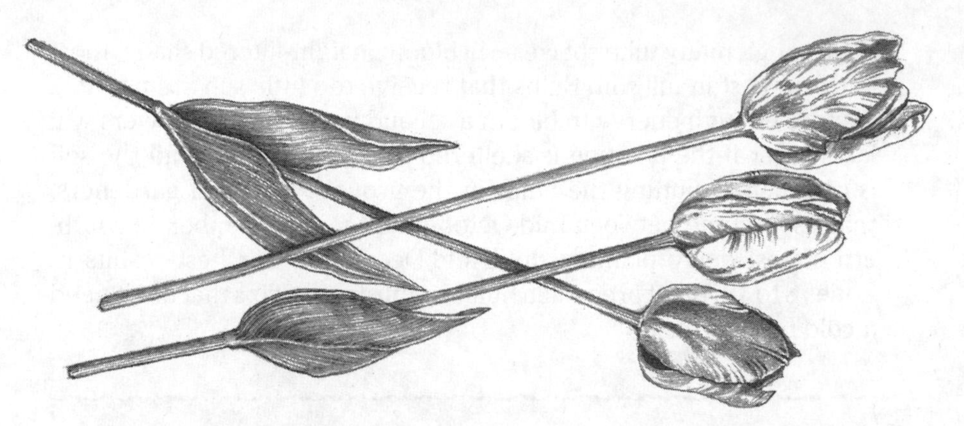

If you plant drifts of tulips, you'll have plenty to cut and add to indoor arrangements. Cut them in the evening with a sharp knife. Then recut the stems at an angle under water, place stems in tepid water, and enjoy the blooms for several days.

4 inches. Keep the pointed growing tip of the bulb up and press the rounded bottom of the bulbs into the earth. Use a slight twisting motion to ensure that the bulbs are in good contact with the soil. If you're planting a lot of bulbs at one time, protect them from prolonged exposure to sunlight, which may induce surface cracks through which fungi and bacteria can enter.

Foiling the Critters

If the neighborhood wildlife has gobbled up many of your tasty tulips in the past, use an encircling barrier of small-gauge chicken wire or hardware cloth around the perimeter of the hole or around groups of bulbs in a large hole. Some gardeners line the entire trench, bottom and sides up to soil level, with an open "box" of ½-inch-mesh hardware cloth. You can even buy small wire cages in which to bury individual bulbs. Smooth these wire barriers into place before you put any soil back into the hole.

Settling into Place

Cover the bulbs with improved soil. Make that a sandy loam, if you have it. Mix some finished compost with the soil you use to fill the hole, and add a pinch of bonemeal per bulb, an excellent source of phosphorus that encourages bloom. Tulips require a good supply of nitrogen, too, so you might also mix dehydrated or thoroughly rotted

DO I HAVE TO DIG THAT DEEP?

Tulip bulbs should be set 6 to 10 inches below ground level, depending on their size. Bulbs that are planted too deeply waste energy working their way up to the light. Those that are too close to the surface are more likely to be damaged by the heaving of soil or eaten by mice, squirrels, voles, or other rodents that consider tulip bulbs a delicacy. Shallow-planted bulbs also tend to divide into many small bulbs, none large enough to bloom, and they may be more vulnerable to the disease botrytis blight.

manure with the soil before you shovel it back into the hole.

Add the soil gently at first, so the bulbs don't get jostled out of position. Fill the entire hole with soil, making sure that fine soil is in contact with the whole surface of the bulb. Mound the soil slightly above ground level because it will sink as it settles.

Water the newly planted bed of bulbs gently and thoroughly. Avoid laying a free-running hose in the bed, which can dislodge the bulbs. Use a sprinkler or soaker hose instead, for gradual penetration to a depth of 10 to 13 inches. Watering helps to encourage root growth. If you can manage to do your bulb planting just before a good soaking fall rain, you won't need to water.

Mulching helps to control weeds and conserve soil moisture. Use leaf mold, compost, shredded bark, or other attractive organic material. One to 2 inches of mulch is enough. If you pile on much more than that, the stems of your bulbs will have too far to go to reach the light. And, if you're as absent-minded as I am, you'll want to stick a waterproof plant label into the ground where you've just planted the tulips so you won't forget and plant something else there.

While you're waiting for the flowers in spring, water your plants if rainfall amounts to less than 1 inch per week. If you want to encourage strong growth, you can top-dress with bonemeal as the new shoots appear.

After the Show

Continue to care for your tulip plants after they bloom. As the flowers fade, snip them off so that the bulbs won't waste energy producing seedpods. Leave the foliage undisturbed until it dies back naturally. As long as it's green, it is producing vital plant food, fattening the bulb for another season of bloom. When the foliage droops, you'll be glad you planted the bulbs deeply because you can now plant annuals (carefully) in the bed without injuring the buried bulbs. Fertilize the bulbs with bonemeal in the fall and again in spring when the leaves start to grow. Mulch them deeply over winter to protect from frost heaving. Then sit back and wait for another beautiful spring.

CHAPTER THIRTY-THREE

Savor Homegrown Soup Beans

If you want to taste some of the finest types of beans—most of them heirlooms intended for drying and especially suited for making baked beans, chili, and soups—then you'll need to grow your own. Cultivars like 'Ireland Creek Annie's', 'Marfax', 'Wild Goose', and 'Wren's Egg' have been carefully saved and passed down through generations of gardeners but can't be found in any store.

Seed catalogs offer only a few of the hundreds of kinds of beans.

Many of the others are maintained by dedicated gardeners working on their own or as members of seed-saving organizations. Beans are the most widely collected of all heirloom vegetables.

By planting a few of these hand-me-downs now and then, you'll not only help preserve and renew part of this heritage, but you'll end up with a supply of easily stored, nutritious, and long-keeping food. Moreover, a shelf or two of glass jars filled with a collection of colorful dried beans—brown, white, black, red, purple, maroon, pink, tan, yellow, and variegated—is every bit as much a winter delight as a supply of canned tomatoes or peaches.

Best Beans for Drying

You can harvest dried beans from any kind of snap beans, even those usually grown primarily for green beans. But many of the best-tasting dried beans, like 'Lazy Wife', are tough and stringy when immature—a defense, you might say, that prevents them from being eaten before they're at their best.

If you're planting especially for dried winter beans, select one of the choice beans developed for drying. Many fine beans are available, in both pole and bush bean types. Pole beans bear more abundantly, and over a longer period of time, than do bush beans. But they bear later than bush beans. Bush beans are the choice of many northern gardeners who want to be sure of a crop in a summer closely bracketed by cool weather and frost. Pole beans, which permit better air circulation among pods, are a good choice in areas where diseases and dampness can pose problems.

Beans like comfortable, warm weather—60° to 85°F—at all stages of their life cycle. And they're highly sensitive to cold—not only to frost, but also to chilling below 50°F. In cold, damp ground, the seeds may rot before they sprout.

Bean seeds are sometimes treated with chemical fungicides, but many catalogs offer untreated seeds in response to the concerns of home gardeners who prefer not to put fungicides in their soil. Wait to plant untreated seeds until your soil thermometer registers 60°F.

Good choices for dried-bean lovers are 'Maine Yellow Eye' (92 days to maturity), a popular good-quality stewing and baking bean; 'Soldier' (89 days), a flavorful white kidney bean from cold-hardy, drought-resistant plants; and 'Agate Pinto' (92 days), a nonsprawling, quick-

HEARTY HOME-COOKED BEANS

Soup beans are at their best in flavorful, slow-cooked dishes like bean soup and baked beans. Here are two of my favorite recipes.

Bean Soup

1 cup dried beans
1 bay leaf
Ham bone or ham hock
2 to 3 cloves garlic
Several peppercorns
1 carrot, peeled and sliced
1 medium onion, diced
1 stalk celery, diced
3 to 4 tablespoons tomato paste OR 1 to 2 cups home-canned tomatoes
Salt or soy sauce to taste

Soak dried beans overnight, in water to cover. The next morning drain off the soaking water. Cook the beans gently in 2 quarts boiling water, along with bay leaf, ham bone, garlic, and peppercorns. When beans are nearly tender, after about 2 hours, add carrot, onion, celery, and tomato paste or canned tomatoes. Season to taste with salt or soy sauce and fish out the bay leaf if you can find it. If the soup is too thick, thin it with chicken stock or tomato juice. *Makes about 3–3½ quarts.*

Baked Beans

2 cups dried beans
1 to 2 cloves garlic
1 medium onion, diced
⅓ cup molasses
1 teaspoon instant coffee
⅓ cup ketchup or tomato paste
Small pieces of ham or bacon (optional)
1 tablespoon prepared mustard
Salt to taste

Soak dried beans overnight, in water to cover. The next morning drain off the soaking water. Simmer the beans in 1 quart boiling water for 15 to 20 minutes. Remove pan from heat and add remaining ingredients.

Cover the bean pot and cook in a slow oven, about 250°F, for about 6 hours. Uncover the pot for the last hour of cooking. If the beans become too dry, add some chicken stock, home-canned tomatoes, tomato juice, or water. Salt just before serving (salt added before cooking toughens the beans). *6–8 servings.*

NOTE: A crockpot is also fine for baking beans.

cooking cultivar of the pinto bean. If your growing season is short, plant 'Jacob's Cattle' (also known as 'Trout' or 'Dalmatian'), the earliest dried bean, maturing in 88 days.

Growing Soup Beans

To hasten germination, I usually soak the bean seeds for several hours before planting. I've read, however, that soaking can damage the structure of a bean seed. I've never had a problem, but if you do, you might try soaking them for a shorter period.

BOOSTER SHOT

Beans, peas, and other legumes produce a better crop and contribute more nitrogen to the soil if, before planting, their seeds are inoculated with a preparation of *Rhizobium* bacteria, available in seed catalogs under various names. The bacteria, which colonize in nodules on the plant's roots, transform nitrogen gas present in the soil air into nitrogen compounds that can be absorbed by the roots—supplying as much as 50 to 70 percent of the plant's nitrogen requirements.

If you treat seeds directly with rhizobia preparations, moisten the seeds just before planting to help the powdered inoculants adhere to the seeds. You can also sprinkle granular legume inoculants into the garden row when sowing the seeds.

Plant bush beans 2 inches apart and 1 inch deep. You can leave them unthinned, as I often do, or thin them to stand 3 to 4 inches apart. The overall yield per square foot is about the same either way. If you've had trouble with diseased bean plants in the past, thin them to a 4-inch spacing to improve air circulation between plants. I plant bush beans in wide raised rows, about four furrows per wide row. Space furrows about 7 or 8 inches apart. With this method, less space is wasted on paths than in single row planting, and as the plants leaf out, their shade helps retain soil moisture and discourage weeds.

Caring for maturing beans is easy, especially if they're left unpicked until they're dried. Just keep them weeded and water them if it's rained less than 1 inch in two weeks.

Supports for Pole Beans

For pole beans, make tripods of poles or ½-inch-diameter saplings lashed together at the top. A tripod is easy to set up: The three poles support each other and are only pushed far enough into the soft soil to stabilize them. Or you can drive a single row of 7-foot poles 12 to 18 inches into the ground. Plant about six seeds around the base of each pole. Whatever your support structure, keep in mind that rough-surfaced poles are easier for the bean vines to climb than smooth ones.

Pole beans seem to like climbing on string even better than on poles. Make a string trellis between steel stakes by suspending weighted strings from a horizontal overhead support. Plant string-supported beans 4 to 6 inches apart.

Keeping Beans Healthy

Beans are subject to a number of fungal and bacterial infections, some of which are transmitted through the seed. (That's why bean seed is grown commercially in dry western states where disease organisms have a harder time getting a toehold.)

You can do a lot to discourage fungal diseases in your garden. Choose disease-free seed and disease-resistant cultivars. Water during the day; evening watering can encourage fungal diseases if the air is still. To cut down on plant-to-plant fungal transmission, avoid working among your bean plants when they're wet. Use a soaker hose to keep water off the leaves. Burn sickly plants or dispose of them in sealed containers. Some people place them in the center of their hot compost pile, where high temperatures will destroy the bacteria. But I'm reluctant to add diseased plants to my compost.

In my area, Mexican bean beetles can chew a bean planting to tatters by midsummer. The beetles look like coppery tan ladybugs. Their soft-bodied larvae are little oval dots of yellow, often found on the underside of leaves. In badly infested areas, release spined soldier bugs (*Podisus maculiventris*) to prey on the pests (see "Resources" on page 300 for a supplier of these helpful predators). Soldier bugs kept my bean vines free of bean beetles last year.

Homegrown soup beans can be every bit as satisfying as a shelf of canned peaches—and as much fun as a marble collection. With a thousand kinds to choose from, you can fill your jars with brown, white, black, red, purple, pink, yellow, or speckled dried beans.

Harvest Time

Dried beans are ready to harvest 12 to 14 weeks after planting. As the plants mature, the beans develop and swell. The pods toughen and then shrink and become limp, tan, and leathery. Leave the beans on the plant until the pods shrink and dry and the plant loses most of its leaves. A mature, ready-to-harvest dried bean will be so hard you can't dent it with your fingernail or teeth. If the weather is wet or the season is short, you can pull the plants after the beans have developed but before the pods are thoroughly dried.

To harvest the beans, pull out the plants before the pods begin to split and spill the beans. Hang them or spread them on screens, where they'll be protected from rain but well ventilated until completely dried.

Threshing and Winnowing

Now to remove the dried beans from their crispy dried pods. If you have only a few dried beans, you can simply shell them by hand. The next easiest way to thresh dried beans is to tie the pods in a pillowcase and tumble it in the dryer, on low for about 30 minutes. The tumbling produces bits of chaff mixed with the shelled beans. Just pour everything into a clean bucket in a brisk wind. The wind does the winnowing, blowing the wispy chaff away while the beans clatter into the bucket.

Another choice is to put the bean pods in a funnel-shaped cloth bag, narrow at the bottom, with openings at both ends. Tie both openings closed, hang the bag up, and whack it with a stick. Then open the narrow end for the beans to fall out. I've threshed dried beans by walking on them, too. Here's how: Spread a clean sheet on the floor, arrange the dried beans on it, cover them with a second sheet, and tread on them. Any of these methods will work. Choose the one that suits you best.

After threshing and winnowing, spread the beans in shallow pans to dry for another week. Dry them thoroughly before you store them, or they can turn moldy. To kill weevil larvae, either freeze the beans for 24 hours before storing them or spread them in a single layer on a baking sheet and keep them in a 175°F oven for 15 minutes. (But don't heat seeds you want to save for planting.) Store the beans in covered jars in a cool, dry place.

CHAPTER THIRTY-FOUR

Create an Apple Doll

Apple-head dolls, like the products of any true craft, are one of a kind. These little characters have wrinkled, leathery faces that look as though they have weathered years of living. All that twinkly-eyed personality, though, develops during a few weeks of drying.

Preserving things by drying is a useful technique that helped to make winter life more comfortable in days gone by. The dried apple doll was a just-for-fun character whittled out of an extra piece of fruit by people who had more time and ingenuity than cash. The mountain people who made these dolls for their children would no doubt be amused to discover that this homespun craft now commands high prices in gift shops. It's more fun to make your own.

Making Just-for-Fun People

One reason apple dolls are such fun to make is that the result is always a surprise. You don't know whom your carved apple will turn into until the drying process is complete.

Fashioning the Head

To achieve realistic proportions, divide the face into thirds. The bottom third ends at the top of the mouth, the middle third extends from the upper mouth to the lower half of the eyes, and the upper eyes and forehead make up the top third of the face. It's fun to carve several heads at a time, using different kinds of features.

Choose good, sound winter apples, such as 'Winesap' or 'Granny Smith'. Summer apples like 'Rambo' and 'Transparent' don't dry well. Got your apple? Here's how to make your doll.

Materials
Apple
Solution of 1 part water, 1 part lemon juice or vinegar
18-inch length of wire, 18 to 20 gauge
String for hanging

Tools
Paring knife
Nutpick

1. Peel the apple.
2. Carve the face. The stem end of the apple is the top of the head; the blossom end, the chin. Make the nose fairly wide and the chin rather prominent. Cut slits for the eyes. Put a few lines in the forehead if you wish. Exaggerate the size and curvature of the mouth. A nutpick makes a handy tool for indenting the flesh on either side of the nose. Press the side of the slender pick against the cheeks to deepen them so the nose stands out.

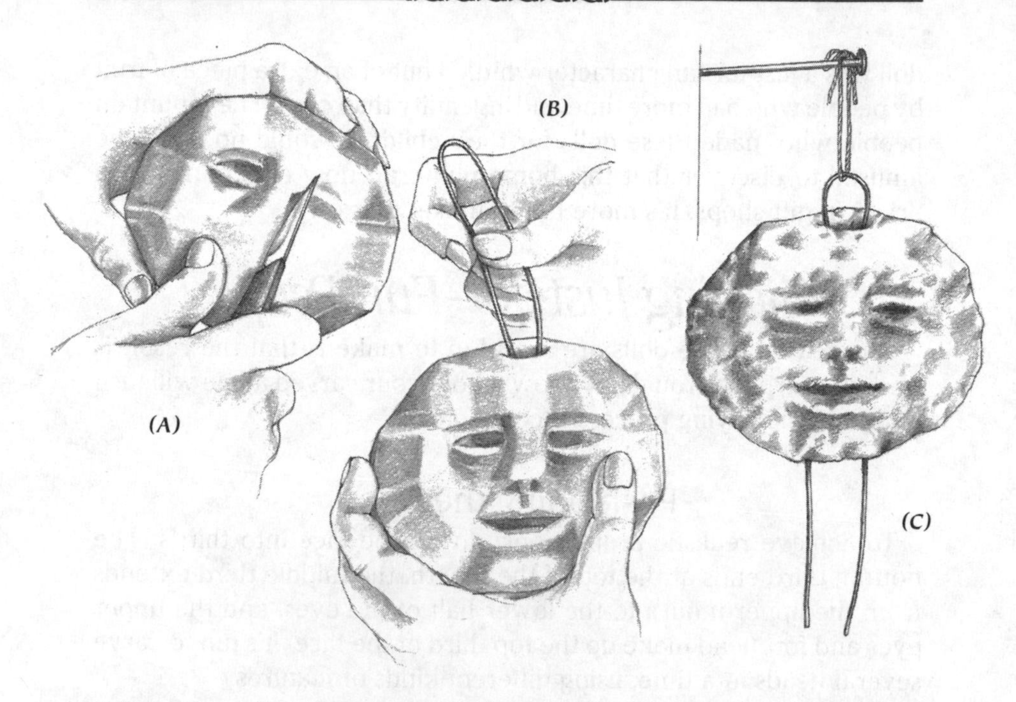

(A) Use a small knife to carve the face of your apple doll. Don't worry if you're not an artist; crude features turn out just as well when the apple dries. Chin, eyes, and nose are the basics.
(B) Insert a long piece of medium wire, bent in half, through the apple. Let a bit of the loop protrude from the stem end. The wires that extend from the bottom will be the form for the doll's body.
(C) Loop a piece of sturdy string through the wire and hang the head in a dry, airy place. After a week of drying, use your fingers to adjust the doughy features to your liking. Then let the head dry for another five weeks.

3. Dip the carved face into a solution of half water and half lemon juice (or vinegar) to help prevent excess darkening.
4. Bend an 18-inch length of wire in half. Poke the ends of the wire through the center of the apple, from the stem end down. Leave a bit of the bend poking above the apple. The wire will be the basis of the doll's body. (If you wish, you can form the body on a wire frame first, then insert the wire into the apple head when it dries. The head won't be as secure, but dressing will be easier. See "Finishing and Clothing" for more details on this method.)
5. Tie a string to the apple stem or to the bent wire so that you can suspend the head freely while it dries. It will become misshapen if it sits on a shelf.

6. Hang the head in a well-ventilated place. The features will be doughy after a week of drying, and you can mold any finishing touches then with your fingers. Complete drying takes about six weeks.

Finishing and Clothing

After the head has been drying for about two weeks, it's time to add eyes. Insert colored (such as blue, black, or brown) glass- or plastic-headed straight pins into the eye sockets. As the apple continues to dry, the skin will shrink around the eyes, giving the face a more realistic look. You can even insert "teeth" in the apple doll's gums if you wish: Use tweezers to poke in uncooked grains of long-grained rice. The gnarled toothless look, though, seems to me to be part of the doll's charm. Glue on cotton, wool, fur, or yarn for hair and beards.

Now let's give the apple doll a body. If you've inserted the bent wire through the head, you'll be fashioning the body onto the remains of that wire. Form the body by padding the wire with a wrapping of cotton rags, old stockings, or T-shirt strips. With an extra length of 18- to 20-gauge wire, fasten on wire arms and wrap them, too. Scraps of worn-out stockings make good skin covering. Then dress the doll, snipping and shaping the fabric as you go. You might give the women a full-skirted calico dress, or sew on a

Homey apple-head dolls are as appealing to grownups as they are to children. A few scraps of fabric and bright, beady eyes bring your creation to life.

bright plaid skirt and cover the bodice with a triangular shawl. Men may be dressed in overalls or a woodsman's outfit with dark pants and plaid shirt. Try giving one a vest, another a red-checkered neckerchief.

You can also make the body separately from the head, leaving a 2-inch prong of bare wire from the body sticking up above the place where body and arms join. Dress the doll completely and then poke this wire "neck" into the dried apple head. This method doesn't fasten the head on as securely as the previous one, but it does make the body easier to dress.

Little scraps of felt make good shoes. Stitch felt pieces together for hands or dry hand-shaped scraps of apples when you carve the heads. Apple scraps make good ears, too. As you've no doubt gathered by now, these dolls are as much for grown-ups as they are for children. If you can bear to part with them, your friends will enjoy propping them by bowls of nuts or apples or sitting them on the windowsill.

CHAPTER THIRTY-FIVE

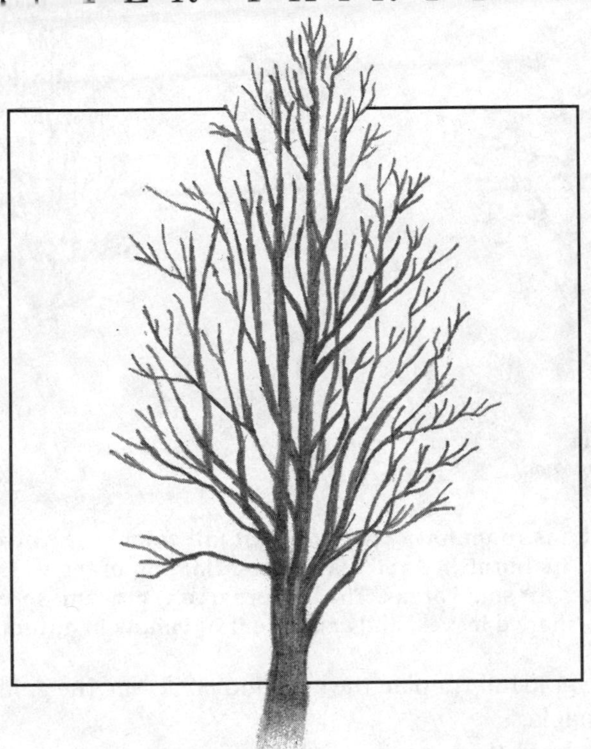

Choose Trees for Fall Color

Every fall, as I feast my eyes on the rich burgundies, golden yellows, and flame oranges of the trees on our mountainside and in our hedgerows, I reflect that this glorious burst of fall color would be reason enough to plant a tree. At the peak of the leaf color season, I'm tempted to walk backward down the lane on my way to the mailbox so as not to miss any of the glory of the gold and garnet mountain. And each year, I watch individual trees that I know will change colors, each in their turn—the crimson swamp

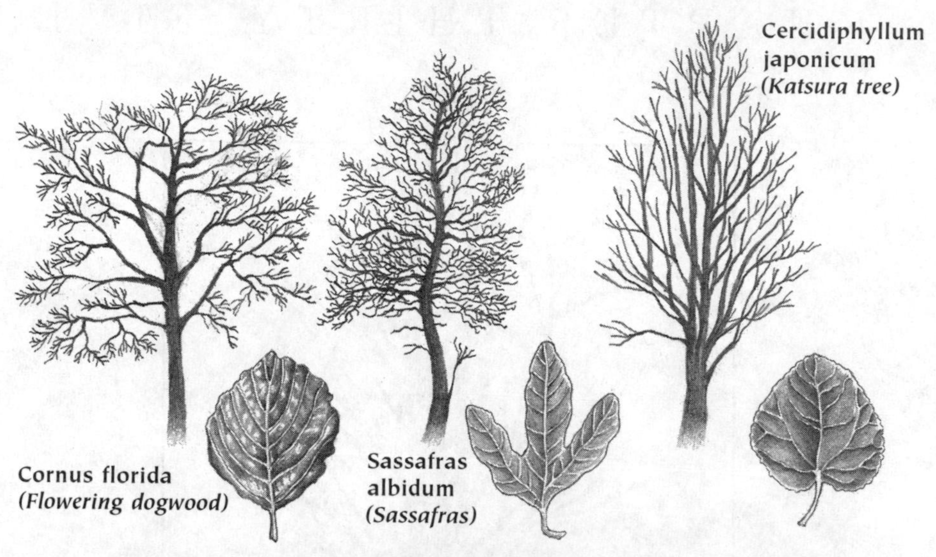

Every yard has room for a spot of bright fall color. The flowering dogwood, with its burnished red leaves, and flaming orange sassafras are good choices for small areas. The katsura tree, a graceful spreading tree with heart-shaped leaves, adds an accent of yellow in autumn.

maple, the gold tulip poplar, the burgundy oak, and the golden yellow Norway maple.

If you've been thinking about planting a tree, why not make it one that will give you extra pleasure in the fall? If you need further encouragement, consider that, according to studies reported by the American Forestry Association (A.F.A.), lawn trees add 5 to 7 percent to the real estate value of a property. In addition, mature trees, by A.F.A. estimates, can provide the following annual benefits: air pollution control worth $50; cooling worth $73; and $75 each for erosion and stormwater control and wildlife shelter. All this, and—with the right selection—fall color, too!

A New Member of the Family

Choose your new trees carefully—they'll be around a long time. Make sure the trees you pick will fit in the site you've chosen—even after they reach their mature height and spread. Select a tree that's right for your conditions. Consider the background of the fall display—will the colors blend or contrast with the brick of your home, or with neighboring trees? Or will the leaves be set off nicely by your neighbor's tall evergreens? Think about what the tree will add to your home grounds at other seasons, too. Red maples, for instance, are breathtaking in fall, but they're just as welcome in spring, when their early blossoms lend a flush of red to bare branches.

Best Bets for Fall Color

The trees suggested here will put on an annual show of color for you—something you can enjoy every day for several weeks, just when garden flowers are fading. To add to your pleasure and to extend the leaf color season, plant several different species—as lawn, property line, or streetside trees. You can plant most of these species in fall or spring, except for a few slow starters that need time to establish their root system. Plant these in spring. (Those trees are noted in the selections that follow.)

Yellow Fall Color

Choose from these suggestions for striking yellow leaves in fall. There's a tree just right for your home grounds.

Betula platyphylla var. *japonica* (Japanese White Birch)

White chalky bark and glossy green leaves make this graceful birch a landscape standout. Leaves turn yellow in fall. Look for the cultivar 'Whitespire', an especially good choice. The bark of this birch doesn't peel like that of canoe birch (*Betula papyrifera*). Don't worry if your young tree has gray bark: White bark doesn't appear until the third year.

Not particular as to soil, the birch needs full sun. 'Whitespire' is resistant to the bronze birch borer, which has shortened the lives of so many lovely European birches. Japanese white birch is heat resistant and fast growing. It is hardy to Zone 4.

Cercidiphyllum japonicum (Katsura Tree)

Katsura trees spread nearly as wide as their 40- to 60-foot height. The heart-shaped leaves are fragrant and turn yellow in fall. These natives of Japan are either male or female. Female trees produce inch-long pods in fall. Plant the katsura tree in rich soil with good drainage. Hardy to Zone 4.

Larix spp. (Larches)

Larches are airy conifers that lose their needles in winter. Choose Japanese larch (*Larix kaempferi*), tamarack or American larch (*L. lar-*

icina), or European larch (*L. decidua*). All have tufts of short needles, ½ to 1 inch long, which grow at close intervals on the stems and shoots. Small cones grow upright on the branches. The mature larch can reach a height of 90 feet.

In fall, the needles turn a soft golden yellow. The soft new growth is a cheering sight in spring. Larches like acid soil and full sun. Good soil fertility will promote faster growth. In the wild, the American larch can be found growing in wet soil. Larches are hardy to Zone 3.

Liriodendron tulipifera (Tulip Tree)

This tree is also called yellow poplar, or sometimes popple, but it's not a poplar at all. It's a member of the magnolia family. The tulip tree is named for its tulip-shaped flowers—open cups of waxy-looking, greenish yellow petals banded with orange near the base. These flowers are quite unusual but are hard to see because they bloom close to the top of the tree. Its ramrod-straight trunk and great height—at least 90 feet in maturity—give the tulip tree a special dignity. The bluntly lobed leaves, about the size of your palm, are nearly straight across the top.

Wait until spring to plant your new tulip tree; this species is slow getting established. Plant in good soil well supplied with moisture but also well drained. Young tulip trees grow quickly. The fall color is a glowing yellow, and the umbrella-shaped seed pods are attractive in arrangements. This tree needs full sun and is hardy to Zone 3.

Orange or Red Fall Color

These trees will add fall color to your landscape in all shades of orange and red—sometimes many combinations on a single tree.

Acer spp. (Maples)

Maples are a popular choice for homeowners, and with good reason. Most species supply plenty of fall color. Two of my favorites are *Acer saccharum,* the sugar maple, and *A. rubrum,* the red maple.

Long-lived sugar maples grow to 70 to 80 feet tall. Their dense, rounded canopy makes them good shade trees. But their fall colors of yellow, orange, scarlet, crimson, often mixed on one tree, are spectacular! You can even tap your tree to make maple syrup once it reaches a trunk diameter of 10 to 12 inches (that'll take 35 to 60 years; sugar maples grow slowly). Give your sugar maple rich soil, on the

NEW RESEARCH ON TREE PLANTING

When it's time to plant the tree you've purchased at a local nursery or ordered by mail, forget all those things you've heard about digging a deep hole and filling in with compost. A tree's roots grow sideways more than they grow deep, so the hole you dig for the new tree should be wide—two times the diameter of the root ball—but no deeper than the root ball. You don't need to fill with especially rich soil, either. Studies have shown that roots of trees planted in small pockets of rich soil often stay confined to that small area instead of ranging as far as they should. Tree specialists have also discovered that trees that bend in the wind develop stronger trunks than those that are immobilized by stakes. If you do stake your new tree, use flexible stakes (such as a sapling) or flexible ties between rigid stakes.

acid side, with a good supply of moisture. The trees do well in full sun but won't mind a bit of light shade. Sugar maples aren't very tolerant of air pollution, so they're not a good choice for an urban garden. They're hardy to Zone 3.

Red maple, also known as swamp maple, tops out at 50 to 80 feet tall, a bit shorter and less dense than the sugar maple. Its buds and flowers are deep red in spring. Moist, acid soil of good fertility suits the red maple, which is found in damp places in the wild. It will adapt to poor soil or part shade and is hardy to Zone 3. Like the sugar maple, the red maple is sensitive to polluted air. Fall color is deep red and red-orange. The red maples on our farm are brilliant each fall, and we watch certain individual trees for their progressive shades of color. They never disappoint us.

Amelanchier laevis (Allegheny Serviceberry)

Also known as sarvis tree, shadbush, and Juneberry, this shrubby tree reaches a mature height of about 30 feet, with multiple trunks growing in a clump. This small tree is easy to fit into a landscaping plan. If you prefer a single trunk, trim off the extra shoots. Allegheny serviceberry is covered with white blossoms in early spring and bears dark purple, edible fruit in summer. In fall, its oval leaves turn orange, yellow, and red.

An adaptable tree, the serviceberry accepts a wide variety of soils and conditions and will even grow in poor soil. Full sun promotes a fuller shape but it will grow in part shade. This tree is hardy to Zone 3.

Cornus florida (Flowering Dogwood)

These lovely trees offer sweeps of white or pink spring bloom. In early fall, the leaves turn deep red through burgundy, sometimes in a dark, muted tone but often brilliant. Red berries stay on into winter, unless a flock of cedar waxwings gets there first. Dogwoods reach a height of 20 feet. Hardy to Zone 4.

Dogwood trees in eastern states have recently been affected by an anthracnose fungus that can kill the tree, usually starting with the lower branches. Trees grown in crowded and stressed conditions are more susceptible. Lawn trees receiving ample water and good air circulation are more resistant. The dogwood tree we transplanted from our woods to the east side of our house several years ago gives us weeks of rich color in fall and is—so far—perfectly healthy. Ask your nursery owner if dogwood blight is a problem in your area. If it is, choose another tree.

Liquidambar styraciflua (Sweet Gum)

This handsome, long-lived tree reaches 60 to 80 feet at maturity. In fall, the interesting star-shaped leaves turn orange-red to rich crimson, shading into burgundy. After the glossy leaves fall, prickly, 1- to 1½-inch seed balls hang on through winter.

Sweet gum grows best in rich soil well supplied with moisture. It prefers full sun and will tolerate a fairly damp location. Hardy to Zone 5.

Nyssa sylvatica (Black Tupelo)

Dark, grayish black bark and leathery, pointed oval leaves make this 30- to 60-foot-tall tree attractive even before it explodes in a burst of fall color. The leaves of black tupelo, also called black gum, turn a rich and beautiful burgundy in fall, with a satiny luster. Birds eat the small blue fruit that hangs on after leaves have fallen.

A swamp tree by nature, black tupelo will accept a wide variety of soil types. It takes a while for roots to settle in, so hold off planting until next spring. Black tupelo grows especially well in loamy acid soil, in either full sun or part shade. Hardy to Zone 3.

Oxydendrum arboreum (Sourwood)

This tree is much beloved for the superb honey that bees make from the nectar of its sprays of small white blossoms. The sourwood has handsome, long, narrow, glossy leaves. In its northern range it averages about 35 feet tall, but farther south, in its southern Appalachian homeland, it can reach 50 to 60 feet. The sourwood tree does grow slowly, however. Fall color is a deep wine red, sometimes scarlet.

Sourwood trees do best in acid soil that is well supplied with moisture but also well drained. They like full sun. Hardy to Zone 5.

NOT ELVES AFTER ALL

Why do leaves change color in fall? I've always liked the story involving elves with paintbrushes myself, but botanists have a different explanation. As you'll recall from your high school biology courses, the chlorophyll in leaves gives them their green color. It is also an essential part of photosynthesis, the process by which plants produce food (plant sugars) from carbon dioxide and water when exposed to sunlight. Chlorophyll is constantly produced in leaves during the growing season. In the fall, however, a scablike abscission layer forms between twig and leaf stem, interrupting the flow of water and dissolved nutrients to the leaf. Without this supply, the leaf's life processes slow down, and its supply of chlorophyll dwindles. As this happens, the green color fades away, revealing other leaf pigments (yellows, reds, oranges, coppers) that were masked by the strong green of the chlorophyll. Some of these pigments were in the leaves all season; others were produced during the warm days and cool nights of autumn. The colorful leaves eventually detach from the tree after the junction between twig and leaf dries completely.

Pyrus calleryana (Callery Pear)

Another spring-flowering tree that also offers glorious color in the fall, ornamental Callery pear cultivars mature into oval-shaped, 30- to 40-foot-tall lawn or street trees. In fall, their leaves turn bright red. Avoid 'Bradford', one of the best-known ornamental pears, because its upright branches with their narrow branch-trunk angles are prone to breaking. Cultivars with stronger branches and somewhat greater hardiness include 'Chanticleer' and 'Autumn Blaze'.

Callery pear trees need full sun but are not particular about soil. They are tolerant of drought and air pollution. Hardy to Zone 4, depending on the cultivar.

Quercus spp. (Oaks)

The northern red oak (*Quercus rubra*) has a broad crown and a pleasing rounded shape, growing to 60 to 80 feet. It has relatively smooth bark and the acorns have shallow cups. The scarlet oak (*Q. coccinea*) is more pyramidal in form and attains heights of 70 to 80 feet. Both oaks are fairly fast-growing, long-lived trees with deep roots, and their leaves have pointed tips. Red oak turns deep, rich red in fall, while scarlet oak turns brighter red.

Oaks take their time getting established, so wait until spring to plant. Put northern red oaks in slightly acid, well-drained soil in full sun. Scarlet oaks like sandy loam and can take a bit of shade. Both are hardy to Zone 4.

Sassafras albidum (Sassafras)

A modest-size tree, growing to 30 feet or so (taller, though, in the South), sassafras is a tree of the fields and hedgerows. Its leaves are remarkable for their variety of forms: Some are plain oval, others are mitten shaped, and still others have small lobes on both sides with a longer central lobe between them. Crushed leaves, bark, and roots of sassafras are aromatic. In fall, sassafras puts on a real show: yellow, orange, salmon, and vermilion, with varied colors and shades often appearing at the same time on a single tree. Birds like to eat the little blue fruit, technically called drupes.

Open ground, good fertile soil with plenty of humus, and full sun make sassafras trees content. This species is hardy to Zone 4.

Bronze Fall Color

This tree is a magnificent selection with striking bronze foliage that lasts well, even into winter. A contrasting background of dark evergreens will heighten the effect.

Fagus grandifolia (American Beech)

American beech, sometimes sold as *Fagus americana,* is a noble, round-trunked beauty, 60 to 80 feet tall at maturity. The beech tree has smooth gray bark, many slender twigs, and graceful branches that may sweep down to brush the ground. Although not brilliantly colored, the richness of their copper or bronze leaves in fall blends well with other autumn tones.

Beeches like good soil—well drained and not highly acid, in either full sun or part shade. An impressive lawn tree when full grown, the beech produces small triangular nuts in burrs that split easily—one of early man's first foods. The leaves often remain on the trees long after those of other species have fallen. Trees are shallow-rooted and slow growing. They're hardy to Zone 3.

CHAPTER THIRTY-SIX

Keep Geraniums over Winter

You know how it is every fall: The flowers in your garden seem to glow with a special brilliance in those last weeks before frost, as though they want to make the most of the time they have left. Your geraniums are flowering abundantly after the heat of the summer. It seems too bad to just let them die with the cold weather.

Happily, you don't need to junk your geraniums after a single season. Our garden geraniums are descended from plants native to South Africa and are really tender perennials. A single plant can live for a good many years if protected from freezing.

Easy Keepers

Geraniums have been popular for a long time, and gardeners and growers have figured out a number of tricks to keep them alive during the cold season. Read through the suggestions that follow, and try the methods that make sense in your house. Always bring in more geraniums than you think you'll need next year; some losses are inevitable. Once you learn how to carry the plants over winter, preparing geraniums for their indoor stay will become another of those comforting rituals of fall, like digging the dahlia roots and planting tulip bulbs.

The Paper Bag Trick

One of the simplest ways to hold this year's geranium plants over winter for replanting in spring is also probably one of the oldest. Dig

WHAT'S IN A NAME?

Our familiar pink, red, and white geraniums of window box and flower bed are really members of the genus *Pelargonium*. This large genus includes some 280 different "geranium" species and hybrids, ranging from the common garden geraniums (*P.* × *hortorum*) to Martha Washingtons (*P.* × *domesticum*) and the wonderful scented types (such as *P. capitatum*, the rose-scented geranium, and *P. crispum*, the lemon geranium).

There is also a *Geranium* genus, but just to confuse matters, the common names of the plants in this genus aren't geraniums. The *Geranium* genus includes the perennial plants sometimes called cranesbills. Some *Geranium* species, such as the spreading, old-fashioned *G. sanguineum*, or blood-red cranesbill, are popular in flower borders; others are favorite springtime wildflowers.

the plants before a killing frost, and shake off the extra soil from their roots. Then enclose them individually in paper bags, roots and all, and hang the bags in a cold, damp cellar or unheated room.

Plant mortality rates are high with this method—often 50 percent or even more—so be sure to bring in plenty of extra plants. Be sure to use paper bags; plastic bags don't allow enough air circulation. This is an easy method—no potting or jostling for window space in the fall. But it's practical only for those who have the requisite cold, somewhat humid, conditions common to dirt-floored basements in old houses. Most modern house basements are too warm and too dry to keep geraniums well.

Take your geraniums out of the bag and repot in early spring when the days start to get longer. Cut the stems back to 3 to 4 inches and keep the plants on a sunny windowsill until planting-out time. If you wait until April or May to put the bareroot plants in pots, they won't look like much until July.

Potted Plants

If your geraniums are in pots, as mine are, you can simply bring them indoors and keep them in bright light, not necessarily direct sunlight. Groom the plants before you bring them in, removing dead leaves and spent blossoms. If the plants have grown leggy or are too large for your sills, cut each branch of the plant back to within a few inches of the main stem.

A cool or even an unheated part of the house will suit your wintering geraniums just fine. My potted geranium plants spend the winter in my unheated greenhouse, which, while somewhat damper, is not otherwise too different from an unheated sunporch. If you can't provide cool quarters, don't despair. To make the transition easier for them, move your geraniums to the house before weather turns cold enough to have the heat on each day. Geraniums are adaptable plants, and though they may sulk at first and shed leaves, they'll soon recover on any bright windowsill in the house.

If your geraniums are growing directly in the garden, move them into pots to bring indoors. It's especially important to cut all stems back to 4 to 5 inches to help compensate for root loss in unearthing the plant. These plants may lose their leaves when moved to the house. Keep the soil on the dry side, especially until new leaves begin to form.

Potted geraniums go through an awkward stage after they're cut back. They take up space for a month or two after pruning before they earn it by reblooming.

A Collection of Cuttings

For thick, vigorous plants with lots of blooms next spring, retire your "mother" geraniums and take cuttings. With the exception of Martha Washington types, most geraniums become spindly and less bushy as they get older. To obtain compact plants for boxes or beds, either prune back your plants hard or start fresh with cuttings.

Your geraniums will live for years if you protect them from cold winters. Unpruned, they'll have a long-legged look. For best results, start fresh with cuttings in fall for bushy, vigorous plants in spring.

You can start taking cuttings in early or midsummer, for new plants that will bloom at your sunniest windows in midwinter. Many gardeners take cuttings from their favorite plants in late summer or early fall. Root your cuttings in a loose, moist mix, and then pot them up. You'll get shapely, easy-to-care-for plants with plenty of bloom.

Here's how to take cuttings.

1. Look for healthy new growth on an actively growing plant. Choose green stems, not brown woody ones, at least 4 inches long.
2. Use a sharp knife to make the cuts, not pruning shears, which might crush the stems. Take a 4- to 6-inch cutting.
3. Remove most of the leaves, leaving three or four at the top of the

cutting. Pinch off all blossoms and buds.

4. To help prevent fungal diseases, swish the cut end of the stem in a solution of 1 tablespoon bleach to 1 quart water, with a few drops of liquid dish detergent added. Set the cutting aside to dry for a few hours. The scabs that form on the cut ends when they dry will also help to discourage the entry of spoilage organisms.
5. Poke the cuttings into pots of damp, but not soggy, soilless potting mix or a mixture of equal parts of vermiculite and perlite. One to three cuttings will fit in a 4-inch pot. You can also root geranium cuttings in jars of water kept in bright, but not direct, light.

Set your potted cuttings on a cake rack over a pan of water, in bright light but not direct sun. The water in the pan will supply some moisture to the rooting cuttings as it evaporates, without waterlogging the mix. Some gardeners put clear plastic bags or clear plastic cups over rooting cuttings. If these coverings are airtight, though, they'll encourage disease organisms. Instead of covering the plants, you can mist them several times a day for the first few days.

Keep the planting mix well moistened while roots grow. Bottom heat will help speed things along. The cuttings will root in three to eight weeks, sprouting new growth and feeling "anchored" when you gently wiggle them. Move them to individual 4-inch pots in February, when longer days begin to encourage active growth.

Through Winter, into Spring

Whether you're keeping rooted cuttings or your original plants indoors over winter, avoid overwatering. Let the soil partially dry before you water the plants again. During the shortest days of winter, you needn't feed your plants while they're just marking time. In spring, when they're growing actively, feed them monthly with any low-nitrogen organic fertilizer. If your plants or rooted cuttings get leggy over winter, prune them back in early spring to encourage bushy new growth.

Harden off your overwintered geraniums just as you would a flat of seedlings: Expose them to sun and wind gradually, keeping them in a shaded, sheltered spot for the first several days. Geraniums are hardy to about 30 °F, so wait till you're sure cold weather is past before you set them out. Although I don't plant my geraniums out in the garden soil until after our final frost in mid-May, I often set a potted geranium in a crock on our east-facing patio as early as the third week in April. In case of severe cold, I cover it or bring it indoors.

Bright, cheerful geraniums are one of the most popular flowering plants, indoors or out. If you learn how to carry them over winter, you can enjoy them both ways.

CHAPTER THIRTY-SEVEN

Mothproof Your Woolens with Herbs

As a child, my friend Carla accidentally locked herself in a freshly mothballed coat closet. That terrifying experience also made her sick—from breathing concentrated fumes of the chemical paradichlorobenzene. If you're sensitive to hydrocarbons and other chemical substances, you don't need such an intense exposure to produce symptoms; fumes wafting from a closet or attic will do it.

Those fumes can affect you even when you can't smell them; mothballs that are snugly enfolded in sweaters and stored in a chest or box or garment bag still release molecules into the air. Even an unopened box of crystals sitting on a shelf can be potent enough to affect someone who is chemically sensitive. The compounds most commonly used in mothballs and moth crystals—paradichlorobenzene and naphthalene—are chemically much like DDT and lindane, two highly toxic insecticides.

A Healthy Alternative

Because both my husband and one of our children have had serious reactions to chemical vapors, we've had to look for other, safer ways of protecting our woolens from moths. Even without evidence of allergy, many folks we know are substituting plant moth repellents for chemicals in an effort to reduce the number of toxic materials in their houses.

The Small but Mighty Clothes Moth

We started by taking a closer look at that tiny pest that can ruin our treasured hand-knit sweaters, heirloom crazy quilts, and favorite wool hiking shirts with a week or two of undisturbed munching. The larva of the webbing clothes moth, *Tineola bisselliella,* attaches silky threads to the material it feeds on. The larva of the casemaking clothes moth, *Tinea pellionella,* spins a tube, which it pulls after itself as it munches through your blanket. Both moths are nondescript creatures, light tan in color, with wings that measure no more than ½ inch from tip to tip. Each adult female lays 100 to 200 eggs, from which small, white larvae emerge. That's when real trouble begins.

These little guys have an awesome ability to digest the protein in keratin—the major ingredient of wool, hair, and feathers. In the wild, your friendly neighborhood wool moth larva lives on shed wool and on the bodies of dead animals, helping in its small way to decompose material that might otherwise pile up to offensive proportions. Although they chomp up and destroy an amount of wool equal to several times their own size, growing to a length of about ½ inch in the process, they don't move far. But one hole is all you need to ruin a good shirt.

AN OUNCE OF PREVENTION

Simple commonsense measures can help to fend off moth damage. My mother always told me to be sure that wool clothes were clean before storing them away, and she was right. Soiled parts of wool clothing are more attractive to the wool moth and its larvae. That spot of gravy, skin oil, blood, or grease is just like a sauce on the moth's favorite food.

Vacuum the corners of your cedar chest or storage closet periodically. Shake out or rewash those scarves and hats that stay in the garment bag year after year without being used. Undisturbed clothing is a likely haven for the egg-laying moth and her mouthy progeny.

Eight hours of exposure to heat above 110 °F or cold under 10 °F will kill any lurking larvae or eggs. Dry cleaning kills them, too. Eggs and larvae can enter your household in that bag of sweaters you buy at a yard sale, or in that handmade cap a friend sends you from her travels. Chill such clothing or send it to the cleaner before adding it to your closet.

Natural Mothproofers

Few studies have been done on any of the traditional mothproofing plants. While we might not have guarantees that they work, or a measurable number of dead larvae to count, the use of plants for moth protection is time honored and widespread. Herbal suppliers report a high percentage of repeat orders on their mothproofing mixtures, so people are voting for the effectiveness of those substances with their pocketbooks.

Apart from any insecticidal essential oils they may contain, herbs with a strong scent may confuse the moth by disguising the odor of the wool. Insects often depend on odor to locate food or to find good egg-laying territory. If the predominant smell in your storage closet is that of pungent, spicy herbs rather than wool, the moth will keep looking for real, recognizable, unprotected wool on which to lay her eggs.

Herbal mothproofers are a healthy, good-smelling alternative to harsh chemicals. Try sachets of strong-scented lavender, santolina, southernwood, and tansy, or use cedar shavings to protect your hand-knit sweaters and heirloom quilts.

Plants and plant products can help keep those wool-hungry larvae out of your sweaters without threatening your health, and they smell much more pleasant than paradichlorobenzene or naphthalene. You can grow some of these moth-repellent plants in your garden.

Lavender

Stems and leaves of English lavender (*Lavandula angustifolia*) are aromatic, but the flowers have the highest concentration of oil—and that's what controls the moths. I've used dried lavender blossoms in an old pine chest where I stored wool blankets.

Lavender is an attractive, shrubby plant growing 1 to 3 feet high, with slender gray-green leaves and wands of small, fragrant, bluish violet flowers. Lavender likes full sun and well-drained soil on the alkaline side. Reliably hardy strains and cultivars are available for northern gardeners. Look for recurrent-blooming cultivars, which produce more flowers in a season. Hardy to Zone 5.

Lavender Cotton

Our great-grandmothers hung bunches of dried lavender cotton or santolina (*Santolina chamaecyparissus*) in closets to repel moths. This is a pretty plant for the herb garden or border, with downy gray-green leaves that resemble coarse lace.

Seeds of this 2-foot-tall perennial are slow to germinate. Start them indoors in pots so you won't lose track of them in the garden. Santolina needs full sun and well-drained, light soil. It tolerates dry, even sandy, soil and is hardy to Zone 6.

Southernwood

Southernwood (*Artemisia abrotanum*) is called *garde robe* in France, a reference to its common use as a moth repellent. This fragrant perennial, which grows 3 to 4 feet tall, has ferny leaves, gray-green in color. When regularly pruned, it forms an attractive hedge.

Southernwood roots readily, so plants are easy to start from cuttings. This can be a long-lived herb. One gardener I know has a southernwood plant that is 20 years old. Southernwood grows well in full sun and ordinary soil and tolerates soil that is poor or dry. It is hardy to Zone 5.

Tansy

Common tansy (*Tanacetum vulgare*) is occasionally used alone as a mothproofer, but it's more often included in herb mixtures for the value of its pungent aroma. It is a 3- to 4-foot-tall perennial with deep green, much-divided leaves and small, golden yellow, flat-topped flowers. Fern-leaved tansy (*T. vulgare* var. *crispum*) has fuller leaves and a more ornamental appearance. Tansy is easy to grow from seed. It likes full sun and well-drained soil, which needn't be especially rich, and is hardy to Zone 4. Tansy spreads vigorously; use sunken strips of edging to keep it in control, or plant it in a wooden half-barrel.

Tobacco

People in the southern Appalachians often mothproof their stored woolens with the tobacco stalks that are left after the leaves have been removed. Tobacco leaves, especially those of the annual wild tobacco (*Nicotiana rustica*), contain even more nicotine than the stalks.

Nicotine kills insects by interfering with the transmission of nerve impulses. Treat this material carefully because it can be absorbed by inhaling and could be toxic if inhaled in large amounts. Wear a dust mask if the tobacco leaves you're handling are very crumbly. Keep them in a cloth bag rather than spreading them loose among your sweaters. Store dried tobacco leaves in a tightly closed container labeled "Poisonous." Nicotine dissipates rapidly when exposed to air.

Tobacco plants are large and imposing. To grow smoking tobacco (*N. tabacum*) or wild tobacco (*N. rustica*), gently press the tiny seeds, uncovered, into the surface of the soil or start indoors in pots or flats. Transplant seedlings into the garden after danger of frost. Prune off the growing tips in midsummer to improve the nicotine content of the lower leaves. Pick the leaves one by one as they start to turn yellow and hang them to dry or spread them on screens.

Wormwood

The aroma of common wormwood (*Artemisia absinthium*) and its content of absinthin, which is highly toxic when eaten, probably ac-

AROMATIC CEDAR

The Rolls Royce of mothproofing arrangements is the cedar-lined closet, a wonderful attic feature of several old houses we've known. My aunt kept wool quilts, fur coats, a nineteenth-century wool suit, and all the family coats and sweaters in such a closet, and the fabrics were not only free of moth damage, but they smelled good, too.

For cedar to be an effective larvicide, the space must be enclosed so the fumes can accumulate. You can make your own cedar-lined closet by attaching cedar boards to a closet with a tight-fitting door. Or line drawers or chests with thin planks of cedar. Sand cedar boards once in a while to release the aromatic oils. In her book *The Weaver's Garden*, Rita Buchanan suggests creating substitute "cedar" chests by treating the inner surface of wooden chests with essential oil of red cedar—or with the equally effective oils of eucalyptus, lavender, or pennyroyal.

When it's time to stash our wool clothes away for the summer, my husband, Mike, planes curly inch shavings from scrap cedar boards that he has milled from trees on our homestead. We stuff these into simple, 10 x 12-inch bags of nylon netting and put one or two into each garment bag.

count for its effectiveness as a moth repellent. It's an attractive plant with silvery, finely cut leaves, but it can retard the growth of neighboring plants.

Seeds of this tall, woody perennial germinate slowly, but cuttings root easily. The deep-rooted plant thrives in either sun or light shade, in well-drained soil of ordinary fertility. It tolerates dry soil and drought and is hardy to Zone 3.

Mothproofing Mixtures

When preparing moth-repellent herb mixtures at home, include a number of different plant materials, both to make the fragrance more interesting and to increase its effectiveness. Lavender, southernwood, and tansy make a good basic mixture. You can make it even more effective by adding cedar shavings, cloves, or patchouli.

I've always assumed that some herbs are included in mixtures more for their fragrance than for any insecticidal properties. But in talking with herb grower Cyrus Hyde of Well-Sweep Herb Farm in Port Murray, New Jersey, I learned that sweet woodruff (*Galium odoratum*) has been used in Germany for hundreds of years not only to impart a sweet vanilla-like scent, but also to guard woolens from moth damage. For mothproofing, Hyde suggests a blend of camphor-scented *Artemesia camphorata,* camphor-scented basil, lavender, patchouli, santolina, southernwood, and sweet woodruff.

Naturalist Euell Gibbons, who had a treasured collection of handmade Scandinavian wool sweaters, protected them with a mixture of cedar shavings, fragrant pine needles, and sassafras root shavings. He spread the dried materials in the bottom of a paper-lined drawer, tacked a layer of thin cloth over them, and then put his sweaters in the drawer.

Here are some recipes to guide you. Unless otherwise noted, all herbs are dried, coarsely crushed leaves. Mix all ingredients together, and spoon the mix into cheesecloth or sachet bags. If you don't have enough herbs to equal the recommended amounts, you can reduce the recipe proportionately. Most of these herbal ingredients are sold in bulk by mail-order suppliers. Several herb merchants offer cloth bags, too, for making your own mothproofing sachets.

Label herb mixtures clearly as moth repellents, so no one will eat them by mistake. Some of the herbal ingredients can cause toxic effects if eaten.

EXOTIC MOTHPROOFERS

In addition to the herbs that you and I can grow in our temperate-climate gardens, several other mothproofers grow in the tropics or subtropics. All of these aromatic plant products are sold by mail-order suppliers (see "Resources" on page 300).

Patchouli, which grows in India, was traditionally used to protect Paisley shawls shipped to England and Europe. The characteristic aroma became a "trademark" of Paisley shawls. Patchouli leaves have also been used to guard valuable stored papers against destructive silverfish insects. You can buy patchouli in dried form or in the more effective essential oil. Tonka beans and oil, from the cumaru tree of South America, Africa, and Ceylon, have a vanilla-like scent. They are usually used in chopped or ground form. Vetiver, the root of a tropical grass from India, and sandalwood, from India, Ceylon, and Malaysia, are included in moth-repellent mixtures in the form of chips and oil.

Pungent Mix
Handful of thyme leaves
Handful of tansy leaves
Handful of southernwood leaves
1 tablespoon crushed cloves

Sweetly Aromatic Mix
2 cups lavender flowers
2 cups rosemary leaves
1 tablespoon crushed cloves
¼ cup dried lemon peel

Spicy Mix
Handful of santolina leaves
Handful of tansy leaves
Handful of mint leaves
Handful of wormwood leaves
1 tablespoon crushed cinnamon stick

Sandy Mush Herb Nursery's Insect Repellent Blend
2 cups southernwood leaves
2 cups lavender flowers and leaves
2 cups wormwood or 'Lambrook Silver' artemisia leaves
½ cup ground cloves
¼ cup ground nutmeg
¼ cup dried citrus peel

How to Use Herbal Mothproofers

You can buy or make simple bags for your mothproofing mixtures. Use a net or cheesecloth bag for coarse mixes, a cloth bag for fine ones. Here are some ideas for how to use your natural mothproofers. Keep in mind that most herbs lose potency after a year. Be sure to replace them with a fresh batch.

- Hang dried sprigs among stored clothing in a closet.
- Tuck small bags in pockets of stored woolens.
- Nestle a bag or two in your sweater drawer.
- Add a stem or two of dried herbs to each sweater box.

If you use natural moth repellents, one thing you won't have to do is to air out your clothes in the fall when you remove them from storage. Instead of that chemical smell, they'll have a spicy, woodsy, or cedar-rich fragrance that will, most likely, be welcome in your closet right away.

CHAPTER THIRTY-EIGHT

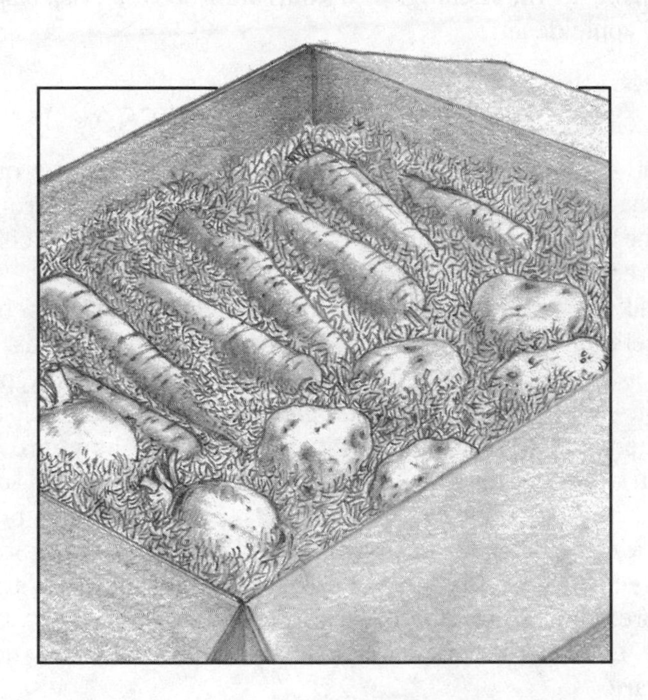

Try Simple Root Cellaring

Of all the satisfactions to be had from growing and keeping vegetables and fruits, surely none is sweeter than selecting from your own stored produce to feed your family in the dead of winter. Even though it's February, and the ground is ringing hard, ice glazes the land, and the trees bend to the howling of the wind, we'll have fresh vegetables for dinner today—not from the store, but from our root cellar. We've just brought up a bowl of potatoes, a pocketful of carrots, a head of Chinese cabbage, a few apples, and a big beet—the makings of a nourishing stew, a crisp salad, and a baked apple desert.

No Fuss, No Muss

All this—and more—can be yours without boiling jars or filling freezer bags. No slicing, no sweetening, no packaging or processing. That's the beauty of the homely, homey root cellar. Natural cold chills and preserves the vegetables in storage.

We still can tomatoes and peaches and we freeze peas, because these methods seem to us the most effective for those foods. But for most root vegetables, some members of the cabbage family, and several fruits—especially apples—you can't beat good old cold storage.

Storage vegetables are a good investment. The homegrown produce you store for winter will contribute to your health and save you money in the days ahead. Apples, beets, carrots, onions, potatoes, squash, sweet potatoes, and turnips are favorite storage foods that should keep without any form of processing until spring. With a little extra care, you can also bank on cabbage, celeriac, celery, Chinese cabbage, escarole, leeks, parsnips, pears, quinces, salsify, and other hearty fare.

Far from being merely inexpensive menu fillers, complex carbohydrates such as those found in vegetables are more valuable than we usually give them credit for. They are an excellent source of fiber, which has been shown to decrease levels of certain cancer-causing substances passing through the intestinal tract. A few specific vegetables, in fact, have been found to counter a toxic substance directly. For example, cabbage, cauliflower, and radishes all help fight the toxic cancer-causing effect of nitrosamines, which may form from nitrites that are routinely added to ham, bacon, and other cured products. So, if you have ham in your freezer, you need some cabbage in your root cellar.

Simple "Cellars"

To provide good storage conditions, some gardeners take a tip from the past and build a simple root cellar, either underground or in the basement, to store quality homegrown food for winter. You can practice an easy version of what we call root cellaring, too, by simply making use of nooks and crannies in your house and outbuildings and by improvising.

Easy-Access Indoor Storage

It's a rare house that doesn't have some odd spot where vegetables can be stored. Insulate the crawl space under a porch to keep potatoes and turnips. An unheated pantry or spare room might be just right for squash and sweet potatoes. You can ripen tomatoes in the basement even if it's heated. Cellar steps leading to the outside provide a graduated range of conditions—cooler at the more exposed top (unless the sun heats the cellar door or air temperatures fluctuate greatly) and warmer near the basement.

One elderly couple we visited made excellent use of the space between their wooden basement steps. Each step riser was the front of a drawer. When pulled out, these drawers revealed a fine stock of onions, sweet potatoes, turnips, and white potatoes. Another family furnished a north-side closet with shelves and insulated the doors to

STORAGE THAT SUITS

As gardeners of old knew, your long-keeping vegetables will take you through to spring if you satisfy their storage needs. Use this list to help you match the conditions of your storage spaces with your crops.

Cold and very moist (32° to 40°F, 90 to 95 percent relative humidity): Beets, carrots, celeriac, celery, Chinese cabbage, horseradish, Jerusalem artichokes, leeks, parsnips, rutabagas, salsify, turnips, winter radishes.

Cold and moist (32° to 40°F, 80 to 90 percent relative humidity): Apples, cabbage, escarole, pears, potatoes, quinces.

Cool and dry (35° to 40°F, 60 to 70 percent relative humidity): Garlic, onions.

Moderately warm and dry (50° to 60°F, 60 to 70 percent relative humidity): Pumpkins, sweet potatoes, winter squash.

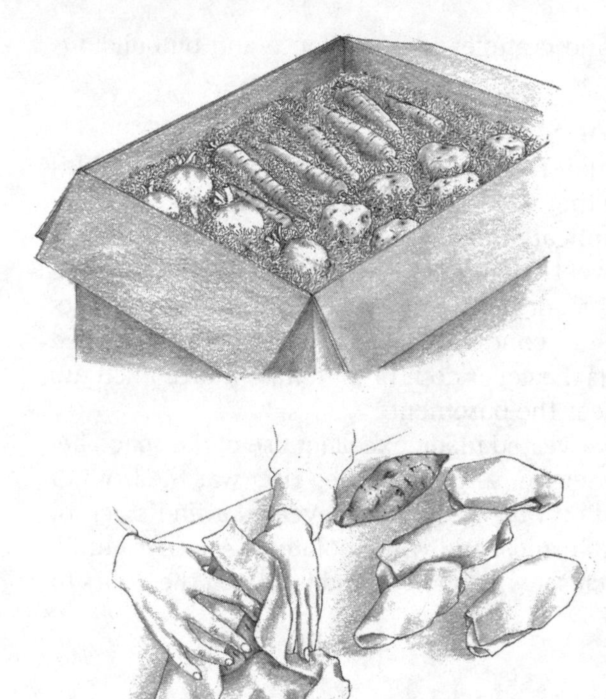

Make a handy modern version of the old-fashioned root cellar by using a cardboard box full of damp sawdust to store long-keeping vegetables like carrots and turnips. Wrap your fall harvest of sweet potatoes in newspapers and keep them cool and dry.

make a small but useful storage spot for root vegetables. Others have found an enclosed porch just right for potatoes and other root crops.

In our old house we had a dirt-floored, unheated basement. This damp, cold location was just right for keeping carrots, Chinese cabbage, leeks, parsnips, potatoes, and turnips. It was too moist for garlic, but not for onions, as long as I kept them off the floor. We kept pumpkins, squash, and sweet potatoes, wrapped individually in newspaper, on shelves and in baskets in an unheated room.

If you have a good moist place to keep your root vegetables, you can simply heap them in baskets and cartons. But if your cellar is medium damp, as ours is, you'll need to protect your vegetables against drying out. Pack them in boxes of damp sawdust to prevent shriveling, or use sand, peat moss, or even leaves for packing. Good air circulation around your packing boxes helps prevent spoilage. Stack the cartons on pallets or slatted shelves rather than directly on the floor.

Going Underground

Here are some small-scale outdoor storage ideas that take advantage of the earth's natural insulation to cool and keep your vegetables.

Mulch blanket. The simplest outdoor vegetable storage method is the time-honored trick of leaving hardy root vegetables right in the row. Cover them with a thick blanket of mulch to keep the ground from freezing solid. Be sure to use a mulch that stays loose and fluffy, like oak leaves or straw, and pile it on at least 6 inches thick. Dig your vegetables until the ground freezes hard, then harvest the remainder of the crop in early spring. You can do this with carrots, parsnips, and salsify.

Cabbage trench. This method of cold storage is almost as easy. Simply dig a trench about 2 feet deep, as wide as necessary to accommodate the vegetables without crowding them. Pack a 3-inch layer of leaves or straw in the bottom of the trench, and then put your cabbages, head down and root up, in the trench. Cover the trench with boards and top with hay or other insulating material. Trench storage is especially good for cabbage, putting them into "solitary confinement" so they cannot affect the flavor of other foods stored close by. Celery also keeps well in trenches. Replant the stalks in the dirt bottom of the trench, roof it with a slanting board to shed water, and pile cornstalks, hay, or other insulation over the boards.

Clamp. A clamp, or earth kiln, is a traditional storage method that's easy to construct. A clamp is a mound of vegetables wrapped with insulating straw and covered with a layer of packed earth. Once a clamp is opened, its entire contents should be removed because it is difficult to repack the mound correctly. For this reason, most home gardeners build several small clamps rather than one large one.

To make a clamp, stake out a 3-foot circle (the diameter of the circle depends on how many vegetables you need to store), and dig a 3- to 4-inch-wide drainage trench around it. Pile a 3- to 4-inch layer of hay or straw on the soil in the center of the circle. Then heap your vegetables in a cone-shaped pile on the straw. Spread straw or hay over the mound of vegetables, and then cover this insulating layer with a 3- to 4-inch-deep outer shell of firmly packed earth. Let a wisp of straw peek through the top to provide ventilation. The first drainage trench remains outside the mound of earth. Dig a second drainage trench around its perimeter. Beets, cabbage, carrots, or potatoes can be stored in a clamp, but be sure to give cabbage its own mound so that the flavor doesn't seep into the other vegetables.

Buried containers. Other underground storage plans may include burying drain tiles or flue liners, trash cans, barrels, or crates, which are then filled with produce. In each case the principle is the same—the fairly constant temperature of the earth below the frost line has a moderating effect and keeps the buried vegetables from freezing. Because underground storage spaces like these are quite damp, this method works well for apples, beets, carrots, potatoes, and other vegetables that like cold, moist conditions, but not for onions, squash, and sweet potatoes.

When burying any container in your ground, it's a good idea to line the hole with rocks to promote drainage, cover the top with hay to insulate it, and add boards on top to prevent the hay from freezing with ice. Bank surrounding soil in a slope to drain water away from the container opening, or dig a trench around the opening to carry rainwater off. Most people tuck leaves, straw, or sawdust between layers of vegetables when putting them in these underground spaces.

Eating with the Seasons

Since we've been root cellaring, we've learned to appreciate our seasonal garden abundance in a new way. We enjoy strawberries when they're fresh, but we don't try too hard to preserve them for January. Apples taste better then, we think. Likewise, we don't eat a lot of beets in summer when fresh peas, tomatoes, and zucchini are crowding our plates. But in winter, we count on beets and the other hardy fare that makes our cold-weather menus as distinctive in their way as our warm-weather meals are. I still do some canning and freezing, but less than I once did, before I learned this easier way to store garden food.

It's a great feeling to be able to go "shopping" in our root cellar for our own hearty baking potatoes; for big, tender beets to cook on a frosty day; for the thick, mellow leeks that do wonders for stews and casseroles; and for the onions and garlic, cabbage, carrots, and turnips that make a cold-weather soup something special. With our homegrown food readily at hand, we are able to eat better and more cheaply than if we depended entirely on shipped-in store produce.

CHAPTER THIRTY-NINE

Build Harvest Figures

Those lolling, pumpkin-headed, leaf-stuffed, homey people-forms called harvest figures that appear on porches in the fall are fun for everyone—children, gardeners, neighbors, and passersby. Many of us adults, I know, take a not-so-secret delight in putting together these creations, ostensibly for the kids, but really just as much for ourselves.

No rules govern the construction of harvest figures, unless you count the unwritten but widely accepted dogma that they should be made entirely of found objects. You would not, say, go to the store to buy a mask or a hat for your harvest figure. Never. These guys are homegrown, hatched in the garden and the closet and the attic and basement where odd leftovers lurk. The pleasure of the art lies in seeing the possibilities in what you have on hand.

Construction Hints

Pumpkins are basic for the head, but you might also fashion a head from a gourd, a squash, or even a melon. Paper bags, pillow cases, discarded plastic jugs, and wooden shingles make good heads, too. The original goblin's head, in Ireland, before pumpkins were introduced, was a large knobby turnip or rutabaga, hollowed out to hold a glowing coal. Bodies are often leaf-stuffed bags clothed in cast-off coats or flannel shirts. Legs may be sticks, iron pipes, long-necked pumpkins, leaf-stuffed stockings, straw-wadded trousers, or perhaps cornstalks or even brooms. Odd gloves see useful life again as harvest figure hands, and funny hats make the creatures seem more human.

Homely harvest figures are a whimsical celebration of the season. A pumpkin head, crookneck squash hands, and old clothes stuffed with leaves make an amiable fellow. Be creative with whatever you have on hand.

You can hang your harvest figure from a tree, lean it against the porch wall, prop it by a lamp post, drape it on a balcony, or seat it on a lawn chair in your front yard. Clothespin fingers, carrot noses, pepper ears, and mop or cornsilk hair are all details that others have used.

As a true folk art, your harvest figure should evolve from what occurs spontaneously to you, rather than from a formula or specific directions or from what others have done, so I'll not give you any more hints. The rest is up to you. See what you can find in the garden and in the attic. Make some silly people and have fun doing it.

How Long Does a Harvest Person Live?

Unlike scarecrows, which are usually left to molder in the garden, flapping wraithlike in the autumn wind, then frosted with a layer of winter snow over their faded clothes, harvest figures are seldom left to disintegrate at the mercy of the weather. These big leaf-stuffed rag dolls appear in September or October, marking the fall season, and are usually dismantled in December when people decorate their homes for the holidays. The clothes go in the rag bag, and the hay or leaf innards on the compost pile, with perhaps the pumpkin head as well. A solid pumpkin, if uncut and not softened by hard frost, could even go on to form the main ingredient in a Thanksgiving pumpkin pie. Of course, if you have an especially mellow pair of overalls and a favorite battered hat, you might want to hang them in the shed so you can rescue them to assemble next year's harvest person, who will have a different head, perhaps, but an equally warm and friendly heart.

Harvest Home

The roots of this homey craft go deeply into our human history. The lighthearted harvest figures that we like to prop on our porches connect us to that time when life was much more precarious and each morsel of food deeply appreciated. Back in the pre-Christian era, the final bundle of produce to be gathered from a growing plot was considered to possess a powerful life force. People saved these "last fruits" of their fields, often counting on them to help make the next harvest bountiful.

Later, in England and in Europe, ceremonies accompanied the gathering of the last crops, with processions and singing and chanting. In a custom that harks back to the ancient idea of Earth as mother, the last-cut bundles of grain were sometimes given a maternal name and arranged and even dressed to resemble a human form. The practice of weaving "corn dollies," decorative woven ornaments made from stalks of dry wheat, probably grew out of this much earlier folkway.

In seventeenth-century Europe, especially in Germany, the ceremonial display of the harvest evolved into the tradition of Harvest Home, celebrated in churches. This was a special service of thanksgiving held in September or October after all the crops had been gathered in. To dramatize the abundance and variety of farm and garden produce, the entire area surrounding the altar of the church was piled with mounds of vegetables, shocks of corn, sheaves of wheat, baskets of fruit, and later, even bread, cakes, and home-canned foods.

Lutheran immigrants brought this custom to America when they settled here, and it is still a live tradition in Pennsylvania and other states where German immigrants settled. In fact, a number of present-day churches have revived the custom. In some Pennsylvania churches the tradition has been practiced continously since the founding of the church. In those early days, the food contributed for the display was given to the poor (and sometimes shared with the minister's family, which was often large and marginally solvent). Today, many churches that continue the Harvest Home tradition invite the contribution of canned and packaged goods, which are then given to area food pantries. The fresh produce is often donated to soup kitchens. In any case, the voluptuous display of Earth's bounty evokes a deeper sense of thanksgiving than mere words ever could.

PART FOUR

Take winter as you find him, and he turns out to be a thoroughly honest fellow with no nonsense in him, which is a great comfort in the long run.

—James Russell Lowell (1819–1891)

WINTER

CHAPTER FORTY

Fashion a Wreath of Greens

Whether your home is a log cabin or a suburban split-level, you can brighten the doorway, walls, and tables with festive reminders of the season. The impulse to light candles and bring in evergreens is a natural one. Ages ago, when the dark, cold winter was mysterious and spring was far from certain, people tried to extend the growing season of light and greenery. They defied the cold, barren, and often hungry days by lighting fires and cutting evergreen boughs to bring inside. As civilization developed, the hanging of greens and keeping of the light took on an increasingly religious symbolism.

Today, as we put up wreaths and relax in candlelight within the security of our own four walls, the green and the glow become a part of the heritage that we'll pass on. Dark still comes early and the ground is cold, but inside we make our own weather and we still make merry together.

A Welcoming Wreath

Begin at the front door with a classic evergreen wreath, beautiful in its simplicity. The wreath is a perennial favorite, and with good reason. Its circular shape and the greens are symbolic of hope and life. And the textured greenery, with or without a smooth red bow, is pleasing to our eyes.

Gathering Materials

You can use greenery of any kind to make a wreath, as long as it resists wilting and holds its leaves. Some homeowners plan to prune their evergreen trees and shrubs in December so they'll have fresh cuttings to use for decorating.

Conifers of many kinds are traditional favorites that keep their freshness. Try arborvitaes (*Thuja* spp.), Colorado blue spruce (*Picea pungens* 'Glauca'), cedars (*Cedrus* spp.), firs (*Abies* spp.), junipers (*Juniperus* spp.), yews (*Taxus* spp.), and graceful eastern white pine (*Pinus strobus*). Hemlocks (*Tsuga* spp.) are good for outside use but shed needles fast indoors.

Broad-leaved evergreens are attractive in holiday decorations, too. English holly (*Ilex aquifolium*) creates a festive look. Perhaps your yard will yield clippings of English ivy (*Hedera helix*), glossy privet (*Ligustrum lucidum*), galaxy (*Galax urceolata*), mountain laurel (*Kalmia latifolia*), Oregon grape (*Mahonia aquifolium*), or Japanese holly (*Ilex crenata*). Boxwoods (*Buxus* spp.) are another good choice, but before you clip away, remember these are very slow-growing shrubs.

If you do not have large amounts of any one plant in your yard or if you want to create a special effect, try mixing two or more kinds of greens together. Use plants with different leaf textures, like boxwood and eastern white pine or Japanese holly and hemlock. The smooth, rounded leaves of boxwood and Japanese holly provide an interesting texture contrast to the leaves of needled evergreens.

Collect greenery a day or two before you need it. Carefully prune several branches off evergreen trees and shrubs. Shape and improve the appearance of the plant as you prune it. Remove crossing branches and thin out areas that are too thick. Stand the cut ends of the branches in water for 1 hour or, better yet, overnight, so they can soak up moisture. This conditioning process will help the greenery last longer. When you are ready to start making your wreath, cut short, 3- to 4-inch sprigs from the the evergreen branches. Start at the tips of branches and side branches, and work your way down.

Constructing the Wreath

You can either purchase a wire wreath base from your local garden center or make one from a coat hanger (see page 152). A 12- or 14-inch wreath base is a good size to begin with. Ready-made wire forms are inexpensive and reusable, and sturdier than a modified coat hanger. But if the wreath-making urge strikes and there's no wreath form at hand, a wire hanger will do just fine.

For a more pleasing rounded shape, make your wreath of many small bunches of greens rather than fewer, longer bunches. To form the wreath, gather together small bunches of evergreen sprigs. Three to four sprigs make a good-size bunch. Wrap a length of flexible floral wire around them to make a compact bundle, and then wire this bundle to the wreath base. Work your way around the circle, covering the wired stems of the previous bunch with the greenery of the next bundle.

Try to angle the bunches in the same direction across the wreath base each time. This way, when you reach the end of the circle, your last bunch will nestle against the first with no stems exposed. For wider wreath frames, you may need to angle bunches in a repeated pattern. For example, if three bunches will fill the width of the wreath base, a fan shape may be appropriate. Angle the inner one toward the hole in the center of the wreath base, the middle one parallel to the wire frame, and the outer one toward the outside of the wire wreath base. Repeat this pattern, working parallel to the wreath base.

The wreath really needs no further embellishment; it's lovely just as it is. But if you want to add more color, wire on crab apples, persimmons (leave fruit on the twig), hawthorn berries, rose hips, pieces of bittersweet, dried red peppers, or pinecones. Wrap wire around the twig holding the fruit (you may like to combine two or more fruits) and then wire the twig securely to the wreath base. You can add a bow, if you like, to dress it up. Red is traditional, but gold and white are also good choices. Bows made of calico or checked fabric have a warm country-kitchen look.

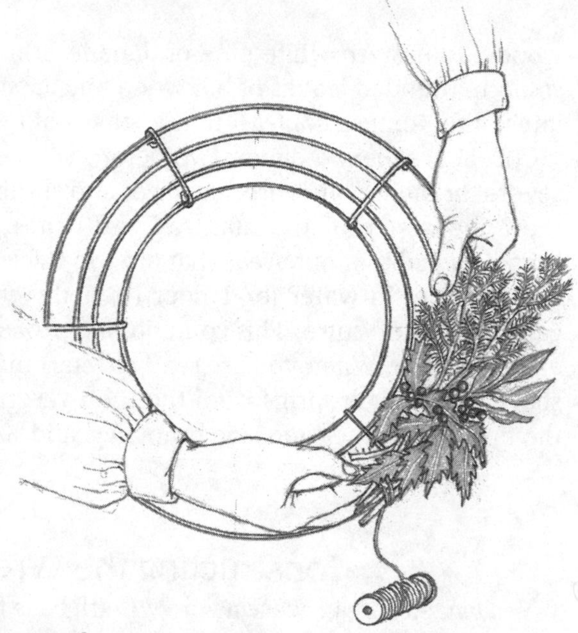

A welcoming wreath is more special when you make it with clippings from around the home place. Use 3- to 4-inch cuttings of evergreens and a purchased wire form to make your wreath. Wire on small bunches of greens, overlapping the previous bundle as you proceed around the circle.

Completing the Circle

Christmas greens have customarily been treated with respect even when the time comes to take them down. In the old days, the wreath was not simply thrown away. It was burned ceremoniously or given to the animals to eat.

Since some greenery and decorations are poisonous, the best use for an old wreath today is to use its clippings for mulch around a favorite plant. Save the wire form for next year's decoration.

CHAPTER FORTY-ONE

Grow Herbs on the Kitchen Windowsill

When frost ends the active growing season, do you miss that last-minute dash to the garden for a pinch of thyme or a sprig of parsley to complete a meal? Have thoughts of fresh chives on your omelet and whole-leaved basil in your stewed tomatoes convinced you that you need some fresh herbs for your winter survival? If you crave herbs year-round, consider growing some of them indoors. Windowsill herbs are more restrained in growth than those picked from the garden in summer. But because they're near at hand, we're more likely to remember to cook with them. Their variety of form and leaf texture adds interest to the indoor scene. When we brush against them as we go about our work, they give us refreshing fragrance without losing a single leaf. Indoor herbs earn their keep.

Getting Started

Well-rooted, container-grown specimens usually adapt better to indoor culture than do larger plants dug from gardens. Herbs that have spent the summer in pots will often do well indoors in winter. If you already have some herbs growing in your garden, you can propagate new plants for potting up. Root a few low-growing branches of rosemary, sage, or other woody herbs by layering. Although any time of the growing season is fine to do layering of woody plants, spring is the best. Dig a shallow hole in the ground near the herb you want to root. Carefully bend down a branch so that a 3- or 4-inch section will lie horizontally in the hole. Remove the leaves from that section. Make a small, slanting cut on the bottom side of the branch. The cut should be shallow, less than half way through the branch. Lay the branch in the hole and pile a few handfuls of soil over the wounded section. Leave 2 or 3 inches of the branch tip uncovered so it will continue to grow. Anchor the branch with a small rock placed where the branch comes out of the hole, or use a bent piece of wire or a twig to hold it in place. Keep the buried section moist but not wet. After a month or two, a healthy set of roots should form near the wound. Cut the branch off just below the new roots. Pot it up and watch it grow.

Your local garden center may keep a stock of herbs on hand, even if the outdoor growing season is over. If the herbs of choice are not available there, try a mail-order nursery.

If you do dig garden herbs for indoor use, cut the top growth of each plant back by one-half to two-thirds before digging, to minimize stress on the roots. Divide bushy plants when potting them up; each division will have more room to send out roots in the pot. To further ease the transition from garden to windowsill, pot up divisions of herbs early enough so that you can safely leave them outside for three or four weeks before bringing them indoors. This will give them time to become acclimated to the pot before the stress of moving into the house.

All-purpose potting mix is fine for filling the containers. If you make your own soil mix, use a recipe of equal parts of good garden soil, finished compost, and vermiculite. Never use garden soil alone for plants in pots. In a pot, even sandy soil packs into a tight, air-excluding mass that is deadly to herb plants.

Let There Be Light

Your indoor herbs will need at least 5 hours of direct sun each day. When bringing plants indoors, I've often covered wide windowsills with my collection. A bookshelf pulled up to the window makes a good perch for herbs, too, or you can use a wheeled cart to follow the sun from room to room. (Some of us will do anything for fresh chives!) Another attractive arrangement is a series of glass shelves mounted next to the window.

Winter days are short and the rays of the far-off sun are at their weakest. If you lack a sunny spot or live in a northern climate, it's a good idea to keep your herbs under fluorescent lights. I've used a fluorescent-light cart with excellent results. Basement light setups are suitable, too, but it's nice to keep herbs closer at hand. Consider attaching pairs of fluorescent lights to the undersides of bookshelves or kitchen cabinets. Both arrangements have worked well for me.

TIPS ON FLUORESCENT LIGHTS

To give your plants a good balance of light, use one cool-white and one warm-white tube in a fluorescent fixture. You don't need the more expensive grow-lights for indoor herbs. After a year of use, however, fluorescent tubes shed less light. Some indoor growers replace the tubes with new ones every year, but for plants grown for foliage and not for flowers—like herbs—you can keep the same lights for two years. Place the plants at least 5 inches but no more than 12 inches from the tubes, and make sure they receive 12 to 16 hours of fluorescent light each day. (You can use a timer to turn the lights on and off.)

I've also used a single fluorescent light fixture sitting on top of the refrigerator. The light was attached to metal legs that straddled the flats.

Growing Conditions and Care

Indoors, herbs appreciate protection from freezing, to be sure, but they don't like to be too hot, either. In our well-insulated, wood-heated house, midwinter temperatures can climb well above 80°F unless I open a window. Most herbs really prefer cool temperatures, more like 60° to 65°F. Like many other plants, indoor herbs like a 5° to 10° drop in temperature at night. These conditions are fairly easy to achieve in a spare room, a kitchen corner, or a sunny, unheated, closed porch. The temperature in those spots is usually fairly constant, with a natural drop at night.

Heated indoor air is unnaturally dry. A humidifier helps add moisture, as does misting at least several times a week. I keep a kettle of water on the wood stove, too. Another way to increase the humidity around your plants is to set the pots on a 1-inch layer of moistened pebbles in a plastic tray. Don't let pots stand in water, though; soggy conditions quickly rot the roots of herbs.

How much and how often you'll need to water your indoor herbs will vary according to the size of the pot, the type of pot, and the prevailing temperature and humidity. Small pots need more frequent watering than large ones, and clay pots need watering more often than plastic. Hanging baskets dry out more quickly than pots standing on pebbles. One good rule of thumb is to water when the soil ½ inch below the surface feels dry.

In their natural habitat, many herbs thrive on fairly lean soil. When confined to pots, however, especially small pots, they need additional nutrients from time to time. Give them a small dose (as recommended on the bottle) of your favorite liquid fertilizer; I use a dilute solution of fish emulsion every four to five weeks in December and January, and every two to three weeks when they're in active growth. In the midwinter months, when windowsill plants receive the least light, use the fertilizer at half-strength. Too much fertilizer makes herbs less flavorful, and herbs grown indoors are generally milder than outdoor specimens anyway.

Herbs are seldom damaged by insect infestations, perhaps because of the repellent effect of their aromatic oils. Indoors is an unnatural place for green plants, though, and problems occasionally occur. Aphids, spider mites, and whiteflies are the most likely pests. Your first line of defense is simply a strong spray of lukewarm water. If that doesn't discourage the invaders, wash the leaves with mild soap—not detergent—and water and rinse them. Or spray with diluted soapy water (1 teaspoon soap per quart of water) or a commercially prepared insecticidal soap such as Safer Insecticidal Soap. (Apply a commercially prepared insecticidal soap as recommended on the label.) Use yellow sticky strips positioned among your plants to trap aphids and whiteflies. The strips are pieces of cardboard or plastic, painted bright yellow and coated with a sticky material. The color attracts insects, which become stuck on the sticky surface. The strips are available from garden centers and mail-order catalogs.

A Cook's Compendium

Bush basil, chives, lemon grass, marjoram, parsley, rosemary, and thyme are some of the most useful and adaptable culinary herbs, and the plants are easily obtained. Here are some tips to help keep these valuable kitchen aids happy on a sunny windowsill.

Bush Basil (*Ocimum basilicum* 'Minimum')

Bush basil grows in a globe-shaped shrubby form, up to 1 foot high. It has rounded, ½-inch-long leaves and white flowers, but it may not bloom indoors. Also called French fin-leaved basil, this cultivar is a better choice for your indoor garden than the larger sweet basil (*Ocimum basilicum*), which requires more light. But even 'Minimum' does best and stays more compact under fluorescent lights than on the windowsill. Like all basils, 'Minimum' is frost-tender, so be sure to protect or move any basil plants grown near a window when nights turn frigid. When you harvest bush basil for cooking, cut off no more than a quarter of the top growth.

Chives (*Allium schoenoprasum*)

Even if you take only an occasional snipping of chives to perk up baked potatoes, the plant is worth cultivating for its piquant, milder-than-onion–flavored green quills. This herb is easier to bring in from outdoors than most others. At the end of the season, divide the chives in the garden by digging a clump and separating the crowded bulblets into smaller clumps. Cut back the foliage to a height of 2 inches. Re-

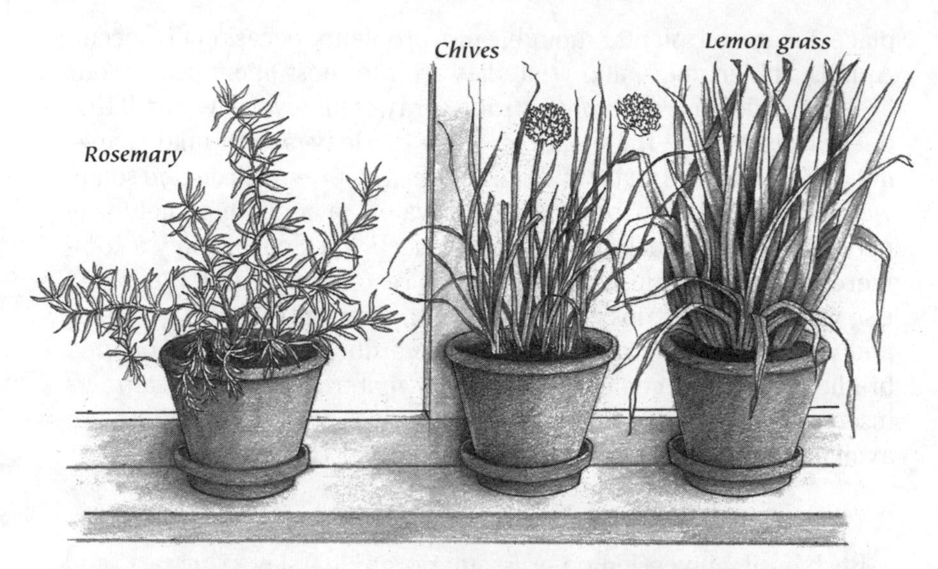

Keep a few pots of herbs on a sunny kitchen windowsill where they'll be handy for cooking. Some of the most flavorful herbs are adaptable to the indoor life. And it's so satisfying in winter to pinch a bit of rosemary for the potatoes or snip some lemon grass for the soup.

plant each cluster of bulblets in a new 5-inch pot with good soil and a fistful of compost. Let the potted plant get settled outdoors for a few weeks before bringing it in.

Like other hardy perennials, chives need a vacation from active growth once a year. If the plants you've brought in stop producing new leaves, withhold water and put them outdoors in a cold frame or bury the pots in soil just up to their rims. The cold will make them go dormant. Bring them back in after a two- to three-week rest. You can also pot up chives in the fall and leave them outdoors to experience their annual freeze before you bring them in. Chives that still grow poorly after a few weeks of dormancy in freezing weather probably need fertilizer.

Lemon Grass (*Cymbopogon citratus*)

Lemon grass grows in clumps of ½-inch-wide grassy leaves that reach up to 3 feet high. Small plants kept indoors will grow to a height of 1 to 1½ feet. Lemon grass rarely flowers.

This tropical native is less tender than basil but cannot tolerate frost. If you have lemon grass growing in the ground, you can divide a clump, after first cutting it back to about 3 or 4 inches, and repot the divisions. Indoors, water infrequently but mist the foliage often. Avoid overfertilizing. Chopped leaves of lemon grass add a delicious lemony tang to soups, drinks, and oriental dishes.

Marjorams and Oreganos (*Origanum* spp.)

These herbs from the mint family most commonly grow 1 to 2 feet high in the open garden, but young plants regularly pinched back stay more compact indoors. Some herb growers suggest that so-called Italian or Greek oregano (*Origanum heracleoticum*) will make more durable windowsill plants than sweet marjoram (*O. majorana*), but if you're using fluorescent lights, you should have no trouble raising sweet marjoram.

Sweet marjoram does well in hanging baskets. It needs plenty of light and doesn't mind a cool location. Growth will slow considerably if the temperature falls below 50°F, though. Avoid overwatering; marjoram is more prone to root rot than oregano. This herb's flavor is best before flowering.

Parsley (*Petroselinum crispum*)

Parsley grows slowly indoors, so you'll need several plants for a regular supply. Curly-leaved parsley (*Petroselinum crispum* var. *crispum*) makes an attractive garnish, but flat-leaved Italian parsley (*P. crispum* var. *neapolitanum*) has a better flavor. For the best indoor parsley, start seedlings in summer and move them to pots when they develop their first true leaves. Or buy young pot-grown plants at your local garden center. In my experience, garden parsley seldom thrives after transplanting because its deep taproot suffers when uprooted.

The perky, 4- to 8-inch-long stems will keep coming all winter if you keep the plant on the cool side and avoid letting it dry out. Parsley grows well outdoors in heavier clay soil, but in pots it needs a porous mix. Grow it under fluorescent lights to keep the plants deep green and compact.

Rosemary (*Rosmarinus officinalis*)

Rosemary adapts to somewhat lower light levels than basil or marjoram; bright, diffused light like that on a windowsill is usually enough. Keep rosemary in a sunny, cool place and water it regularly. If you allow the soil to dry out completely, the plant may go into a rapid and irreversible decline. Rosemary needs very good drainage and can be subject to root rot if the soil retains too much water. I always include compost in my potting mixture and have had no rosemary root-rot losses. If you have trouble, add some perlite to improve drainage. Rosemary likes neutral or alkaline soil, so if your potting mixture tends to be acidic, add a few crushed eggshells (a source of calcium) or a generous pinch of limestone to each 4-inch pot.

Thymes (*Thymus* spp.)

Thyme is a low-growing, often creeping plant with more than 400 kinds. The best thymes for culinary purposes, according to Cyrus Hyde of Well-Sweep Herb Farm, in Port Murray, New Jersey, are English, French, and German winter thymes, oregano thyme, and porlock (all are types of *Thymus vulgaris*); lemon thyme (*T.* × *citriodorus*); and caraway thyme (*T. herba-barona*).

Young plants—seedlings or newly rooted starts—are the best way to start thyme in pots. Thyme makes a good "groundcover" at the base of a taller potted plant like lemon grass.

Thyme needs excellent drainage. It's a good idea to add ¼ cup of perlite to each 4-inch pot of soil mix. Avoid overwatering.

Even with the best of care, thyme may turn woody when grown indoors and lose its tiny rounded leaves in late winter. But by then, the pungent leaves will have enlivened many a turkey stuffing and otherwise ordinary pea soup.

CHAPTER FORTY TWO

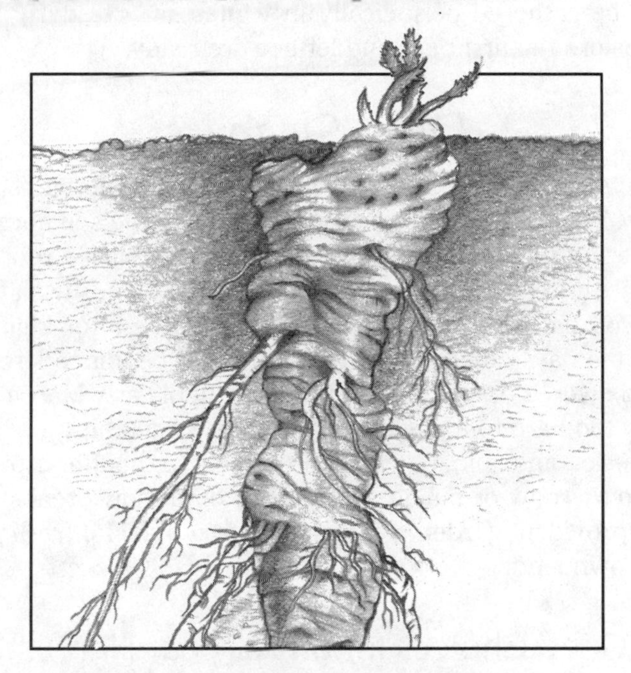

Extend Harvests with Hibernating Vegetables

On the surface, the winter landscape appears lifeless, except perhaps for the birds that dart from the feeder to the weeds in the field. Snow blankets the lane, the hills, the pasture, and the lawn. The wind is fierce, days are short, and nights are frigid.

Yet there is life in the garden. Vegetables lie in wait in the ground all winter. They are mature specimens grown last fall and left in the earth to be gathered periodically in winter and regularly in early spring, before the first peas and lettuce are ready.

Deep Sleepers

Safe in the earth from the cold of winter, root vegetables stay crisp and tasty. The trick for the gardener is keeping the soil above them from freezing solid. Mulching the ground above buried root vegetables with a good foot of straw or with bags of leaves usually keeps the soil soft enough to dig for a month or more after killing frost. Then as the days begin to lengthen, the cold begins to strengthen, and for six weeks or so, from mid-January until early March, the soil is usually too hard to allow digging for root vegetables.

Kale, leeks, and spinach can still be picked, though, especially if protected by snow or mulch. And whenever a thaw breaks winter's grip, the provident gardener can dig in the cold soil for fresh produce from his own land.

Good Choices for an All-Year Harvest

Hibernating vegetables like these will give you a taste of spring long before it's in the air. As you plan this year's garden, keep next winter in mind. Fresh greens and root vegetables provide relief from winter's doldrums.

Be sure to mark with care all rows from which you plan to dig root vegetables. A few feet of snow can hide your treasure from you.

Carrots

Generously mulched carrots usually keep well in the soil all winter. The hardiest carrots are those with a thick root and large core. Sometimes mice burrow under the mulch and gnaw on the roots. Spread a piece of hardware cloth over the row before piling on the mulch to make it more difficult for the mice to find your buried carrots.

I know a pair of determined New York State gardeners who have managed to keep even turnips in the ground for all-winter eating. Most of us content ourselves with storing turnips in the root cellar, but my friends' trick will let you store turnips or carrots in the garden. They mulch with a foot of dry hay, covered by a sheet of plastic weighted down with stones, soil, or boards. When they dig, they start from the ends of the bed and work quickly to prevent chilling of the remaining vegetables.

Horseradish

The thick, tough roots of horseradish do most of their growing in late fall and remain in good condition until spring. Eating quality declines when new growth begins, so dig the roots in time to make horseradish sauce for your Easter eggs or as early in spring as you can spade the ground. To enlarge your patch, plant 1- to 2-inch chunks cut from the very top of the root. Set them 2 or 3 inches deep in the soil. Space chunks 8 to 10 inches apart in a bed. Planting can be done any time the soil can be dug.

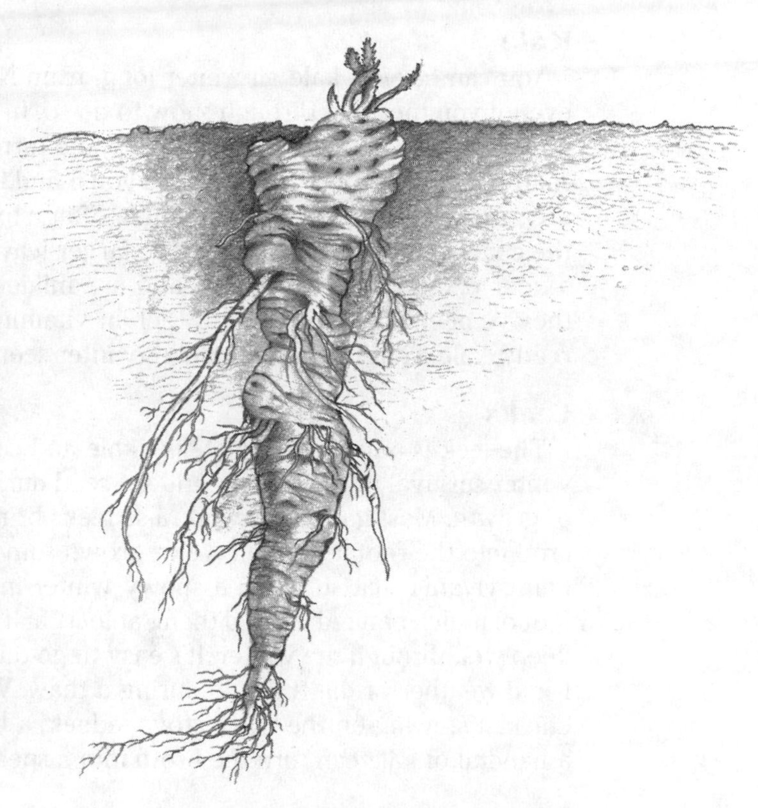

Zip up winter meals with a grating of fresh horseradish. The thick roots are tastiest when top growth is still asleep. Mulch your planting deeply with a foot of straw or loosely piled leaves, and uncover to dig a bit of root.

Jerusalem Artichokes

These crisp, nut-flavored tubers have thin skins and sometimes spoil in the refrigerator or the root cellar, but they keep well in the ground. Their flavor is best after frost. I most appreciate perennial Jerusalem artichokes in March, when even home-canned food has become dreary. Be sure to dig the tubers before they sprout new top growth, usually sometime in April. After sprouting, they'll be tough.

Kale

You can harvest kale all winter long, from November until April, even if you must dig through snow to do so. In the bitter cold of the northern states, the leaves may droop and turn dark, but when you snap them off and take them inside you'll find that they're alive and green and ready to enrich your dinner after a brief steaming. Cut out the coarse midrib when serving the larger leaves. Young leaves are tender enough to serve whole and are milder than cabbage once they've been touched by frost. Rich in vitamins A and C, and ever ready, kale from the garden makes winter seem less harsh.

Leeks

The leek is a hardy biennial, like kale and carrots. All three have winter survival in their genes and set seed during their second year of growth. Most gardeners who raise leeks bring at least part of the crop into the root cellar, but we've grown some unmulched leeks in Pennsylvania that survived a snowy winter in good shape. With a foot of mulch banked around them, at least half a row of leeks should keep well through the winter. It's easy to go out and chop one off in frigid weather or dig the bulb during a thaw. When there's a pot of chicken stewing on the wood stove, a leek, a bunch of carrots, and a handful of kale can turn the broth into a special soup.

Parsnips

The parsnip's long germination period and low seed vitality can be forgiven when you consider that it not only remains edible but actually improves in flavor as freezing weather turns more and more of its starch to sugar. March-dug parsnips are the sweetest of all, a treat that the new countryman soon learns to anticipate. I bring parsnips into the root cellar in December, but I always leave some well-mulched roots in the row for spring digging. Dig the wintered-over crop before new spring growth begins. A few, small sprouted leaves emerging from the crown are the signal to get the roots out of the ground and into the root cellar or freezer within a week or two.

Salsify

Salsify fares better in the ground than in the root cellar because its long, thin roots shrivel after a few days in the air. Like the parsnip, its flavor is improved by frost. Salsify is usually served sliced in soups, baked in butter, or shredded and mixed with egg and flour and then fried to form mock seafood patties. As with parsnips and leeks, salsify is planted in spring for a fall and winter crop.

Spinach

Spring-planted spinach fades quickly, but fall-planted spinach can produce a double crop. The secret is in the cooler nights and shorter days—and in the choice of cultivar. 'Winter Bloomsdale' and 'Cold Resistant Savoy' are bred for winter hardiness. Last year, I planted spinach in early September and the plants produced enough greens for some good salads before hard frost. I tossed a few bags of leaves over the row in early December, and snow soon covered them with a few more inches of insulation. In January, I picked enough leaves from the snowed-in plants for another salad. In mid-March, eight weeks before the spring planting was ready, the wintered-over spinach began to produce tender, new green leaves.

CHAPTER FORTY-THREE

Brighten Your Home with Holiday Plants

Indoor plants link us with the world of growing things while winter weather keeps us indoors. Their green color refreshes us—and they even help improve the air quality in our heated houses. Some houseplants have such brightly colored flowers and fruit that they can serve as Christmas decorations.

Your local garden center is sure to be well stocked with holiday plants for indoors. Or you can start your own from seed or cuttings from a friend's plant. Many houseplants live a long life and need only a bit of care to come into glory for the holiday season.

The Indoor Life

Bright flowers and fruit are always welcome indoors, and they seem to add a special touch to the holiday season. But life indoors is an unnatural environment. The dry, heated air can be difficult for houseplants. In general, houseplants prefer a cool, bright location, away from direct sources of heat.

Festive Favorites

You may already have some of these holiday favorites. But if your friends don't, remember that a living plant makes a welcome gift, especially if it's one you started yourself from seed or a cutting. Here are a few tips to help you keep your plants at their best over the holidays and to start new plants for yourself or for gifts.

Araucaria heterophylla (Norfolk Island Pine)

This plant makes a perfect living Christmas tree for anyone whose space is limited. Norfolk Island pines—whether tiny tabletop trees or 3-foot specimens in tubs on the floor—lend themselves to delicate decorations like tiny, shiny balls or small-scale origami figures in bright colors.

To keep these indoor trees in good shape all year long, keep them out of direct sun. Coolish temperatures between 50° and 70°F are best. Once a week, or whenever the soil feels dry ½ inch down, let the plant stand in a bucket of water until the surface of the soil feels moist. Keep the watering can away; these plants are especially sensitive to overwatering.

Capsicum annuum (Ornamental Pepper)

To retain the bright red, deep black, or purple fruit on these delightful plants, keep them in a sunny but cool place, 55° to 60°F. If blossoms drop off without forming fruit, the air is probably too dry. Try spraying the flowers daily with a fine mister. Or fill a shallow tray with 1 inch of gravel and fill with water. Set the pots on the moistened

Christmas cactus (*Schlumbergera bridgesii*) brings welcome flowers to the winter windowsill. Treat it like a poinsettia, controlling the amount of light in autumn, for another season of bloom next Christmas. New plants are easy to start from cuttings and make welcome gifts.

gravel but make sure they do not stand in water. Drafts, too, may cause fruit and flowers to drop. Water as often as necessary to keep soil evenly moist but never soggy. You can start plants from seed in mid- or late summer. They make cheerful gifts.

Hedera helix (English Ivy)

Immortalized in the Christmas carol "The Holly and the Ivy," these plants became holiday favorites. Ivies come in a wide variety of leaf shapes, colors, and sizes, and most houseplant growers have at least one cultivar. For a festive effect, try grouping several ivy plants in a basket or making a centerpiece of ivy surrounded by fruit. Set an especially graceful plant on a mantelpiece, flanked with candles.

Ivies, in general, like bright, indirect light rather than strong, direct sun. Let the soil dry before watering but then give the pot a good soaking. Under hot, dry indoor conditions, spider mites sometimes attack the plants. To prevent this trouble, wash or spray the leaves with water about once a week. If spider mites appear, spray with a mix of ½ teaspoon liquid household soap per quart of water and keep the plants on the cool side: 50° to 60°F is ideal.

Ivies are easy to start from cuttings. Root snippings from your most vigorous plants in water to produce tiny "table favor" ivy plants that are fun to tuck in with food gifts.

Kalanchoe blossfeldiana (Kalanchoe)

To bring one of these pretty, red-flowered succulents into bloom, give it long nights by draping it with a black cloth or tucking it into a dark closet for 12 hours each night. Start this about three months before you want the plant to bloom. These plants need bright light in a draft-free but not stuffy place. Let the soil dry out between waterings. To make gift plants, take cuttings with a razor blade or sharp, clean knife, from a stem that has no flowers. Root cuttings in water under fluorescent lights.

Manettia spp. (Firecracker Vines)

These climbing plants with their bright tubular flowers do well on a sunny windowsill. The red flowers, tipped with yellow, make it easy to see where the plant gets its common name. Keep plants potbound and give them a spot with good air circulation. Water only when soil is thoroughly dry. Avoid chemical sprays of any kind; the leaves are usually sensitive to foreign substances.

Schlumbergera bridgesii (Christmas Cactus)

Although these jungle natives do well in full sun during the summer, they are short-day plants that need controlled light to bloom for the holidays. To bring them into flower by Christmas, start in October or early November to give them 12 hours of uninterrupted darkness each day for six to eight weeks. Cover the plants with a black cloth or put them in a dark closet. Cool night temperatures and scant watering help to induce flowering, too.

When the plants are in bloom, keep the soil evenly moist but never soggy. They need less water than most houseplants but more than other cacti. Take cuttings from new growth and root in moist sand or vermiculite to start gift plants.

Sinningia speciosa (Gloxinia)

Spectacular glowing red, rich purple, or velvety white blossoms appear on gloxinias at Christmas time. The tubular flowers bloom in profusion over a long period of time if the plant receives the care it needs. Provide 18 hours of light daily (fluorescent tubes are a must) and a temperature no lower than 62 °F. Give your plant a twice-weekly application of fertilizer, such as fish emulsion. Be sure to prepare the concentrations as suggested on the label. Feed the plant only when it's growing and blooming. Keep the soil moist; a wilted plant has a hard time recovering. In heated homes, gloxinias appreciate the additional humidity provided by a tray of pebbles in shallow water, set under the pot. Gloxinias lose their leaves and go dormant after flowering, but you can bring them back to life after their rest. Keep dormant plants cool and dry for five to six months until signs of new growth appear in the spring. Then repot and return to watering.

GROW YOUR OWN GLOXINIAS

If you find the richly colored flowers and velvety leaves of gloxinia appealing, you might like to try growing your own from seed or rhizomes. You can buy the tubers of gloxinia (*Sinningia speciosa*) at some garden centers and from mail-order catalogs. Plant the tubers ½ inch deep in 6-inch pots and count on six months until bloom. While you're waiting, keep the soil evenly moist but not soggy. As soon as sprouts appear, place the pots in bright filtered light. To grow gloxinias from seed, press the fine seeds lightly into your potting mix and do not cover with soil (light helps them to germinate). The seedlings sprout in two to three weeks at 70° to 75°F. Feed them dilute liquid organic fertilizer solution three times a week. (Make the mixture twice as weak as suggested on the label. For example, if your fertilizer recommends 2 tablespoons fertilizer per gallon of water, only put in 1 tablespoon.) The plants will form tubers and should bloom within the year.

CHAPTER FORTY-FOUR

Wassail Your Fruit Trees

Ages and ages ago, even before the early days of recorded time, people believed that they had to take action of some kind to keep the seasons turning. The dark, short days before and after the winter solstice (and, later, the 12 days after Christmas) became a time of great significance. People gathered to pray for the return of the sun and for good harvests and kind fortune in the days ahead. Rich traditions of feasting, merrymaking, visiting, and hanging evergreens in homes have grown up around this "low" time of year, making it instead a high point in the dark, cold season.

Make Merry with a Wassail Party

One of those traditions, wassailing the apple trees, combines merrymaking, pranks, feasting, and rituals to ensure good crops. Practices and dates vary according to local custom. In some European towns, wassailing of the apple trees took place on Christmas Eve. In parts of England and Wales, processions of villagers visited each orchard on Christmas morning. Elsewhere in England and on the continent, Twelfth Night, the 12th evening after Christmas, was the traditional time. January 15 and January 17 were customary in other areas. So you can see that custom (from somewhere) will be on your side if you want to stage a wassailing party on any date between December 21 and January 17.

Because wassailing rituals varied, too, you can include in your plans elements from any of the wassailing traditions that would suit your situation—an evening of family fun or a party for friends or a get-together to cement neighborly ties.

Cider for Guests and Tree

Often the celebrating company would carry a large bowl of cider to the orchard. Gathering around the most fruitful tree in the orchard, they would each drink a cider toast to the tree. Then they either sprinkled the remaining cider on the tree or dipped the tree's branches in it. Sometimes a pail of cider with roasted apples added was placed in the orchard. Celebrants would dip a cup in the brew, drink some, and toss the remaining cider and apple fragments on tree after tree until each tree had been recognized, addressed by name, and admonished to bear well.

WHAT IS WASSAIL?

In Old England, wassail was a salutation that was customarily spoken when giving a guest a cup of wine. It meant "Be whole" or "Have health." By gradual association, wassail took on the meaning of a beverage used for toasts. Later, its meaning expanded to include the revelry and rituals surrounding traditional well-wishing, whether at parties for people or cheering sessions for fruit trees.

Gather friends and family and wassail your favorite apple tree with a toast of hot spiced cider on Christmas Eve. It's a nice tradition and just may reward you with a good harvest next year.

Often the merrymakers would thump on the trees with sticks, or shake them. They would sometimes blow horns and almost always sing one of several ancient tree-blessing songs. In parts of England, where a small bird was thought to represent the spirit of the tree, people would leave small pieces of bread or cake, dunked in cider, in the fork of the tree "for the robins." In southern Germany, people would shake the crumbs from their Christmas tablecloths around the roots of their fruit trees.

In some places, the men would encircle and toast the trees while the women locked the doors of the house. Inside, the women would put a piece of food on a spit to roast over the fire. The men then had to guess the identity of that mystery morsel (squirrel? woodchuck? beet? onion?) before the women would agree to unlock the doors and invite them in to the merry meal that almost always followed the wassailing ritual. One custom you probably won't be tempted to adopt was the ancient one of going nude to the orchard on Christmas Eve and wrapping ropes made of straw around the fruit trees (again, to encourage fruitfulness).

Apple trees were the usual objects of the merry toast, probably because they were more numerous and more important to the local economy (cider was a staple beverage in the old days). But other fruit trees were included in the celebration. So, even if you have just a single pear tree, or a plum or a cherry, you can have fun and maintain tradition by wassailing your fruit-bearer. And, who knows—we no longer apologize for talking to our houseplants—perhaps all that attention showered on your trees will have some effect!

TRADITIONAL WASSAILING RHYMES

Here are some old-time rhymes for you and your merry company to recite as you toast your trees. You may be inspired to make up your own; it's easy to get the idea from these.

Wassail the trees, that they
may bear
You many a plum and
many a pear;
For more or less of fruit they
bring
As you do give them
wassailing.

Here's to thee, old apple tree,
Whence thou mayst bud,
and then mayst blow
(bloom)!
And whence thou mayst
bear apples enow!
Hats full! Caps full!
Bushel, bushel sacks full!
And my pockets full too,
huzza!

Apples and pears and right
good corn,
Come in plenty to everyone;
Eat and drink good cakes
and ale;
Give earth to drink and she
will not fail.

Stand fast, root, bear well,
top;
God send us a yowling crop,
Every twig, apple big;
Every bow apples enow;
Hats full, caps full, bushel
sacks full,
And my pockets full too!
Hooray!

Apple tree, apple tree,
I wassail thee
to blow and to bear
Hat-fulls, cap-fulls, three
bushel bagfulls,
And my pockets full too,
hip, hip, hurrah!

Health to thee,
Good apple tree!
Well to bear pocketfulls, hat
fulls,
Peck-fulls, bushel-bag-fulls.

CHAPTER FORTY-FIVE

Plan a Garden for Ethnic Cuisine

My three-year-old grandson told me that his family grows eggplants for making ratatouille. When I was his age I didn't even know what an eggplant was, much less ratatouille! But like many other children today, he's also familiar with tacos, guacamole, pizza, and pasta. When even young kids know there is more to supper than hamburgers and chicken noodle soup, we who influence the menu by what we plant in the garden may have more freedom than we realized.

Broaden Your Garden Horizons

You needn't be a starched-apron gourmet chef to appreciate the ways in which our food choices are enlivened by other cultures. Any adventurous cook with a garden enjoys a wide array of options. You can raise vegetables that are hard to find in stores and, because your produce is homegrown, it's superior in quality and freshness.

As you page through the crop of catalogs, keep in mind your favorite ethnic dishes and plan to include some of their makings in next year's garden. Here are some specialty foods you can grow that will spice things up in your kitchen and make your ethnic cuisines even more authentic.

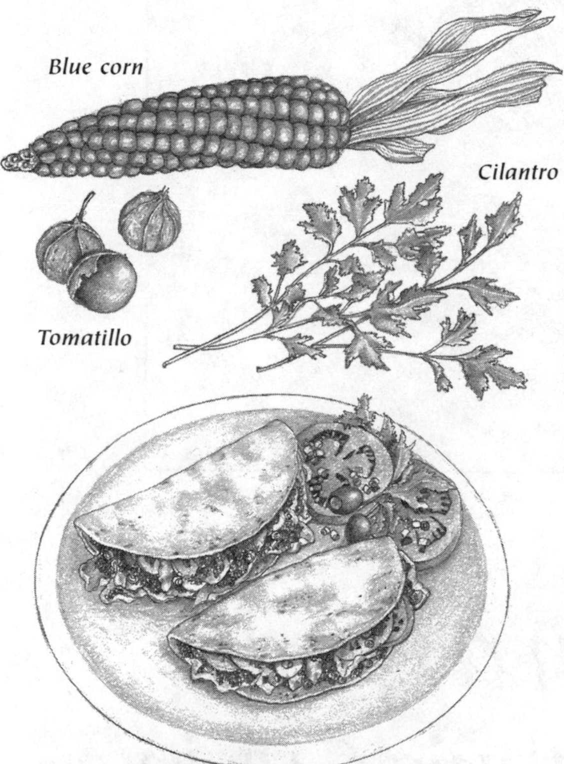

If you're a fan of Mexican cooking (and who isn't?), grow your own vegetables and seasonings for tacos, enchiladas, and other treats. Blue corn is an old variety favored for tortilla making, and pungent cilantro is a must in salsas. Tomatillos add fine flavor to sauces.

Mexican

Mexican dishes are a staple in many home kitchens. Children seem to take quickly to this style of cooking and eating. The following vegetables and herbs add authentic flavor to your south-of-the-border meals.

Amaranths (*Amaranthus* spp.)

This ancient Mexican food is rich in symbolism from that country's centuries of civilization. Amaranth seeds were used in Aztec rituals, and amaranth candy is still sold at festival time in Mexico. Try vegetable amaranth steamed or cooked in soup, or grow high-protein grain amaranth to add to bread, to pop, or to make sprouts.

Amaranth likes warm weather, so plant the seeds ¼ inch deep in the garden after the last frost. Space rows 2 feet apart for grain amaranth and 1½ to 2 feet for vegetable amaranth. Thin grain amaranth to 10 inches apart and the vegetable type to 6 to 8 inches apart. Don't discard thinnings; you can use them in soups or salads. The leaves taste best before flowering. Grain amaranth grows from 4 to 8 feet tall, depending on the species. Most species grown for greens are about 3 feet tall. For greens, a 2- to 3-foot-wide, 4- to 6-foot-long bed provides plenty for two to three people.

Blue Corn (*Zea mays*)

Blue corn only seems strange until you taste it. Then its full, mellow flavor wins you over. Although some people eat blue corn fresh when it's young, it is grown mostly for grinding into flour for tortillas.

Plant seeds at about the time of the last spring frost, spacing them 1 inch apart in 2½- to 3-foot-wide rows. Thin plants to 12 to 14 inches apart. For grinding, harvest ears when the kernels are dry and hard.

Chili Peppers (*Capsicum annuum* var. *annuum*, Longum group)

Chilies put the spark in Mexican sauces (Chinese sauces, too). For chili rellenos, try 'Anaheim', 'Colorado', 'Numex Big Jim', and 'Ancho' cultivars. 'Santa Fe Grande', hot 'Jalapeño', and hot, hot 'Serrano' go a long way in sauces. 'Cherry', 'Gold Spike', and 'Caloro' are often pickled. Small chilies strung in ristras to dry add homey warmth to a kitchen. Hot peppers may be picked any time they're large enough to use. Most are even hotter after they turn from green to red. Grow chilies as you would grow bell or other peppers. See the instructions listed for peppers on page 266.

Cilantro (*Coriandrum sativum*)

Cilantro, the leaves of coriander, is just what you need for a true Mexican salsa. It is used in many other ethnic cuisines, too, including oriental and East Indian dishes. I consider it an acquired taste, but once you've enjoyed a few memorable Mexican meals, especially south of the border or in the American Southwest, the good memories cilantro recalls will add another dimension to your cooking.

For a continuous supply of green leaves, sow seeds every two to three weeks, starting in spring around the time of the last frost. Thin the plants to stand 2 to 3 inches apart. You can start cutting the leafy tops when the plants are about 6 inches tall. They go to seed in about 60 days. A 3-foot stretch of a row should be plenty for family meals.

Epazote (*Chenopodium ambrosioides*)

Epazote is a 3- to 4-foot-tall herb with a distinctive, authoritative flavor. It is often cooked with black beans and is sometimes brewed for tea. Plant epazote seeds at the end of May. Once the days grow longer, epazote sprouts promptly and grows quickly. Sow the small seeds sparsely and thin them to a final spacing of about 2 feet apart. Use epazote sparingly at first until you decide how much of it you like in soups and sauces. Use epazote only as a garnish, as large quantities may cause harmful side effects.

Tomatillo (*Physalis ixocarpa*)

Tomatillo is another authentic salsa ingredient. This green, husk-enclosed berry is related to the smaller, sweeter ground cherry that grows wild in many farm fields. Treat tomatillos as you would tomatoes, starting seeds in flats indoors about six to eight weeks before the average last spring frost. Transplant seedlings to pots, and start hardening them off two weeks before the last spring frost. Plant them outside after frost. Space plants about 20 inches apart. The grape- to walnut-size fruit, removed from the husk, is cooked in sauces or served raw in salads.

Chinese

Chinese cooking is popular and healthy, too. Fresh vegetables and leafy greens are a big part of most dishes. Try these selections in your home garden.

Asparagus Beans (*Vigna unguiculata* subsp. *sesquipedalis*)

Asparagus beans, or dow gauk, are long, slim beans that grow on vigorous vines and flourish in hot weather. They're often served chopped and steamed or stir-fried. Plant seeds ½ to 1 inch deep about two weeks after your last frost date. Sow in June for an August harvest. Support the vines with strong poles or a trellis, and pick the beans when they're about 16 inches long.

Chinese Cabbage (*Brassica rapa*)

Chinese cabbage comes in two forms: bok choy (also called pak-choi), a loose cluster of leaves; and pe-tsai (also called wong bok or Chinese celery cabbage), a solid, cylindrical head. Both types are wonderful for stir-fries, egg rolls, and other delicious concoctions.

Most cultivars of Chinese cabbage grow best as fall crops from seed started in July because they tend to go to seed in warm weather. Check catalogs for special slow-bolting cultivars to try for spring. Plant in rich soil and thin the cabbages to stand 12 to 15 inches apart. Transplanting may make these plants go to seed, so transplant carefully and only if necessary. The plants are hardy and their flavor is especially good after frost.

Engtsai (*Ipomoea aquatica*)

Green engtsai, a relative of the morning glory, is also called water spinach or kankon. Its hollow stems and pointed leaves add flavor to soups, salads, and stir-fries all summer from seed planted in early spring. Plant the seeds to a depth three times their thickness; space them 1 foot apart. Engtsai requires plenty of moisture and thrives in wet soil.

Mustards (*Brassica* spp.)

Mustards add zest to Chinese cooking, and many are available, in a wide range of pungency. Young 6-inch leaves are tasty in stir-fries and salads. All of these leafy plants are hardy and at their best in cool weather. Plant seeds ¼ inch deep in early spring and again in July and August. Thin the plants to stand about 8 inches apart.

Snow Peas (*Pisum sativum* var. *macrocarpon*)

These slender, crisp pods make oriental dishes memorable and are easy to grow. Plant seeds as soon as the ground can be worked. Place well-branched sticks or netting along rows for support. Space the seeds 1 to 2 inches apart and do not thin. Pick the peas while the pods are still flat, before the peas start to swell. Taller varieties like 'Oregon Sugar Pod II' and 'Mammoth Melting Sugar' have better flavor than the dwarf cultivars.

Italian

Italian cooking is a long-time favorite all across America. Pastas and sauces made from fresh-picked vegetables and seasonings are tastier than anything that comes in a box or a can. Consider these specialties for your Italian recipes.

Basils (*Ocimum* spp.)

Any basil marries well with most Italian dishes, especially those containing tomatoes. For an extra measure of authenticity, try some special Italian basils like *Ocimum basilicum* 'Napoletano', with large, crinkled leaves and excellent flavor; *O. basilicum* 'Genova Profumatissima' or perfume basil, a vigorous plant with intense flavor; or *O. basilicum* 'Fino Verde Compatto', a compact, 1-foot-tall plant with small leaves. Start basil indoors in pots, or plant outside after the last frost. Basil is frost-tender and thrives in warm soil. Space plants 9 to 12 inches apart; 6 to 8 inches for 'Fino Verde Compatto'.

Broccoli Raab (*Brassica rapa*, Ruvo group)

Broccoli raab is a nonheading broccoli grown for its tender top shoots and pungent flower buds, which are cooked before serving. Plant seeds in early spring and again in summer for a fall crop. Space plants 10 to 12 inches apart.

Broccoli 'Romanesco' (*Brassica oleracea*, Botrytis group)

Broccoli 'Romanesco' is an old, mild Italian selection with a sculptured, light-green, pointed head that looks like the top of a seashell. The slow-growing crop does best when planted in June for a fall harvest. Space plants 20 to 24 inches apart, water regularly, and fertilize monthly.

GARDENS AROUND THE WORLD

Mexican, Chinese, and Italian cuisines are among the most popular ethnic cooking, but your choices as a gardener-cook can include other regional specialties, too. Grow grape leaves, eggplants, and spinach for Greek specialty foods; cucumbers to combine with yogurt to make East Indian raita; and native American grinding corns for pones, crackers, corn bread, and mush. And, of course, you'll want to grow those garden basics—tomatoes, onions, and potatoes—that appear in many foods throughout the world.

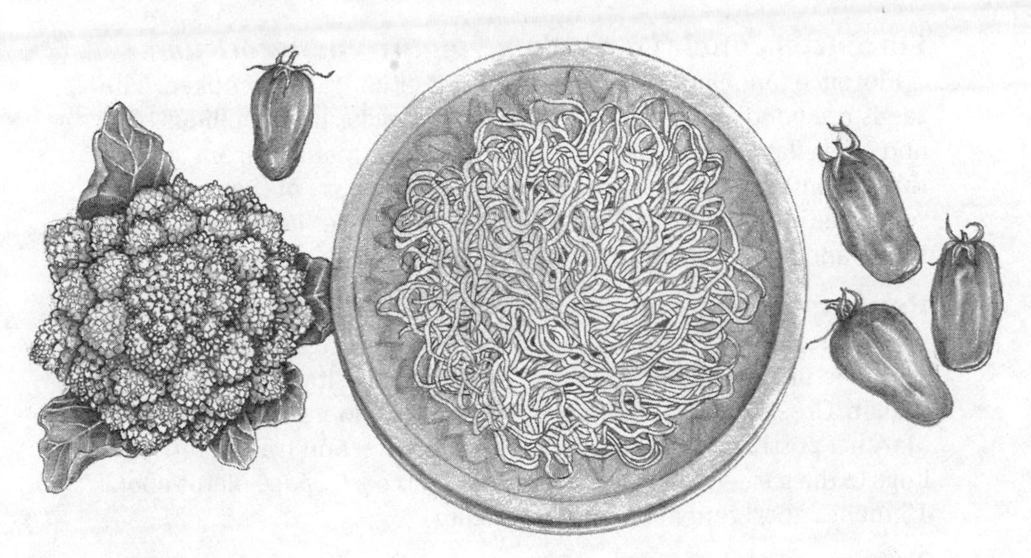

Broaden your Italian-foods repertoire with special vegetables, like cone-shaped broccoli 'Romanesco' and meaty plum tomatoes, which make a tasty topping for pasta primavera or a good addition to hearty sauces.

Chicory (*Cichorium intybus*)

Chicories of all kinds give piquancy to Italian meals. Some, like 'Catalogna', are served cooked; others, especially the radicchios, are eaten in salads.

Radicchios are planted in July for a fall harvest, and some varieties may be left in the row under mulch all winter. Space plants about 8 inches apart. The leaves are green in summer. To obtain the red-leaved, loose-headed radicchio of trendy restaurant fame, cut the plants back in fall. The new growth produced in those cold, short days will be red.

Escarole (*Cichorium endiva*)

Escarole has rounded green leaves growing in an open rosette. In its fringe-leaved form, it is called endive. Escarole has a slightly bitter, though agreeable, taste that adds zest to salads. Plant it in July for a fall harvest; the flavor is best in cool weather. For a milder taste, blanch the plants in September by gently tying up the outer leaves with a soft cloth. To prevent rotting, untie the leaves when it rains and let the leaves dry thoroughly before retying. Escarole is hardy and, if covered, lasts until January in the row. Serve it cooked or in salads.

Florence Fennel (*Foeniculum vulgare* var. *azoricum*)

Florence fennel, or finocchio, is served either raw or cooked. The seeds are good to eat, too. This celery look-alike has a bulbous base and anise-flavored stalks, leaves, and seeds. It matures from seed in three months. For a more tender bulb, hill the base of the plant with soil when the bulbs become about 2 inches wide. Leave the upper stems and leaves uncovered. Space plants 10 to 12 inches apart.

Peppers (*Capsicum* spp.)

Peppers, too, are a vital part of Italian menu magic. Special Italian varieties include 'Italia', 'Italian Pepperoncini', 'Italian Sweet', and 'Italian Green Frying'. Start pepper plants indoors in February or March if possible, although April is not too late, and transplant seedlings to the garden after the danger of frost is past. Space plants about 15 inches apart and avoid overfertilizing.

Tomatoes (*Lycopersicon esculentum*)

It's hard to imagine pasta without tomatoes. Any tomato is good with Italian sauces and salads, but some special kinds include 'Principe Borghese', a small, plum-shaped fruit grown for drying; 'San Marzano', a meaty paste type; and 'Super Italian Paste', a large, long, pointed paste tomato. As with all tomatoes, start plants indoors in April and transplant them outdoors after the danger of frost is past.

CHAPTER FORTY-SIX

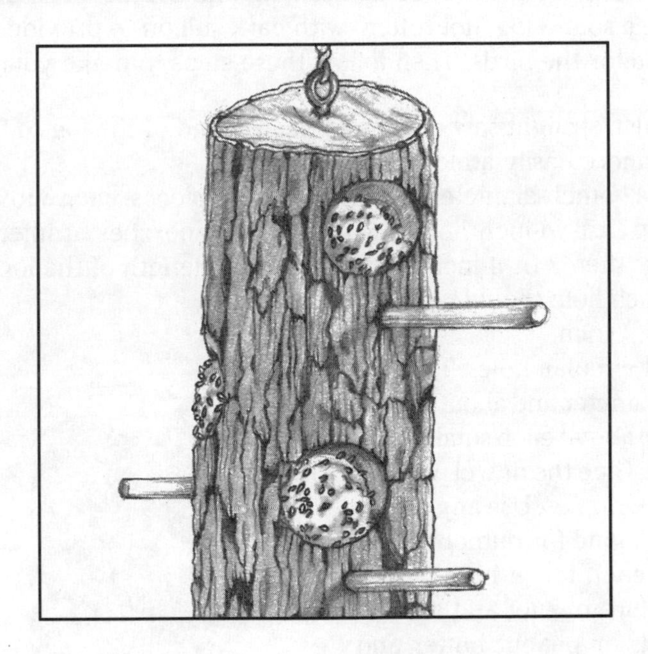

Put Up a Yule Log for the Birds

Just as many pet owners enjoy giving their animal friends a tasty holiday treat, bird lovers like to provide something special for their feathered visitors, too. This simple bird feeder can be a family project, with children choosing the log and helping with the gluing, filling, and hanging, and adults doing the drilling. You might want to make some for gifts, especially for housebound loved ones who would enjoy watching the birds from a window. If your loved one cannot get outside to care for the yule log, bring it inside for refills and work together to mix the materials and fill the feeder.

A Five-Step Project

Find a small log about 18 inches long and 2½ inches in diameter. Choose a sound log, not rotten, with bark still on to provide a better foothold for the birds. Then follow these steps to make your feeder.

1. Make a straight saw cut across the top end of the log so that you can more easily attach a hanger to it.
2. Cut a ¼-inch-diameter dowel rod into six pieces, each 3 to 4 inches long. Drill ¼-inch holes for these dowel perches at intervals no more then 3 or 4 inches apart along the length of the log. Depth of each hole should be about ⅜ to ½ inch.
3. Drill circular holes 2 inches in diameter and about ½ inch deep above each small perch hole. Glue the dowel perches in their holes. Use any waterproof glue for outdoor use.
4. Fill each large hole with a mixture of suet and smaller seeds or peanut butter and cornmeal. (Don't use peanut butter alone; it tends to gum up the birds' mouth parts. Use as much cornmeal as you can without making the mixture crumbly.)
5. Insert a sturdy screw eye into the top end of the log and thread a length of plastic-coated wire or twine through the eye to make a hanger. You could insert a hook into the log instead of a screw eye and use it for a hanger. Suspend the feeder from a branch or roof edge. Fasten the feeder to a roof overhang by inserting a hook into the overhang and hanging

A log full of holes makes the perfect feeder for spreadable bird treats like peanut butter and cornmeal or suet and seeds. These high-fat foods provide plenty of fuel during cold weather. Add dowels for handy perches, and hang the feeder from a branch where you can watch the action.

the feeder from the hook. If you hang the feeder from a branch, loop the plastic-coated wire or twine around the branch.

Refill your feeder as necessary. Cold weather will preserve the mixture for several months. If the birds haven't finished off the mixture by the time warmer weather arrives, replace the food with a fresh mixture.

To make the yule log more festive looking, especially if you're making it for a gift, you can attach sprigs of greenery, berries, and even a waterproof ribbon bow at the top. Plain and simple or fancied up, the yule log will soon attract neighborhood birds to the feast.

CHAPTER FORTY-SEVEN

Read an Almanac

Who isn't curious about the future, edgy about the coming winter, touched by tales of shipwrecks, dramatic rescues, and brave pets, and thoughtful about what happened on a given day 100 years ago? Almanacs are for everybody. I love them—the lists, the tables, the 1898 servant's daily work plan, the history of badminton, the American Indian prayer, the list of unsung heroines, and the discussion of outdated measuring terms (you'll learn, for example, how many barleycorns make up an inch).

A Second Opinion for the Gardener

Apart from the rich mix of miscellany, which may be predictable in scope but contains new details each year, almanacs can be useful tools for the gardener. Although their weather forecasts might not always hit the mark, at least they offer you an opinion when you are planning your garden and trying to guess whether spring will be early, cold, dry, or all three.

Every almanac has its moon-sign table, which guides those who plan their plantings by the phases of the moon. You'll also find nuggets of gardening advice scattered among the tables and predictions. Perhaps there'll be a cabbage trivia quiz, advice on how to save plants in a drought, or directions for cooking with flowers.

American Almanacs

Almanacs live a long life. Some of those published in the United States have been around for nearly 200 years. Even in these hi-tech days, the friendly little books keep a following of loyal readers.

ROOTED IN THE PAST

Early almanacs were written frequently by astronomers or astrologers, sometimes by scholars, and often by physicians who prescribed herbal treatments for common maladies. A surviving manuscript from Egypt, printed during the time of King Rameses II (1290–1223 B.C.), lists religious festivals, designates lucky and unlucky days in black and red, and predicts the fortunes of children according to their birthdays. Much later, Christopher Columbus and other navigators used almanacs to plan their voyages. In the days before drugstores, calendars, National Weather Service forecasts, and gardening magazines, people needed all the help they could get to keep track of holidays, tides, and the changing positions of the sun and moon, and to treat annoying and often frightening illnesses. Almanacs provided a wealth of information and moral support. Peering ahead at the weather helped bolster people for the trials of uninsulated winters and satisfied their natural human curiosity about the future.

If all you want from an almanac is advice for planting your garden according to the phases of the moon, Ed Hume's slim annual *Moon Sign Planting Dates* offers the essentials in two dozen pages. It includes monthly lists of the most propitious days to perform a wide range of garden chores.

But if you enjoy a delightful mix of amusing and informative stories along with weather forecasts and gardening timetables, try one of these old-timers. You can find them for sale in garden centers, bookshops, and hardware stores.

The Old Farmer's Almanac

The oldest American almanac is *The Old Farmer's Almanac,* founded by Robert Thomas in 1792. In addition to the traditional weather forecasts and moon, time-, and tide tables, it offers such things as best fishing days for the year, killing-frost times for 62 cities, mathematical puzzles, and articles on catfish, home remedies for hiccups, and the evolution of the barn. The almanac contains a fair number of ads, but as commentator Charles Kuralt has said, "Publications come and go with their ads for designer gowns. *The Old Farmer's Almanac* offers remedies for aching feet. That's why it's lasted for 190 years."

"Our readers don't like us to alter anything," says Jud Hale, editor of the almanac. "When we changed printers and the new moon signs were very slightly different—a barely noticeable difference—a reader wrote to complain!"

The detailed, month-by-month weather forecasts for each region of the country are prepared without reference to the thickness of squirrels' tails or the color of woolly bear caterpillars' fur. Surprised? So was I. *The Old Farmer's Almanac,* it turns out, employs meteorologist Dr. Richard Head to calculate weather data. The almanac spends about $100,000 a year on its weather forecasts. "This is not a gag," editor Tim Clark says. "We are serious about it. But we try not to be solemn about it.

"Back in the 1700s," Clark continues, "almanac founder Robert Thomas made general weather forecasts for New England, based on his own secret formula, which is allegedly kept in a black box in our offices. Dr. Head's forecasts are often checked against this formula."

"We claim 80 percent accuracy," states Clark, "perhaps because it

Many gardeners plant their garden according to the phases of the moon, one reason to add an almanac to your stack of gardening helps. But moon signs are just the beginning—almanacs are chock-full of useful advice, oddball tidbits, and plenty of good reading to take you through the long winter nights.

is traditional for almanacs to do so. But it's really impossible to keep any statistically significant records of our forecasts' success, because we cover such a large area. We've had some memorable flops. Still, people are remarkably nice to us. Although they often complain when the local weather service predictions are wrong, they let us know when we're right!"

American Farm and Home Almanac

The next-oldest almanac is the *American Farm and Home Almanac* (and its sister publication, *Farmer's Almanac*). Good reading-aloud fare in past issues of *Farm and Home* included "The Tale of the 12-Toed Wizard of the Green Mountains," minutes from the meetings of a nineteenth-century fire company, recipes, weather lore ("Six weeks after you hear crickets chirp in the summer, look for frost"), and an essay on driftwood fireworks.

In addition to the monthly table of days, illustrated with appealing old woodcuts, this almanac carries general weather predictions for the year. "Our weather forecast is based on an old formula from 1881," says editor Ray Geiger, who adds the title "Philom" (from *philomath,* "lover of learning") to his byline. "A retired astronomer does our planetary calculations, and we provide weather predictions for several other almanacs, as well."

Associate editor Pete Geiger likes to tell about the letter he received from an Illinois man requesting a copy of the almanac to help him prepare the $25,000 snow-removal budget for his town. "We get questions about which weekend is a good time for a garage sale," Geiger adds, "and, of course, we're the bride's best friend."

Baer's Almanac

Baer's Almanac, founded in 1825 by Pennsylvanian John Baer, was published in German as well as English from 1830 to 1917. "In Pennsylvania German homes, it was customary to have a Bible and an almanac," says editor Gerald Lestz. "As people moved west, they took the almanac with them, and now it is sold all over the United States and Canada."

Many residents of Pennsylvania Dutch country take moon signs seriously. For example, "the first day of Virgo," says Lestz, "is the best day to plant flowers. The sign of Uranus on the calendar is considered an indication of a change in the weather, usually for the colder. And the sign for the moon, when it appears in conjunction with a square sign we call the Icebox, means a snowstorm is coming."

Baer's subscribes to the *American Farm and Home Almanac*'s weather service. "Our weather forecasts are always right for some part of the world," Lestz stoutly maintains. "Sometimes our almanac is right and the weather is wrong."

Baer's Almanac also carries seed-planting tables, compiled by both the U.S. Department of Agriculture and Amos Applesschnitz, and a table for foretelling the weather. Past issues contained brief essays on "More Than You May Care to Know about Money," butterflies, the blizzards of '88, and regional food specialties. "We love trivia," says Lestz, "and we put in as much as we can get away with."

Blum's Farmer's and Planter's Almanac

Founded in 1828, *Blum's Farmer's and Planter's Almanac* contains more ads and somewhat less lore than *Baer's. Blum's* includes the standard information—weather tables, planting advice, fisherman's calendar, and a moon-sign gardening guide. A typical issue may also carry information on how to make an inexpensive rain gauge, a list of armchair exercises, a list of medical specialists and what they treat, and "The Rule of 72," which tells you how to determine when your

KEEP YOUR OWN GARDEN DIARY

Accumulated wisdom is what almanacs are all about. You can keep your own collection of helpful gardening information, tailored to your own climate and circumstances. Just jot down notes on a calendar or in a notebook. Here are some things to keep track of in your garden diary.

Planting dates. These are especially helpful if you're trying to stretch the season by planting as early as possible. They also make good reminders for summer plantings.

Cultivars. Write down the exact names of the vegetables and flowers that you plant and then, later, note those you want to plant again.

Yields. It's so easy to forget how many bushels of potatoes you lugged in last year. Keeping track of yields will help you plant just what you need—and give you a good reason to do some end-of-the-season gloating, too!

Costs. If you're raising food to ease the budget, or if you just enjoy the satisfaction of getting a good bargain, then it's nice to have these figures down in black and white to show how much you're saving.

Soil improvements. When we write soil improvements down on our large feed-store calendar, we can see at a glance what part of the garden we most recently enriched, so we don't overfeed one section and neglect another.

Garden gaps. When I'm roaming the borders with a basket of bulbs in the fall, I'm glad that I made notes in the spring about where we had gaps in our spring plantings.

Inspirations. If it occurs to you in midsummer that a clump of peonies would be perfect right there by the porch, write it down.

Resources. Keep phone numbers handy for sources of free manure or mulch, the saw sharpener, and food banks that need surplus produce.

Chance observations that delight. When the wild geese return or the Christmas rose blooms, when you sight a comet or hear the first spring peepers, when you pick the last fall rose—write it all down.

invested money will double (hint: divide 72 by the rate of interest).

A short piece on chiggers hints at the almanac's slightly regional slant—*Blum's* is published in Winston-Salem, North Carolina—but its weekly weather predictions cover New England to the Pacific Coast. A seed-planting table with separate sections for New England, the South, the Midwest, and central-western states is useful and comprehensive.

A Year's Worth of Knowledge and Fun

Old almanacs had holes punched in their upper left-hand corners so that they could be hung on the wall for convenient browsing. Some still come with holes. Whether you hang it or stack it with your phone book, keep your almanac handy. It may be a long shot, but where else could you find at least an educated guess about the weather, months in advance? The well-formulated mix of statistics, history, lore, whimsy, down-home recipes, and sometimes-awful jokes will amuse and instruct you—and perhaps even help you win your next trivia game.

CHAPTER FORTY-EIGHT

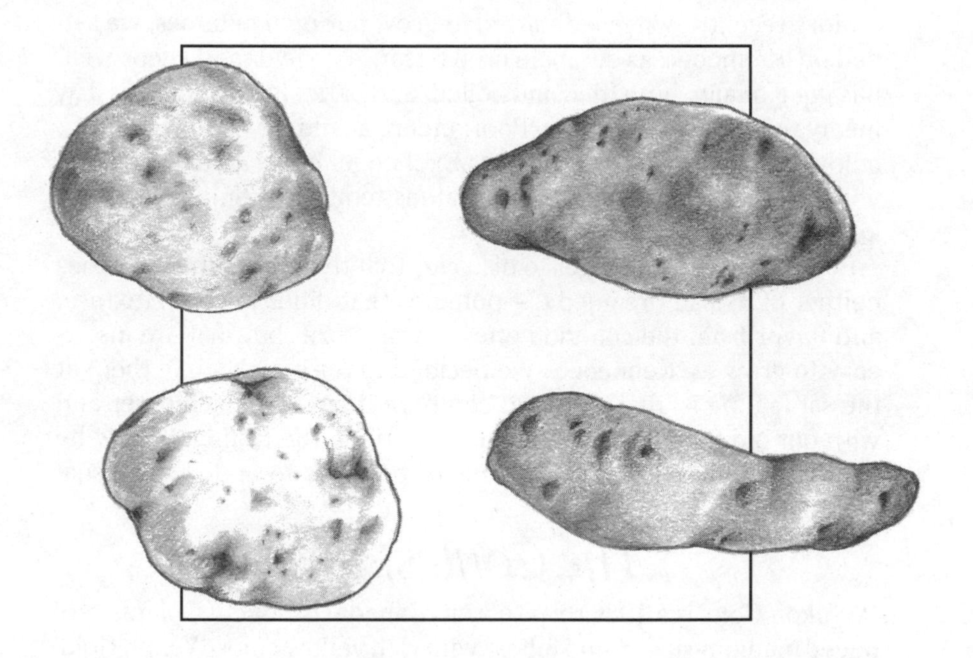

Shop Catalogs for Gourmet Potatoes

Until I married Mike, I never expected much from potatoes. I considered them a background food, and I never thought of a potato as having flavor. I soon found, though, that potatoes were important to my husband. Having grown up in Poland at a time when food was scarce, he considered potatoes soul food. His mother raised potatoes. They were the backbone of family meals. So I learned to cook potatoes carefully, with respect, and I learned the difference between the two or three kinds of potatoes sold in stores.

More recently, when we started to grow our own potatoes, we settled on 'Kennebec' as our main crop because it yields and keeps well, has good quality both fried and boiled, and bakes into a delicious dry, mealy morsel. We also grew 'Poorlander', a cultivar obtained from a fellow member of the Seed Savers Exchange. It has an excellent flavor when boiled, although the potatoes tend to be small with little knobby toes and noses.

It took me a while longer to discover that there are other potatoes neither of us had dreamed of—potatoes that differ in color, texture, and flavor from the common ones sold in stores but that are just as easy to grow as 'Kennebec'. We decided to raise a bunch of them at the same time so that we could compare them with each other and with our old favorite. Mike volunteered to do the tasting. I knew he would. We chose seven new kinds of potatoes to add to our usual planting.

The Contestants

'Yukon Gold' is a 1980 release from Canada. Productive plants produced medium-size, round tubers with rich yellow color. 'Yukon Gold' stores well, unlike some other yellow potatoes.

'Yellow Finn' is an older cultivar that, for us, produced a fine yield of 10 to 13 yellow-fleshed potatoes per plant even before the foliage died back. Many yellow potatoes tend to run small. We'll give ours an extra helping of compost next year.

'Fingerling Salad' potatoes have moist, waxy, yellow-fleshed, finger-size, narrow tubers with many thumb-size extras. For us, this cultivar yielded well—about 12 to the hill. The tubers tend to sprout at the tip while still in the ground, but sprouts are easy to snap off when harvesting. These potatoes are not great keepers. Tuck a bag of them in the crisper of your refrigerator for replanting next spring.

Blue potatoes, shocking purple when you dig them, are a real challenge to anyone's preconceived notion of the True Potato. Ours yielded only four to five small potatoes per hill and many had scab disease. We'll feed them more generously if we grow them again.

'Rosa', a cultivar popular with home-garden testers in New York State, has round, white-skinned, purple-eyed, late-season, multi-

YELLOW POTATOES

Yellow potatoes aren't new—only rediscovered, as immigrants from Europe have shared some of their old favorites. In fact, a history of the Landreth Seed Co., the first seed company in America, notes that in 1811 the company offered the first all-white variety of potato. Until that time, potatoes had been available only in yellow.

purpose tubers. They were not as productive for us as some others. We got five to seven small-to-medium spuds per hill. The thin skin of 'Rosa' makes careful curing important. To cure potatoes, spread them out in a single layer in an area out of the sun but with good air circulation. Leave them to cure for a week or two. This helps the potatoes develop thicker skin, which makes them keep better.

'Irish Cobbler', an old variety, is early, has good-quality tubers, but is not an especially good keeper. We dug four to five medium-size 'Irish Cobblers' per hill.

'Butte', introduced in 1977, yielded long, blocky-shaped beauties that looked like super versions of the usual supermarket baking potatoes. They were productive, with good tuber size and excellent quality. 'Butte' is noted for good vitamin C and protein content.

Planting the Contestants

To prepare the seed potatoes for planting, I cut large ones into two to three pieces, each having at least two eyes (buds). I spread the cut pieces out in shallow cardboard cartons and kept them in a well-lit room for a week so they could heal over and develop sprouts before planting. If a seed potato was egg-size or a bit larger, I left it whole.

We planted all but 'Yukon Gold' on the same day, April 6. (We had planted 'Yukon Gold' about a week earlier.) Mike and our son, Greg, hoed 2- to 3-inch-deep furrows in the soft, tilled ground, where we had plowed under well-aged sheep manure the previous fall. After I spread compost (a good handful per seed potato) in each trench,

Greg's wife, Tish, settled the seed potatoes into the earth, cut side down. Greg raked back the loose soil over the planted furrows and tamped it gently. It was a warming spring ritual that helped us emerge from the lethargy of March. After the harvest, we all enjoyed the potatoes more because we had worked on them together.

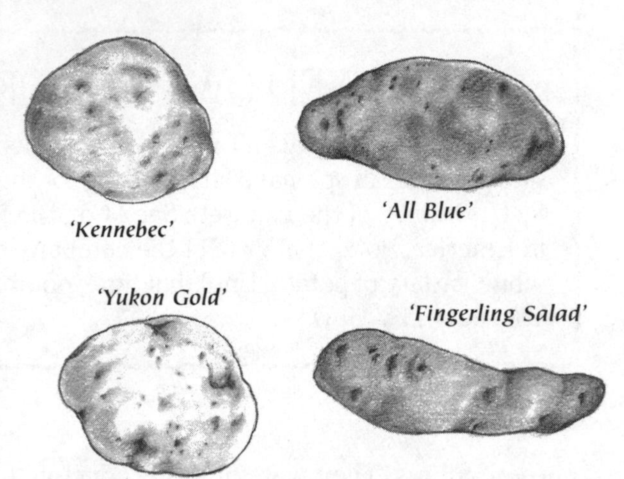

Potatoes come in all shapes and sizes—even in different colors. We sampled a variety, from our favorite 'Kennebec' bakers to the lavender-fleshed but tasty blue types and the appealing 'Yukon Gold', which looks as if it's already buttered. 'Fingerling Salad' cooks quickly and peels easily for hot or cold potato salads.

By April 24, we were writing to Greg and Tish that "the potato plants are showing their first crinkled leaves aboveground." When the plants were 14 inches tall, I tilled between the rows and then immediately hilled up the fine, loose soil around both sides of each row. (We planted about 275 feet of row.) We started to harvest the first potatoes in mid-July.

The Test

When we had a good representative sampling of each crop, we held our official Potato Trial Day. As a boy, Mike had eaten potatoes plain—no butter or gravy. "My mother would peel the potatoes," he remembers, "then boil and drain them and pop them into a hot brick oven to dry until they cracked open and you could see the shiny starch crystals." Thus, the cooking rules for the trial were established.

I steamed medium-size tubers of seven unpeeled varieties for 25 minutes and then dried them all for 10 minutes in a 350°F oven. I served the potatoes as is, with no butter to mask the flavor. Mike's impressions of the potatoes were based on flavor, color, texture, and appearance. I did not identify any of them until after he had evaluated each one. To clear his palate, he ate 'Sweet 100' cherry tomatoes between helpings.

On our first trial day, Mike sampled only steamed potatoes. The next time, he compared two different baking potatoes, both oven-baked for 1 hour at 400°F with special potato nails (found in kitchen and grocery stores) inserted for speedy, even cooking.

The Steamers

Mike was the picture of a happy man, with seven kinds of steaming, fresh-cooked spuds spread out before him. First he tried 'Irish Cobbler' and pronounced it to his liking—mealy and dry. "The texture is good," he said. "I'd call the flavor neutral." When Mike took a bite of the 'Yellow Finn' potato next, his expression changed to one of interest. "Smooth texture here, almost as though it had been buttered, and a pleasant flavor." After a few cherry tomatoes, Mike summoned the courage to try the blue potato, which when cooked had pale lavender flesh and grayish skin. Not a very appetizing sight, but he bravely chewed on a forkful. Good flavor, he judged, and more moist than the others without being watery.

Back on more familiar ground, Mike took a stab at 'Rosa' and compared it with two of our favorites. "This one tastes as good as 'Kennebec', a bit better than 'Irish Cobbler'." On to 'Yukon Gold'. "This is a good flavor, even before you chew it. It tastes as though it had been buttered. I like the rich yellow color, too." Mike was impressed enough to suggest we grow it again.

After sampling more of each kind, Mike ranked the cultivars for flavor as follows: 'Yukon Gold' was best, followed by the blue potato, then 'Rosa', 'Kennebec', 'Irish Cobbler', 'Yellow Finn', and 'Fingerling Salad'. "With butter and with my eyes closed, it would have been harder to detect differences," he added. "They're all good."

The Bakers

Even for a potato lover like Mike, eight kinds of potato in a day might have been too much of a good thing, so we saved our baked potato bake-off for the following day. The two contenders were 'Butte' and 'Kennebec'. Both—thanks to a long, cool spring—were gorgeous, large, smooth, long potatoes.

Both kinds baked to a delicious, appetizing mealiness. 'Butte' had the best texture—super-dry, almost crystalline mealy flesh. 'Kennebec' is still our choice for an all-purpose potato, but we agreed that, for a baker, 'Butte' is even better. We plan to grow 'Butte' again to see whether it will be as productive as 'Kennebec' and to enjoy more of those marvelous, crisp-skinned baked potatoes.

A CLASS BY ITSELF

The 'Fingerling Salad' potato, we decided, is in a class by itself. Because of its waxiness, it couldn't compete with the more mealy boiling and baking potatoes on their own turf. For its own special purpose, it's outstanding. "Now that I've tasted these," concluded Tish, "I won't be content with generic potatoes in potato salad again." She's right. These little fingerlings cook quickly, peel easily, and hold their shape when sliced into salad. Their rich, creamy color gives the potato salad an appetizing appearance. They're pretty good fried, too, but they really shine in potato salad.

Tips for Tasty Potatoes

You'll save some flavor and vitamins by peeling boiled potatoes after they're cooked. I try to use just enough water to last the 20- to 25-minute cooking period, then dry the potatoes briefly in a hot oven before serving (easy in winter when the wood cookstove is always on).

Potatoes baked bare have a much finer flavor and texture than those wrapped in aluminum foil before baking. Foil-wrapped potatoes are actually steamed, and they can't compare with a true baked potato.

Other factors besides cultivar and cooking method can affect potato flavor, too. Potatoes that turn green after exposure to the sun have developed surface concentrations of the toxin solanine. They taste bitter and should not be eaten.

Fertilizer can also affect potato quality. According to studies done in Finland, high-nitrogen fertilizer results in lower starch content and therefore less mealiness. Potatoes that received heavy amounts of nitrogen fertilizer also tended to discolor more readily in both their raw (cut) and cooked states.

And finally, storage conditions can affect potato flavor. "In one case," says John Schoenemann, a vegetable production specialist at the University of Wisconsin, "potatoes that were stored in a basement near a pile of musty old newspapers picked up the musty flavor." As you've probably discovered if you've ever kept potatoes in the refrigerator, prolonged storage at low temperatures can make them taste sweet. The cold triggers the conversion of some of the potato's starch to sugar.

Which potatoes will we grow again? We have our list all ready for next year. We'll give blue potatoes another try someday, but we doubt whether they'll become a staple like the others. 'Kennebec' is still there, and we've added 'Yukon Gold', 'Butte', and 'Fingerling Salad' potatoes. Each, we thought, was outstanding in its class. We haven't stopped experimenting, though. There are more yellow varieties we want to try. Meanwhile, we have a supply of eight kinds of nutritious tubers to satisfy Mike's every whim.

CHAPTER FORTY-NINE

Sprout an Avocado Houseplant

If you've treated yourself to an avocado to liven up midwinter salads, save the seed. It will grow into a handsome, long-lived houseplant with large, oval leaves and gracefully drooping branches.

To prepare the seed for sprouting, keep it in a warm, dry place for a day until the brown outer skin cracks. Then peel off the skin and plant the seed, wide end down, in potting soil in a 4- to 6-inch pot.

Avocados germinate more readily when the seed is exposed to light, so leave the top ½ inch of the seed above soil level.

Keep the soil moist until the pit cracks to reveal a sprout. It can take as long as a month or two for the sprout to appear. When the plant starts to grow, you can fill in the top of the pot with soil. Keep the plant in a sunny window once it develops a sprout, and water it when the soil feels dry.

Unpruned plants grow tall with a single stem, branching only when they reach 4 feet or so. For a bushier plant, cut off the top 2 inches of stem and leaves when the seedling is around 6 inches tall. Prune 1 inch or so off the ends of new shoots to encourage even more bushiness. Before the plant gets too big, prune again as needed to keep your new plant in bounds.

As the plant grows, roots will fill the pot and start to grow out of the drainage hole. Each time this happens, repot it in successively larger containers.

Avocados do well indoors, but they appreciate a summer vacation in the garden if it's convenient to move them outdoors. Carry the pot to a sheltered, shaded spot when the weather turns reliably warm, and bring it back inside in early fall. A platform with casters makes it easy to move large avocado plants around. It's best to put your avocado in a bright, unheated room for a couple of weeks until it acclimates to indoor conditions again.

CHAPTER FIFTY

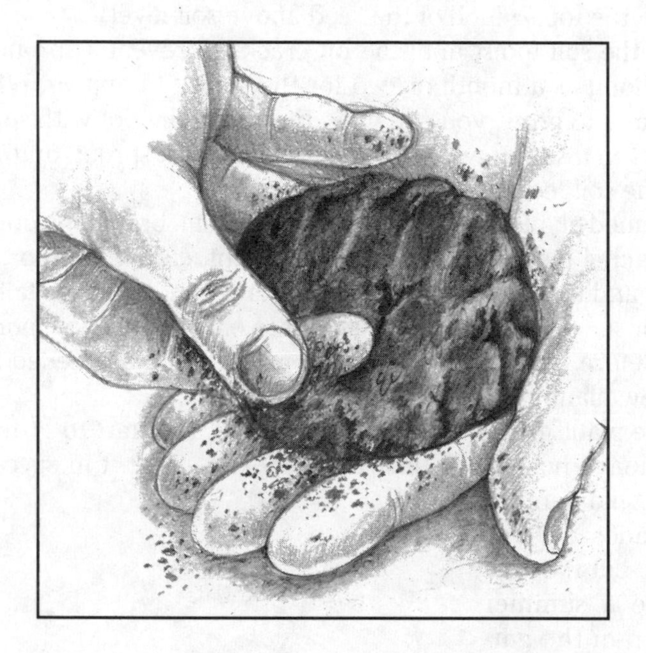

Resolve to Follow the Rules of Good Gardening

Are you looking for ways to improve your garden, to get bigger harvests and healthier plants? A good way to start is by eliminating some bad gardening habits. Many gardeners find it all too easy to follow certain gardening practices that seem to come naturally but are actually counterproductive. Steering clear of even a few of these pitfalls can make as much difference in your garden plot's productivity—and in your own satisfaction—as a load of fertilizer, a season of perfectly distributed rainfall, or a two-week delay in the first frost.

Resolutions Born of Seasoned Experience

I've made more than my share of blunders in many seasons in the garden. Most gardeners outgrow these bad habits after a few seasons, but even the best still goof up occasionally.

Here is my hard-learned list of Gardening Resolutions.

I WILL LET THE SOIL DRY BEFORE I DIG.

Any gardener who denies having done some premature digging either has a short memory or lives in the tropics. Those of us whose gardens gradually emerge from snow and ice in spring know all too well that eagerness to start planting something green. But if soil is dug or stepped on while still sodden, it tends to pack and form large clods, often ruining the soil structure for the season.

When that planting urge strikes, start a few seeds in flats. Wait to dig the garden until a ball of soil will crumble in your hand. Use the same restraint in summer after a hard rain.

If you hand-dig your garden, you can work it several days earlier than your neighbor who rotary-tills, and he'll be ahead of the farmer who plows. The heavier the equipment, the drier the soil must be to avoid compaction.

I WILL BE CAREFUL NOT TO PLANT SEEDS TOO DEEPLY.

Burying seeds beneath too much earth is so easy to do, especially when the soil is chunky and not finely worked. Remember this rule of thumb: Cover seeds with soil to a depth of three times their diameter.

Seeds planted too deeply may die soon after sprouting because they have been through an overwhelming struggle to reach light and air. Lacking air and warmth, they may fail to germinate at all.

I WILL TRY TO SOW SEEDS THINLY.

"Less is more" may be true in the garden, too. Our problem here seems to be that we lack confidence. We empty a whole packet of seeds in a small space, thinking that at least some of them will grow. But all too often, most of them grow! In their search for air and light, they develop tall, weak stems that never fully recover even after we've thinned the surplus seedlings.

Some plants, like peas and parsnips, should be seeded rather thickly, but most others are habitually over-crowded. Consult a good gardening book or read the seed packet to determine recommended seed spacing. I've found it especially easy to sow cabbage, radish, leaf lettuce, and carrot seeds too thickly. Sometimes I mix fine seeds with sand or coffee grounds to space them out. Seed-planting devices can help you sow thinly, too, by controlling the flow of seeds.

Resolve to stay out of your garden—no matter how tempted you are!—until your soil passes the crumble test. Squeeze a handful and see how easily it crumbles. If it sticks in a muddy lump, the soil's too wet to work.

I WILL BE SURE TO THIN CROWDED SEEDLINGS.

I know, you'd like to let all of the sprouts in your garden live. So would I. But in most cases, if you don't thin, all of them will be stunted. A crowded plant can't develop to its true potential. Eat the thinnings, or pot them and exchange them with your neighbors. If you have no takers, add the excess plants to your compost pile.

I WILL LABEL MY PLANTED SEEDLING FLATS AND RECORD PLANTINGS ON MY GARDEN CALENDAR.

Somewhere there are a few well-organized gardeners who always have perfect row labels and plant records. The gremlins who knock over labeling stakes and mix up trays seem to make repeated visits to my garden. But record keeping is important: Only when you have clear records of what and when you've planted will you know which cultivars to order and when to plant next year. I keep a felt-tip pen and a generous supply of plastic plant labels on my potting bench.

I WILL STEP AROUND PLANTING BEDS, NOT ON THEM.

I know a gardener who feels so strongly about this that she posts a "Keep Off" sign in her garden. She's right: Raised planting beds encourage better root growth because the soil is loose and well aerated. Footsteps compact the soil and drive out air, thus putting a damper on the growth of roots that thrive in the oxygen-rich spaces between soil particles. Walk only on the paths and reach over the beds, and your plants will show you that they feel the difference.

I WILL ROOT OUT WEEDS BEFORE THEY GET BIG.

The time to attack weeds is when they still look too puny to amount to anything. Young weeds are easily uprooted with a hoe or tiller. Established weeds often have deep taproots or prickly stems that make them hard to pull. Clearing out early weeds is also a boon to young seedlings.

I WILL NOT ADD TOO MUCH FERTILIZER OR OTHER SOIL ADDITIVES TO MY GARDEN.

Some fertilizer is good, but more isn't necessarily better. Avoid giving too much nitrogen-rich fertilizer, such as chicken manure, to flowering plants, root crops, and fall storage crops as harvest time approaches. Excessive nitrogen promotes leafy growth at the expense of fruit development. And if you spread rock phospate, greensand, or a bagged blended organic fertilizer on your soil, stick to the recommendations on the bag.

People who have wood stoves often overdose a garden with wood ashes. Once you've spread the recommended annual 20 pounds per 1,000 square feet, put the rest around the fruit trees and in the pasture, or save it to use on icy walks. Treat fruit trees by dusting the ashes on the soil out to the drip line. Leave a couple of inches free from ashes around the tree trunk. Also note that too much ash may affect soil pH or induce mineral imbalances.

I WILL WATER DEEPLY.

Watering the garden every evening after dinner can be good therapy for the gardener, but it's not so good for the plants. When the soil is often sprinkled on top but never deeply soaked, plant roots tend to remain in the upper few inches of soil where they are vulnerable to searing midsummer heat and drought. If plants are watered less often and more thoroughly, they develop longer roots, and so are more likely to survive drought. Aim to supply 1 inch of water a week. Be sure to water thoroughly so the soil is soaked to a depth of 4 to 6 inches.

I WILL PICK CUCUMBERS AND OTHER ENTHUSIASTIC VEGETABLES FREQUENTLY TO KEEP THEM PRODUCTIVE.

Okra and cucumbers, and, to a lesser extent, zucchini, tend to stop producing if their fruits are allowed to become large. Pick okra and cucumbers every other day, even if you don't need them, to encourage continued production. You can freeze okra slices for hot soups, and make cucumber puree for cold yogurt-dill-potato soup. Get into the habit of picking zucchini in the fingerling stage. You can use more of them that way, they're tender and quick cooking, and at season's end you're less likely to end up with unusable baseball bats.

I WILL USE ENOUGH MULCH TO DO THE JOB.

It's a mistake to put down just a little mulch. It looks good for a few weeks, but then weeds poke through. Insufficient mulch gives your plants much less drought protection, too. How much is enough? If you're using hay or straw, 8 to 10 inches; newspaper, three to six sheets; grass clippings, 4 inches when first spread (it will compact later to about 2 inches); and wood chips, at least 6 inches.

You can also combine mulches. Tomatoes, for example, can be mulched with a couple of layers of newspaper and 2 to 3 inches of wood chips on top. If you choose wood chips for mulching around vegetables and plan to till the soil at the end of the season, you may want to rake the wood chips into the path before tilling because they break down slowly.

To discourage pests and rot, keep mulch about 1 inch away from stems of flowers and vegetables and deep mulch about 6 to 12 inches away from woody stems of shrubs and trees.

CHAPTER FIFTY-ONE

Make Gardening Easier for Someone You Love

What does a gardener do if his leg is in a cast, her back won't bend, his arm is stiff, or her steps are unsteady? When physical problems interfere with kneeling, stooping, and digging, those time-honored gardener's qualities of ingenuity, adaptability, and determination can help to compensate for difficulties.

The garden, in fact, becomes more important than ever to the person whose stroke or arthritis or other body limitation interferes with

A sturdy, waist-high raised bed is within easy reach for planting and weeding. Landscaping timbers, joined with metal rods and brackets at the inside corners, make a long-lasting frame and a sturdy seat.

mobility. The soul-satisfying work of caring for plants, controlling a small corner of one's environment, is good medicine for one whose arms or legs aren't always obedient to command. The exercise is good therapy, too, which helps to keep the whole body in condition and to strengthen and limber muscles that need stimulation. Gardening can be just what the doctor ordered; horticultural therapy is, in fact, a recognized professional specialty.

Adapt the Garden and the Gardener

Gene Rothert, a registered horticultural therapist at the Chicago Botanic Garden, has a realistic approach that has helped many experienced gardeners to continue gardening, and new enthusiasts to start, despite handicaps. "Adapt the garden," says Rothert, "adapt the gardener, and adapt the plants."

Bring the Garden within Reach

It's not difficult to adapt the garden. Small changes can make a significant difference. Most obvious, and probably most helpful to the largest number of gardeners, is to build raised garden beds that are high enough to be worked without stooping or that are easily reached from a wheelchair.

A Pennsylvania gardener who suffered a stroke at age 59 designed a 3-foot-high, 4 × 12-foot garden bed enclosure made of landscaping logs, overlapped log-cabin style at the corners. Without bending or depending on his nonfunctioning left arm, he can plant and tend an assortment of vegetables, including tomatoes, broccoli, lettuce, onions, peas, and peppers, even a dwarf apricot tree, and a rose bush.

Put a simple machine to work for you by using pulleys to hang your plants. Lower the plants to within reach for watering and maintenance, then raise them up again.

Another inventive gardener, Bill Andrews of Pawtucket, Connecticut, devised a 4-foot-wide, waist-high, octagonal, raised-bed enclosure. It has helped him to keep on gardening after a leg amputation confined him to a wheelchair. Andrews calls his easy-access bed the "No-Bend Garden," and he sells it as a kit. He also offers a separate automatic watering system designed to fit the unit.

Here are some other ideas for bringing plants within reach.

- One determined porch gardener had her hanging plants put on pulleys so that she could raise and lower them easily to water, fertilize, and remove dead flowers.
- A Minnesota nursing home converted a discarded open-top store freezer to an accessible garden for its residents. They had the 20-foot case set on concrete blocks at delivery time, drilled drainage holes in the bottom, and painted it green.

- Simple, sturdy 12- to 14-inch-deep wooden boxes set on legs of a convenient height raise gardens to an accessible level.
- A garden atop a waist-high retaining wall might be well within reach of a gardener who can't stoop.
- For raised-planter gardening on a small scale, try clay flue tiles. They're attractive, rot-proof, and come in several heights (24-inch is especially good). Group them on a patio for easy access.
- Grow-Bags, double polyethylene soil-filled bags, may be set anywhere handy—on walls, tables, even in carts—for small-scale plantings. Cut the bag open and pop the plant right into the bag.
- The Patio Tower Garden, a 4-foot-high redwood structure, takes only 2 square feet of patio space but provides 46 easy-to-reach linear feet of growing space.
- Another possibility is using halved whiskey barrels.

An advantage to all of these raised-garden arrangements is that they tend to warm earlier in spring and stay warmer late in fall. They're easy to cover, too, when frost threatens. And they provide good drainage. If all plantings are in containers that are relatively shallow, it's best to stick to annual flowers and vegetables because roots of perennial plants might be injured by winter freezes. Deeper planter boxes like those described in the list above should provide enough mass to buffer winter's cold as far north as Zones 4 to 5.

Designing the Garden for Ease of Use

Garden layout can be an enabling factor, too. If possible, keep garden beds close to the house and to stored tools, or build a little toolshed in a convenient place. Gardeners who use wheelchairs or sit-scooters to get around the garden will need wide, firm, smooth paths. Thick grass, soft soil, and uneven brick are difficult to negotiate on wheels or with unsteady feet. Make sure paths slope gently—not more than 1 inch every 15 inches. Curved paths are easier to follow than those with sharp corners.

For the gardener whose strength or dexterity is severely limited, caring for a few plants is absorbing and therapeutic. But for one who wants more extensive plantings, it's best to avoid growing everything in small pots, which dry quickly and must be watered often. In any size garden, an automated watering system can be a wonderful help.

Learning New Ways

The gardener's adjustment can be a matter of attitude, appliances, or both. Concentrate on remaining abilities and strengths. What can your loved one reach, hold, or turn? Encourage him or her to feel free to do things in a different way.

If energy is limited, decide where to concentrate your efforts. You might, for example, suggest that he hire someone to mow the lawn so that he will have more time and strength left to tend the garden. Encourage your loved one to be realistic about her strength and set time limits. It's better to take frequent breaks than to work too long at a time and get exhausted—a temptation familiar to all gardeners who find themselves eager to "just finish this row."

Small aids can expand the possibilities. Consider some of these.

- A 4-foot broom handle lashed to the last 4 feet of a hose to stiffen it makes watering easier.
- A scissor-action pickup tool to pick up dropped seed packets and wayward sticks is handy in the garden.
- A carpenter's apron with plenty of deep pockets reduces the number of things dropped and keeps tools handy.
- A basket tied to a walker can hold hand tools or bring in the harvest.
- A whistle on a cord around the neck is a sensible precaution to summon help in case of difficulty.
- A cordless phone puts help or advice at the gardener's fingertips during an extensive weeding session.

Planting for Easy Access

Your choice of plant materials can make it easier to garden without strain, too. Select insect- and disease-resistant flowers and vegetables whenever possible, so there will be less need to hover over them plucking bugs and treating diseases. If bending is a problem, plant pole beans; trellis tall peas, cucumbers, and other climbing plants; and stake or cage tomatoes rather than letting them sprawl. Easy-to-see purple beans are a boon to gardeners with vision problems.

The harvest of flowers, vegetables, and fruit counts for a lot—surmounting difficulties and working with growing things satisfies the spirit and strengthens the body, and those red, ripe tomatoes are pure enjoyment.

MAIL-ORDER GARDENERS' AIDS

A number of helpful tools are available from mail-order catalogs. Here are a few products that you might find useful. A key to mail-order sources is listed in parentheses. The addresses for these sources follow the product list.

- The Easy Kneeler, with sturdy side handles for support, becomes a bench when you turn it upside down. (2,4,6,7)*
- The Garden Scoot has a swiveling, tractor-type seat and large wheels to help you get where you want to go. (2,4,7)*
- The swan-neck hoe has a long handle and a curved neck that's a real backsaver. (2)
- The E-Z Oriental Hand Tool has a twisted blade that requires less effort than a trowel does to make planting holes for seedlings. (1)*
- Left-handed pruning shears, made by Felco, are a boon to the naturally left-handed gardener, as well as to the one who must adapt to left-handedness because of injury or illness. (3,6)
- Long-handled grass shears help you to trim lawn edges without stooping. (2,3,6)
- Seed-planting devices made to be used while standing upright or those that measure seed in small preset amounts make planting a row an easy job. (4,5)

*Sources listed may offer a product similar to the one described.

Sources

1. The Cook's Garden, P.O. Box 535, Londonderry, VT 05148
2. Gardener's Supply Co., 128 Intervale Rd., Burlington, VT 05401
3. A. M. Leonard, Inc., 6665 Spiker Rd., P.O. Box 816, Piqua, OH 45356
4. Mellinger's Inc., 2310 W. South Range Rd., North Lima, OH 44452
5. Park Seed Co., Cokesbury Rd., P.O. Box 31, Greenwood, SC 29647
6. Smith & Hawken, 25 Corte Madera, Mill Valley, CA 94941
7. Stokes Seeds, Inc., P.O. Box 548, Buffalo, NY 14240

CHAPTER FIFTY-TWO

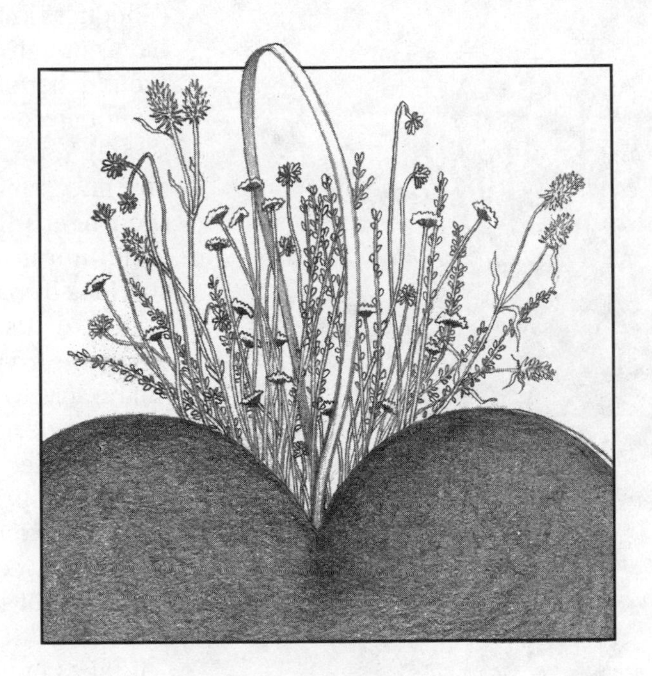

Create a Wordless Valentine

Years ago, a friend sent us a charming Swedish paper craft at Christmas time. I hung it on the Christmas tree and later made some myself to send as valentines. You might want to make a number of them in different sizes and hang them in a window.

You'll need stiff red paper, white glue or rubber cement, thread, and dried weeds or small dried flowers, such as statice. I've always

Simple homemade gifts say "I Love You" without needing any words. Fashion your valentines from colored paper, and add a bouquet of dainty dried weeds and flowers for a romantic touch.

used weeds for mine. (Goodness knows we have enough of them around here on our mountainside homestead!) You can usually find dried weed seed heads in good condition in winter. Just look in your own backyard. Also check along the roadsides, but be sure to get the owner's permission before collecting on private property. Or raid that bouquet of dried field weeds that you brought indoors last fall.

It takes only a few minutes to make one of these wordless valentines. Here's how.

1. First, cut two identical heart shapes from stiff red paper. Mine are usually 2 to 3 inches across at the widest part . . . purposely small, to be in scale with the delicate weeds.
2. Spread glue all around the edges of one paper heart. Then arrange a few stems of tiny dried weeds at the top of the heart, pressing them into the glue. Add a loop of thread at the center.
3. Finally, fit the second paper heart on top of the first, pressing around the edges to bond the two hearts together. It's all right if there's a slight gap at the top, as long as the flowers and the thread loop are securely glued on.

USDA PLANT HARDINESS ZONE MAP

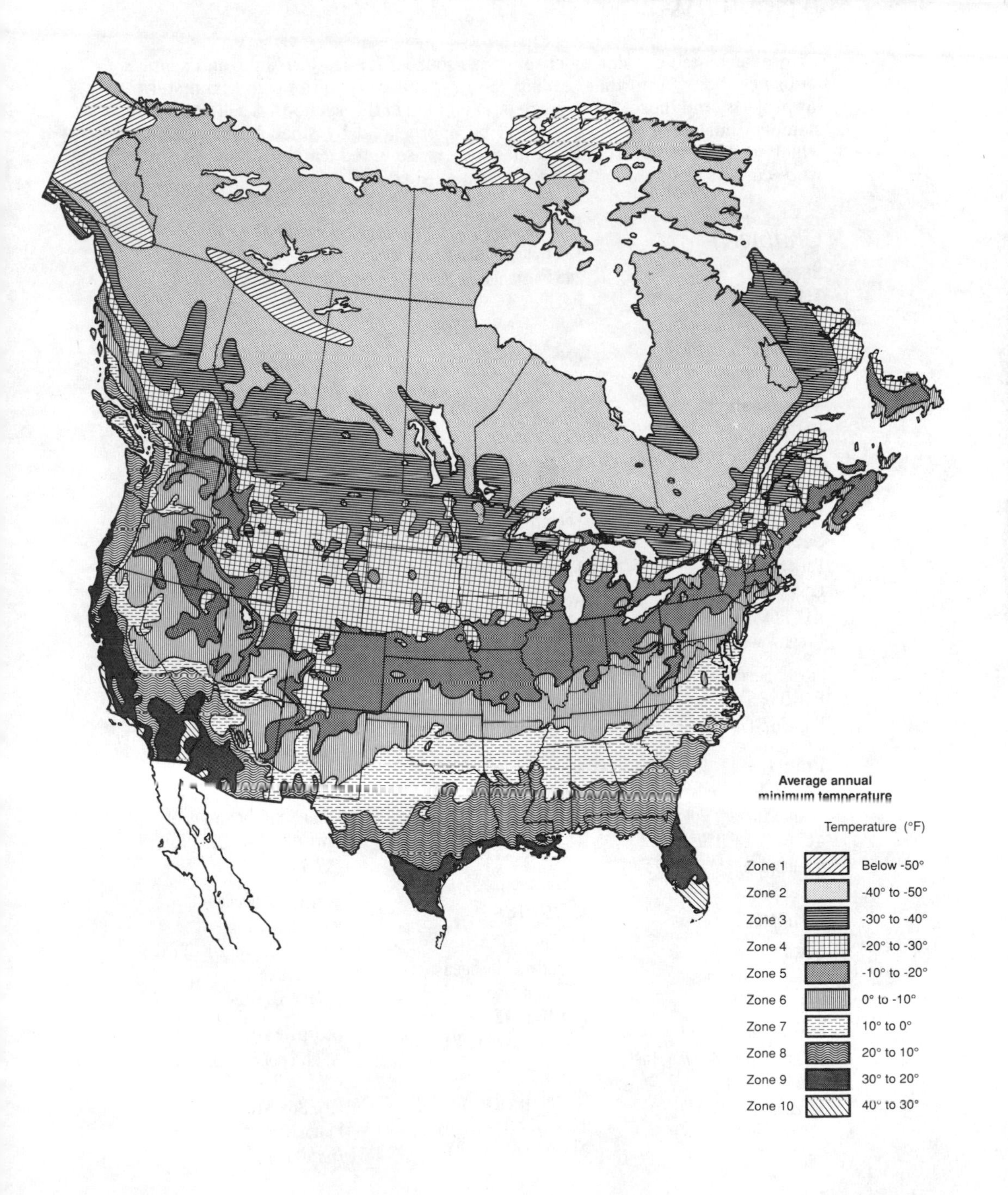

RESOURCES

Here, arranged chapter by chapter, are sources for seeds, plants, and supplies and suggestions for further reading. (Some chapters require no special materials for projects, and those chapters are not included in this section.) A self-addressed, stamped, business-size envelope will be appreciated by small businesses from which you request information. Unless otherwise noted, catalogs are free. Prices were current at the time this book was published.

Chapter 1

Seeds

The Country Garden
P.O. Box 3539
Oakland, CA 94609
($2)

Stokes Seeds, Inc.
P.O. Box 548
Buffalo, NY 14240

Chapter 2

Seeds

Park Seed Co.
Cokesbury Rd.
P.O. Box 31
Greenwood, SC 29647

Stokes Seeds, Inc.
P.O. Box 548
Buffalo, NY 14240

Plants

Henry Field Seed and Nursery Co.
415 N. Burnett St.
Shenandoah, IA 51602

Chapter 3

Seeds

Stokes Seeds, Inc.
P.O. Box 548
Buffalo, NY 14240

Thompson & Morgan, Inc.
P.O. Box 1308
Jackson, NJ 08527

Plants

Van Bourgondien Bros., Inc.
245 Farmingdale Rd.
P.O. Box A
Babylon, NY 11702

Wayside Gardens
1 Garden Ln.
Hodges, SC 29695

Chapter 4

Seeds

Thompson & Morgan, Inc.
P.O. Box 1308
Jackson, NJ 08527

Plants

Park Seed Co.
Cokesbury Rd.
P.O. Box 31
Greenwood, SC 29647

Book

Thomas, Graham Stuart. *Plants for Ground-cover.* 3rd ed. Portland, Oreg.: Timber Press, 1990.

Chapter 5

Seeds

Abundant Life Seed Foundation
P.O. Box 772
Port Townsend, WA 98368
($1)

Nichols Garden Nursery
1190 N. Pacific Hwy.
Albany, OR 97321

The Rosemary House
120 S. Market St.
Mechanicsburg, PA 17055
($2)

Chapter 6

Seeds

The Cook's Garden
P.O. Box 535
Londonderry, VT 05148
($1)

Shepherd's Garden Seeds
30 Irene St.
Torrington, CT 06790
($1)

Chapter 7

Seeds

Johnny's Selected Seeds
310 Foss Hill Rd.
Albion, ME 04910

Peace Seeds
2385 S.E. Thompson St.
Corvallis, OR 97333
($3.50)

Territorial Seeds
P.O. Box 157
Cottage Grove, OR 97424

Chapter 8

Supplies

A. M. Leonard, Inc.
6665 Spiker Rd.
P.O. Box 816
Piqua, OH 45356
Hedge clippers

Mellinger's Inc.
2310 W. South Range Rd.
North Lima, OH 44452
Hedge clippers

Chapter 9

Bulbs

Fox Hollow Herbs
P.O. Box 148
McGrann, PA 16236
($1, refundable with order)

Kalmia Farm
P.O. Box 3881
Charlottesville, VA 22903

Chapter 10

Seeds

W. Atlee Burpee and Co.
300 Park Ave.
Warminster, PA 18974

Seeds Blum
Idaho City Stage
Boise, ID 83706
(First catalog, $3)

Supplies

Gardens Alive!
5100 Schenley Place
Lawrenceburg, IN 47025
Sabadilla dust, Bt, nematodes

Peaceful Valley Farm Supply
P.O. Box 2209
Grass Valley, CA 95945
($2) Natural insect controls

Association

World Pumpkin Federation
14050 Gowanda State Rd.
Collins, NY 14034
In charge of competition to locate largest pumpkin

Chapter 11

Seeds

DeGiorgi Seed Co.
6011 N St.
Omaha, NE 68117
($2)

Johnny's Selected Seeds
310 Foss Hill Rd.
Albion, ME 04910

Pinetree Garden Seeds
Rt. 100
New Gloucester, ME 04260

Chapter 12

Plants

Brittingham's Plant Farms
P.O. Box 2538
Salisbury, MD 21801

Hartmann's Plantation, Inc.
P.O. Box E
310 60th St.
Grand Junction, MI 49056
($2.25) Both rabbiteye and highbush blueberries

Chapter 15

Plants

Companion Plants
7247 N. Coolville Ridge Rd.
Athens, OH 45701
($2)

Cricket Hill Herb Farm Ltd.
Glen St.
Rowley, MA 01969
($1)

Well-Sweep Herb Farm
317 Mt. Bethel Rd.
Port Murray, NJ 07865
($2)

Chapter 16

Seeds

The Country Garden
P.O. Box 3539
Oakland, CA 94609
($2)

Nichols Garden Nursery
1190 N. Pacific Hwy.
Albany, OR 97321

Southern Exposure Seed Exchange
P.O. Box 158
North Garden, VA 22959
($3)

Chapter 17

Seeds

Nichols Garden Nursery
1190 N. Pacific Hwy.
Albany, OR 97321

Redwood City Seed Co.
P.O. Box 361
Redwood City, CA 94064
($1)

Seeds Blum
Idaho City Stage
Boise, ID 83706
(First catalog, $3)

Chapter 18

Books

Hils, Ralph J. *Market What You Grow.* Atlanta, Ga.: The Chicot Press, 1989.

Wallin, Craig. *Backyard Cash Crops.* 2nd ed. Friday Harbor, Wash.: Homestead Design, 1989.

Chapter 19

Supplies

Necessary Trading Co.
P.O. Box 305
422 Salem Ave.
New Castle, VA 24127
($2)

Peaceful Valley Farm Supply
P.O. Box 2209
Grass Valley, CA 95945
($2) Beneficial insects, seeds, monitoring supplies

Book

Carr, Anna. *Rodale's Color Handbook of Garden Insects.* Emmaus, Pa.: Rodale Press, 1979.

Chapter 20

Seeds

W. Atlee Burpee and Co.
300 Park Ave.
Warminster, PA 18974

Hastings Seeds
1036 White St. SW
P.O. Box 115535
Atlanta, GA 30310-8535

Shepherd's Garden Seeds
30 Irene St.
Torrington, CT 06790
($1)

Chapter 21

Seeds

W. Atlee Burpee and Co.
300 Park Ave.
Warminster, PA 18974

The Country Garden
P.O. Box 3539
Oakland, CA 94609
($2)

Thompson & Morgan, Inc.
P.O. Box 1308
Jackson, NJ 08527

Chapter 22

Supplies

A. M. Leonard, Inc.
6665 Spiker Rd.
P.O. Box 816
Piqua, OH 45356
Shade fabric

Mellinger's Inc.
2310 W. South Range Rd.
North Lima, OH 44452
Shade fabric

Chapter 23

Seeds

Garden City Seeds
1324 Red Crow Rd.
Victor, MT 59875-9713
($1)

Pinetree Garden Seeds
Rt. 100
New Gloucester, ME 04260

Shepherd's Garden Seeds
30 Irene St.
Torrington, CT 06790
($1)

Chapter 25

Supplies

A. M. Leonard, Inc.
6665 Spiker Rd.
P.O. Box 816
Piqua, OH 45356
Stakes, bamboo, ties

Mellinger's Inc.
2310 W. South Range Rd.
North Lima, OH 44452
Stakes, bamboo, ties

Chapter 26

Plants

Carroll Gardens
P.O. Box 310
444 E. Main St.
Westminster, MD 21158
($2)

Rocknoll Nursery
7812 Mad River Rd.
Hillsboro, OH 45133
($1)

Shady Oaks Nursery
700 19th Ave. NE
Waseca, MN 56093

Book

Schenk, George. *The Complete Shade Gardener.* Boston: Houghton Mifflin Co., 1984.

Chapter 27

Cornhusks

The Corn Crib
R.R. 2, Box 164
Madison, MO 65263
Send SASE for information.

Chapter 28

Bulbs

Delegeane Garlic Farms
P.O. Box 2561
Yountville, CA 94599

Kalmia Farm
P.O. Box 3881
Charlottesville, VA 22903

Southern Exposure Seed Exchange
P.O. Box 158
North Garden, VA 22959
($3)

Association
The Garlic Seed Foundation
Rose Valley Farm
Rose, NY 14542
Membership $10/year; includes newsletter

Book
Engeland, Ron L. *Growing Great Garlic.* Okanogan, Wash.: Filaree Productions, 1991.

Chapter 29

Books
Garner, R. J. *The Grafter's Handbook.* New York: Oxford University Press, 1979.
Kaufman, Peter, et al. *Practical Botany.* Text ed. Englewood Cliffs, N.J.: Prentice-Hall, Reston, 1983.

Chapter 30

Seeds
DeGiorgi Seed Co.
6011 N St.
Omaha, NE 68117
($2)

Park Seed Co.
Cokesbury Rd.
P.O. Box 31
Greenwood, SC 29647

Plants
Kurt Bluemel, Inc.
2740 Greene Ln.
Baldwin, MD 21013
($3)

Garden Place
6780 Heisley Rd.
Mentor, OH 44060
($1)

Limerock Ornamental Grasses Inc.
RD 1, Box 111C
Port Matilda, PA 16870
($2)

Books
Darke, Rick. *Ornamental Grasses at Longwood Gardens.* Kennett Square, Pa.: Longwood Gardens, 1990.
Greenlee, John. *The Encyclopedia of Ornamental Grasses.* Emmaus, Pa.: Rodale Press, 1992.
Otteson, Carole. *Ornamental Grasses: The Amber Wave.* New York: McGraw Hill Publishing Co., 1989.

Chapter 31

Seeds
Garden City Seeds
1324 Red Crow Rd.
Victor, MT 59875-9713
($1)

Johnny's Selected Seeds
310 Foss Hill Rd.
Albion, ME 04910

Stokes Seeds, Inc.
P.O. Box 548
Buffalo, NY 14240

Chapter 32

Bulbs
Dutch Gardens
P.O. Box 200
Adelphia, NJ 07710

John Scheepers Inc.
P.O. Box 700
Bantam, CT 06750

Veldheer Tulip Gardens
12755 Quincy St.
Holland, MI 49424

Chapter 33

Seeds
Abundant Life Seed Foundation
P.O. Box 772
Port Townsend, WA 98368
($1)

William Dam Seeds Ltd.
P.O. Box 8400
Dundas, Ontario L9H 6M1
($2, refundable with order)

Johnny's Selected Seeds
310 Foss Hill Rd.
Albion, ME 04910

Supplies
Gardens Alive!
5100 Schenley Place
Lawrenceburg, IN 47025
Spined soldier bugs

Association
Seed Savers Exchange
R.R. 3, Box 329
Decorah, IA 52101
($1 for information)

Chapter 35

Trees
Vernon Barnes and Son Nursery
P.O. Box 250
McMinnville, TN 37110

Musser Forests Inc.
P.O. Box 340
Rt. 119 North
Indiana, PA 15701

Northwoods Nursery
28696 S. Cramer Rd.
Molalla, OR 97038

Chapter 36

Plants

Davidson-Wilson Greenhouses
R.R. 2, Box 168
Crawfordsville, IN 47933-9423
($2)

Lake Odessa Greenhouse
1123 Jordan Lake St.
Lake Odessa, MI 48849

Shady Hill Gardens
821 Walnut St.
Batavia, IL 60510-2999
($2, refundable with order)

Chapter 37

Plants and Supplies

The Herbfarm
32804 Issaquah-Fall City Rd.
Fall City, WA 98024
Bagged, ready-to-use mixtures for mothproofing

Indiana Botanic Gardens
Box 5
Hammond, IN 46325
Dried plant materials

Richters
P.O. Box 26
Hwy. 47
Goodwood, Ontario L0C 1A0
($2.50)

The Rosemary House
120 S. Market St.
Mechanicsburg, PA 17055
($2)

Sandy Mush Herb Nursery
Rt. 2
Surrett Cove Rd.
Leicester, NC 28748
($4, refundable with order)
Cloth bags to hold homemade herb mixtures

Chapter 38

Book

Bubel, Mike and Nancy. *Root Cellaring.* 2nd ed. Pownal, Vt.: Storey Communications, Garden Way Publishing, 1991.

Chapter 41

Plants

Dabney Herbs
P.O. Box 22061
Louisville, KY 40252
($2)

Dutch Mill Herb Farm
6640 N.W. Marsh Rd.
Forest Grove, OR 97116
Send long SASE for catalog. Only ships lavender; offers more herbs at farm.

Wrenwood of Berkeley Springs
Rt. 4, Box 361
Berkeley Springs, WV 25411
($2)

Chapter 42

Seeds

The Cook's Garden
P.O. Box 535
Londonderry, VT 05148
($1)

William Dam Seeds
P.O. Box 8400
Dundas, Ontario L9H 6M1
($2, refundable with order)

Johnny's Selected Seeds
310 Foss Hill Rd.
Albion, ME 04910

Chapter 43

Plants

Betsey's Briarpatch
1610 Ellis Hollow Rd.
Ithaca, NY 14850
Send long SASE for catalog. Specializes in cacti and succulents.

Logee's Greenhouses
141 North St.
Danielson, CT 06239
($3, refundable with order)

Sunnybrook Farms Nursery
P.O. Box 6
9448 Mayfield Rd.
Chesterland, OH 44026
($1)

Chapter 45

Seeds

Abundant Life Seed Foundation
P.O. Box 772
Port Townsend, WA 98368
($1)

Evergreen YH Enterprises
P.O. Box 17538
Anaheim, CA 92817
Oriental vegetable seeds

Horticultural Enterprises
P.O. Box 810082
Dallas, TX 75381-0082
($1) Pepper seeds

Native Seeds/SEARCH
2509 N. Campbell Ave. #325
Tucson, AZ 85719
($1)

Plants of the Southwest
Route 6, Box 11-A
Sante Fe, NM 87501
($1.50)

Sunrise Enterprises
P.O. Box 330058
West Hartford, CT 06133
Oriental vegetable seeds

Chapter 47

Books

American Farm and Home Almanac
Geiger Brothers
P.O. Box 1609
Lewiston, ME 04240

Baer's Agricultural Almanac
John Baer's Sons
Box 328
Lancaster, PA 17603

Blum's Farmer's and Planter's Almanac
Blum's Almanac Co.
3301 Healy Dr.
Winston-Salem, NC 27103

The Old Farmer's Almanac
Yankee Publishing Inc.
P.O. Box 520
Dublin, NH 03444

Chapter 48

Seed Potatoes

Becker's Seed Potatoes
R.R. 1
Trout Creek, Ontario
P0H 2L0
Canadian customers only

Ronniger's Seed Potatoes
Star Rt.
Moyie Springs, ID 83845
($2)

Wood Prairie Farm
RFD #1, Box 164
Bridgewater, ME 04735

Book

Bollen, Constance, and Marlene Blessing. *One Potato, Two Potato: A Cookbook.* Los Angeles: Pacific Search Press, 1983.

Museum

The Potato Museum, P.O. Box 791, Great Falls, VA 22066

Chapter 51

Supplies

W. Atlee Burpee and Co.
300 Park Ave.
Warminster, PA 18974
Patio Tower Garden

Books

Moore, Bibby. *Growing with Gardening: A Twelve-Month Guide for Therapy, Recreation, and Education.* Chapel Hill, N.C.: University of North Carolina Press, 1989.

Please, Peter, ed. *Able to Garden: A Practical Guide for Disabled and Elderly Gardeners.* London, England: B. T. Batsford, 1990. Available for $22.95 from Abundant Life Seed Foundation, P.O. Box 772, Port Townsend, WA 98368.

Relf, Paula Diane. *Gardening in Raised Beds and Containers for Elderly and Physically Handicapped.* Blacksburg, Va.: Virginia Polytechnic Institute and State University, August 1987.

INDEX

Note: Page references in *italic* indicate tables. **Boldface** references indicate illustrations.